P9-ECO-749

Japan and China as Charm Rivals
Soft Power in Regional Diplomacy

In international relations today, influence is as essential as military and economic might. Consequently, leaders promote favorable images of the state to attract allies and win support for their policies. Jing Sun, an expert on international relations and a former journalist, refers to such soft power campaigns as "charm offensives."

Sun focuses on the competition between China and Japan for the allegiance of South Korea, Taiwan, and other states in the region. He finds that instead of adopting a one-size-fits-all approach, the Chinese and the Japanese deploy customized charm campaigns for each target state, taking into consideration the target's culture, international position, and political values. He then evaluates the effectiveness of individual campaigns from the perspective of the target state, on the basis of public opinion polls, media coverage, and the response from state leaders.

A deep yet comparative study, *Japan and China as Charm Rivals* enriches our understanding of soft power by revealing deliberate image campaign efforts and offering a method for assessing the effectiveness of such charm offensives.

JING SUN is assistant professor of political science at the University of Denver. Before coming to the United States in 1999, he worked for various Chinese media outlets.

Japan and China as Charm Rivals

Soft Power in Regional Diplomacy

Jing Sun

The University of Michigan Press • *Ann Arbor*

Copyright © by the University of Michigan 2012
All rights reserved

This book may not be reproduced, in whole or in part, including illustrations, in any form (beyond that copying permitted by Sections 107 and 108 of the U.S. Copyright Law and except by reviewers for the public press), without written permission from the publisher.

Published in the United States of America by
The University of Michigan Press
Manufactured in the United States of America
⊚ Printed on acid-free paper

2015   2014   2013   2012   4   3   2   1

A CIP catalog record for this book is available from the British Library.

Library of Congress Cataloging-in-Publication Data

Sun, Jing.
    Japan and China as charm rivals : soft power in regional diplomacy / Jing Sun.
        p.   cm.
    Includes bibliographical references and index.
    ISBN 978-0-472-11833-5 (cloth : alk. paper) —
    ISBN 978-0-472-02845-0 (e-book)
        1. China—Foreign relations—Japan.   2. Japan—Foreign relations—China.
    3. East Asia—Foreign relations.   4. Strategic rivalries (World politics)
    I. Title.

    DS740.5.J3S76   2012
    327.51052—dc23

                                                                2012011047

To Meiqin—My Dearest Piàopiào

Contents

Acknowledgments

To me, the "acknowledgments" part, which often precedes the text of a book, embeds a sense of sweet irony. After all, an author won't need to worry about such a ceremonial beginning until the very end—that is, if luck could carry him this far. The triumphant symbolism certainly excites me. But as I am writing the acknowledgments—finally—I find myself immersed in appreciation. I am thinking of all the people who have shaped my life and made this book a reality. While the rest of the book is about what I found out, this part is about them.

The first person I think of is my father, Sun Shujun, who passed away in October 1999, only two months after my American journey had started. My father, though a factory worker, inspired my interest in the study of politics. The considerable lapse between his departure and this book's arrival has only allowed me to better understand him as my pathfinder. Even today, upstream against the passage of time, I can still see myself as a little boy, waiting anxiously for the sound of his bicycle and dashing to him when he appeared. His bag was always filled with newspapers and books, most of which were about history and politics. Thanks to him, the first adult book I finished was the Chinese version of *The Memoirs of Richard Nixon*—an odd choice for a third-grader. But to me, it marked the amazing beginning of my intellectual voyage. I only wish my father could see my book. Though he would not understand a word, I knew he would be pleased and proud nonetheless. In fact, he already was.

I thank my mother, Fu Yi, who has endured too much and enjoyed too little. Her life has defined sacrifice and perseverance. She taught me to fight for my own fate, no matter how the odds might be stacked against me. She also encouraged me to take Japanese as a second foreign language when I was just a pupil. I see my eventual profession as a political scientist with a focus on Japan as the best gift jointly bestowed on me by my parents. I also thank my elder brother, Sun Lei, who has been my buddy and my teacher through all these years. But most important, he has been my fierce protector. In his eyes, his younger brother could never grow up. Maybe he is right—I don't need to when I am with him.

I thank my wonderful parents on my wife's side, Rui Hekai and Gu Yueqin. They are more than in-laws; they have accepted me and loved me in every meaningful way as their own child. Rui, a professor and a scientist, spent a long time living and doing medical research in Japan. I have often been amazed by how well he understands the country on which I am supposed to be an expert. But most impressive is Rui's impeccable character. Despite his age and the hardships that the People's Republic has brought to its intellectuals, he has remained morally untainted. He has passed on to me not only his vast knowledge of Japan but also his fundamental belief in the goodness of human nature. He is brave enough to be an idealist, and I only hope to obtain half his audacity in doing so. Gu, for her part, cares first and foremost about my health. She has made my life in Shanghai comfortable so that I could focus on my work. Simply put, she has indulged me with love.

In the professional world, I am indebted to many people who have helped me grow as a scholar. I thank my graduate adviser, David Leheny, who never fails to inspire me with his originality, diligence, and humor. I was fortunate to have him as my mentor. I thank the members of my dissertation committee: Mark Beissinger, Katherine Cramer-Walsh, Edward Friedman, and Zhongdang Pan. They all helped me become a more qualified scholar. I particularly thank Friedman, who has been an exemplary scholar and a model for me in so many ways. I also thank Naomi McGloin and Akira Miura for helping me improve my language skills. I will always remember my days in their classes. In Colorado, I thank my wonderful colleagues at the University of Denver for their support: David Ciepley, Lisa Conant, Peter Hanson, Setsu Kawada, Christina Kreps, Seth Masket, Anne McCall, Susan Sterrett, Nancy Wadsworth, Spencer Wellhofer, Yunbo Yi, and Duan Zhang. I thank Tom Knecht, a wonderful former colleague who has since moved to California, for his continued friendship.

While conducting research on this topic, I received constructive comments from many scholars, including Lowell Dittmer, Ingrid d'Hooghe, Ikuro Fujiwara, Linus Hagström, Narushige Michishita, Dechao Sun, Jian Wang, Tsuneo Watanabe, Daqing Yang, Suisheng Zhao, and Jianrong Zhu. I thank the reviewers at the University of Michigan Press for their insightful comments and sharp criticisms, all in the good spirit of improving the quality of this manuscript. I particularly thank June Teufel Dreyer, who took the unusual step of setting up personal contacts with me after the acceptance of this book. She has since offered me numerous suggestions and new pieces of information that were greatly helpful in my revisions. At the University of Michigan Press, I owe a huge thank you to editor Melody Herr, who has provided trust, patience, and above all unwavering faith in the value of my research. I was lucky to have such a highly professional and passionate manager for this project. I also thank Susan Cronin for guiding me through the labyrinth of manuscript preparation, and Ellen Goldlust-Gingrich for copyediting the manuscript. At the institutional level, I thank the University of Denver for offering crucial financial aid to assist my research. I also thank the library system of the University of Michigan for providing travel grants so that I could use their vast collections.

There are plenty of people to thank on the other side of the Pacific. Saoru Kato and Ikuko Toyonaga served as wonderful faculty sponsors at the University of Tokyo and Waseda University, respectively. Masao Hirotani, Wang Kuan, and Dong Ling made my life in Tokyo much easier. I thank the Japan Foundation for financially supporting my fieldwork. On the Chinese side, I thank my friends Feng Wen, Wu Tao, and Zhang Hua, among others, for their support through all these years. I thank my teachers, Liu Jiuping and the late Chang Mingchu for their inspiration and support. I owe huge thanks to many people in the government and journalists for agreeing to be interviewed. Although they have to remain anonymous, they have my most sincere gratitude. Despite the support I have received from all these sources, any errors remaining in the book are my sole responsibility.

When I wrote down the first few words of this manuscript in September 2007, our son, Colin, was still more than three months away from coming to this world. Now he has been filling my life with wonder and laughter for more than four years. Our daughter, Eva, has since joined him. It will be years before my children will bother to open this book and see what their father has put down. But when they reach this page, as they eventually will, I want them to know that my love for them will always be deeper than they could ever imagine. I thank them for making me a fuller person.

I save my most important thanks for last—my wife, Rui Meiqin, affectionately known as Piàopiào to family and friends. Seventeen years have passed since our teenage paths first crossed on the campus of Fudan University. During these years, she has been my classmate, girlfriend, wife, and now the mother of our children, with each change merging our lives closer.

While it has been a story of joy to me, the journey has brought far more bittersweetness to her. I cannot even imagine the scope of her sacrifices to make our love thrive, beginning with quitting her comfortable job in Shanghai, leaving her indulging parents, and coming to the other side of the globe, where only a used frameless mattress and two chairs were awaiting her. But Meiqin has accepted all these changes with grace. She loves to smile, and her smiles always bring me back to the years when we were chatting on Fudan's green lawns and at its little cafes. She did not fail to lighten me up then, and she still succeeds now. She has never lost faith in my potential, not even when I had doubts. Instead, she hugs me and says, "Bènbèn, everything will be fine because Piàopiào is with you."

Yes, thank you for being with me and sharing my life all these years, Meiqin. This book is for you—my friend, my wife, my soul mate, my dearest Piàopiào.

Introduction:
"Peaceful Rise" vs. "Beautiful Japan"

The idea for this book came to me in a rather random way. In December 2006, a news story, "Dragon May No Longer Fit to Serve as China's Symbol," caught my attention. Professor Wu Youfu, also the party general secretary of the Shanghai Foreign Studies University, was urging the Chinese government to consider a new national symbol to replace the dragon—a mythical creature widely used by Chinese and foreigners alike to symbolize China. Wu contended that "dragons are perceived as domineering and aggressive giants in the Western world." To associate China with such an image might hurt the credibility of China's "peaceful rise" thesis. Wu also urged his Chinese compatriots to reconsider calling themselves *long de chuan ren* (dragon's descendants), a term made popular by a 1980s hit song.[1]

The article, once posted on the Internet, attracted countless visits. In fact, its controversy convinced QQ, China's most popular instant messaging provider and a major infotainment Web portal, to set up a forum, "So—We Are No Longer Dragon's Descendants?" The majority of those who weighed in sounded critical of Wu's idea. Han Han, a young antiestablishment writer of a widely read blog, argued sarcastically that if "ability to please" was to be the prime quality of China's national mascot, a golden retriever would be an excellent choice.[2]

Whatever their point of view regarding the dragon, Chinese leaders find animal-related metaphors attractive. At his 2005 annual press conference, for example, Chinese premier Wen Jiabao likened China to a "friendly elephant" (though that animal is a traditional symbol of India).[3] The creature's gigantic yet placatory posture makes it an ideal candidate for China's charm incarnation.

For whatever reasons, the dragon was not chosen as the mascot for the Beijing Olympics. In late 2008, with the Hollywood animated movie *Kung Fu Panda* chopping up box offices everywhere and two pandas delivered to Taiwan, the debate picked up new momentum. In an article published by numerous media outlets, Yuan Yue, a popular Shanghai Television talk show host and the CEO of a major polling organization, proposed the panda as China's new national symbol. Yuan praised pandas for being "cuddly," "cute," and "basically having no negative connotations," whereas dragons looked "imperial and aggressive."[4] The online responses, however, showed the public far less enthusiastic about calling themselves "panda's descendants."[5]

Beijing probably will not officially enshrine an animal as China's state mascot any time soon. In fact, media outlets choose to go after such stories at least in part because of their sensational component.[6] However, there is no doubt that the Chinese government has been attempting to project a nonthreatening image to the rest of the world. On various international occasions, Chinese leaders have made frequent references to the country's "peaceful rise [*heping jueqi*]," a concept first coined by the former vice president of the Chinese Communist Party School, Zheng Bijian. Realizing that the word *rise* still bears a sense of forcefulness and thus is not reassuring enough, the Information Office of the Chinese State Council formally changed the term to "peaceful development [*heping fazhan*]" in a December 2005 government white paper.[7]

As I began to trace signs of China's campaign to refurbish its official and anecdotal image, stories about another country's similar efforts entered my vision. At about the same time that Chinese netizens were debating which creature was most qualified to symbolize their country, an annual review of the year's best-selling books in Japan showed that a political book, *Utsukushi kuni he* (Toward a Beautiful Nation), was in fourth place.[8] The author, Abe Shinzō, became prime minister in September 2006. At the age of fifty-two, he was the youngest politician to assume this post in postwar Japanese history. With his popularity rate at over 70 percent and his book sitting atop the charts, the nation apparently had high expectations for this young and aspiring politician. Even Pupu, a brand of ice cream that Abe claimed to crave, saw its sales grow.[9]

Abe's tenure, however, turned out to be a chain of disasters. One minister took his own life, a few others resigned amid scandal, and most significantly, in what political scientist Gerald Curtis has termed Abe's Hurricane Katrina, social security records disappeared for more than fifty million pensioners. The young prime minister saw his popularity rate dip to just over 30 percent, and under his leadership, the Liberal Democratic Party lost the August senate election by a humiliating margin. In September 2007, a thin, pale Abe announced that he would resign. He spent most of the remaining days of his premiership in a hospital ward.

Despite his short-lived tenure in office, Abe's vision for a "beautiful Japan" has more enduring implications. First, he was not alone. Asō Tarō, a like-minded conservative who became prime minister in 2008, was another vocal proponent of emphasizing Japan's charm. Known as an *otaku* (comic book geek) and devouring comic books even while in office, Asō seemed to have no problem embracing this somewhat derogatory title. In a speech delivered at the Digital Hollywood University in 2006, Asō, then serving as foreign minister, urged professionals in the Japanese digital industry to boost Japanese pop music, animation, and fashion to help a national political cause. He exhorted his audience that the Japanese

> have a grasp on the hearts of young people in many countries, not the least of which being China. What you are doing through your work is something that we over at the Ministry couldn't do if we tried. And that is why I say that you are the people who are the new actors involved with bringing Japanese culture to the world. . . . To put this another way, one part of diplomacy lies in having a competitive brand image, so to speak. Now more than ever, it is impossible for this to stay entirely within the realm of the work of diplomats. It is necessary for us to draw on assistance from a broad spectrum of people who are involved in Japanese culture. And so, I am speaking to you here today to urge you to join with us in polishing the Japan "brand."[10]

In addition to Abe's vision for a more beautiful Japan and Asō's speech about branding the country, popular attention to the power of Japan's imagery is also present in media representations. Douglas McGray, an American freelancer, became an instant celebrity in Japan after he wrote a piece, "Japan's Gross National Cool," in which he provided a long list of achievements that has made Japan cool—the country's high level of technological sophistication, state-of-the-art industrial design, and globally acknowledged achievements in films and literature, among many others. Even a decadelong economic stagnation, McGray contended, had done little to tarnish Japan's image.[11]

There is, however, an implicit tension between McGray's acclaim and politicians' increased efforts to construct a more beautiful Japan. If Japan has always been cool, why are its leading politicians feeling the urge to revamp its image? In whose eyes is Japan not cool? How have Japan's neighbors responded to its wooing effort?

The contrast between Japan's popularity campaign and China's branding effort highlights some larger issues that arise from such comparisons. First, whereas Japan has been a solid electoral democracy for more than six decades, China has consistently defied the global trend toward democratization. In fact, according to democratization scholar Larry Diamond, China's rise has contributed to the slowing down and reversing of democratization movements elsewhere.[12] Hence, analyzing a powerful democracy and its neighboring giant nondemocracy's charm offensives leads to intriguing questions: How do China and Japan promote their international images? What can their similarities and differences tell us about the relations between diplomatic wooing and the political nature of a regime?

The two processes are not only comparable but also interactive. Enhancing popularity ideally should be about better self-advertisement. In practice, however, one way to increase one's attractiveness to an audience is to belittle a third party.[13] Japan and China have yet to make peace with their pasts. To what extent has a zero-sum mentality influenced their efforts to construct positive state characters, and do their respective charm offensives contain components of Othering?

In short, Japan and China are democracy and nondemocracy, materially interdependent yet emotionally antagonistic, qualities that make a comparison of these two countries an excellent way to explore diplomatic wooing in different settings and how international competition has been embedded in this process.

Soft Power and New Contextualizing Possibilities

Image, branding, charm, wooing—all these terms inevitably lead to the growing literature on soft power, a concept first coined by political scientist Joseph Nye in his 1990 book *Bound to Lead: The Changing Nature of American Power*. When policymakers, media professionals, and scholars in both China and Japan discuss their countries' charm offensives, they frequently use the terms *ruan shi li* and *sofuto pawā*, the Chinese and Japanese translations, respectively, for "soft power." A January 2011 search for *ruan shi li* at Baidu.com, China's top search engine, located more than fourteen million entries. A similar search at Yahoo! Japan, that country's top search engine, found nearly four million entries. Although these numbers can tell us little about the depth of popular understanding of soft power, they do offer hints about the breadth of its usage.

The idea of soft power has made important contributions to the study of international relations yet is also superficial and is overused. The term can describe almost anything with the possible exception of the use or the threat of use of military power. Are all of the tens of millions of people discussing soft power talking about the same thing?

What is soft power? According to the concept's inventor, it is "not force, not money," but "shared values."[14] Soft power is "the power over opinion" and "the power to inspire dreams and desires."[15] Instead of intimidating others into compliance, a country exercising soft power will achieve that goal by launching charm offensives, convincing other countries to perceive the wooing country as an example and voluntarily follow its preferences.

Nye's concept adds a fresh perspective to our understanding of international relations. The adjective aside, the word *power* has intellectual connections with classical international relations (IR) theories, which are unmistakably power-based. Early IR theorists offered few thoughts on charm's role in diplomacy. Indeed, what determines a country's place in the jungle of survival is not whether the country is liked but whether it is credibly feared.[16] Security is the fundamental goal for every country. Economic prosperity and military strength, though desirable qualities themselves, are crucial means for protecting and enhancing a country's security. Smaller countries can maintain their existence as long as their leaders appreciate the ultimate wisdom of knowing their countries' places vis-à-vis others and being content with that place.[17] The nature of such power is unapologetically coercive, threatening, and static. "He who has the sword makes the rule" becomes an enduring pattern of international relations.

Soft power dismisses the role of swords and highlights that of roses. It is essentially about enhancing interest through diplomatic wooing. To be sure, some IR theorists prior to Nye also pointed out the importance of fascination and attraction.[18] But Nye was the first to succinctly summarize these sporadic thoughts into a power-related concept. His key contribution lies in adding new contextualizing possibilities for our analysis of power. IR theorists have long argued that power is not fungible.[19] That is, power in one issue area cannot be easily transformed into power in a different issue area. For example, the formidable military deterrence of the United States is irrelevant in disputes with Canada and Mexico. Power's lack of fungibility means that analysis of it has to be contextualized.[20] According to Nye, one way of contextualizing is to differentiate between hard and soft uses of power. Power struggles among states include not only "hard" contests characterized by coercion, saber rattling, actual use of force, and the like but also charm offensives—that is, nation-states attempting to become more legitimate, reassuring, attractive, reliable, and convincing.

One can further juxtapose soft and hard uses of power with issue areas in international relations. One possibility, as Nye suggests, is to dissect IR into a three-level hierarchy. At the top are military issues, where hard power factors continue to dominate. In the middle are economic issues, an arena that Nye perceives as tilted toward hard power concerns yet less frightening than guns and missiles and hence softer. The lowest level consists of transnational issues such as environmental changes and exchange of ideas. In Nye's words, a country "must win both horizontally and vertically."[21] The lower the level in this hierarchy, the more mutually dependent a country finds its relations with other countries and the more important it is for the country to achieve goals by soliciting willing cooperation rather than by intimidation.

Ever-accelerating economic and social integrations have expanded middle- and lower-level issues while shrinking those at the highest (and hardest) tier. Threat or actual use of physical force is becoming increasingly costly and ineffective, even when relations are structurally imbalanced, as the U.S. war effort in Iraq and NATO's increasingly difficult campaign in Afghanistan demonstrate.

As a result, force is losing relevance as a hard power resource, particularly in governing relations among major powers. Germany's relations with its European Union (EU) neighbors are a case in point. As long as the country's de facto leadership role is caged in the EU's multilateral framework, no members of the EU need fear the rise of the Fourth Reich.[22] In fact, when Polish prime minister Jaroslaw Kaczynski used the Holocaust to justify more voting shares for Poland vis-à-vis Germany, fellow EU members dismissed his proposal as "crass, amateurish, and deplorably nationalistic."[23] Kaczynski's failure paradoxically reflects EU member states' lack of urge to contain Germany. The country's postwar reputation has won confidence and trust. Even in places such as the Taiwan Strait, where threats are real and costs are high, a web of economic penetrations among major players has effectively tamed extreme moves by any one actor.[24] Nye and like-minded scholars argue that as the possibility of achieving results by threatening or conquering declines, the wooing dimension of international relations has become more important. States used to get what they wanted by using or threatening to use force. Now they try to achieve their goals by convincing and attracting.

Unresolved Problems

Since its genesis, the rapid adoption of the term *soft power* by both scholarly and popular discourses has attested to its attraction: simple, vivid, and instantaneously sensible. Yet the fast-expanding terrain of the term's usage also makes it easy to neglect or in some cases exacerbate its unresolved problems. Conventional wisdom has placed too much attention to popular culture and too little to the state, leaders, and history. As a result, there is a growing gap between soft power in theory and soft power in practice. A difference exists between how the concept ought to be read and how it has been read and executed in diplomacy.

This confusion is triggered by an implicit prodemocracy bias. That is, mainstream scholarship sees a democracy as logically a better candidate for promoting soft power as a consequence of the universal appeal of the values it embodies: openness, human rights, and freedom. Indeed, Nye asserts that soft power is a staple of daily democratic politics and that narrow values and parochial cultures are less likely to produce soft power.[25] In other words, a democratic state ought naturally to be more attractive than a nondemocratic one.

Based on this assumption, one would wonder why the Chinese government would get excited about soft power. Beijing ought to shudder at even the mention of the term. After all, few in the world, including China's citizens, would see the country as a democracy with an enviable human rights record. Quite the contrary is true. But the passion the term has stirred up inside China is real, and *ruan shi li* has joined the Chinese diplomatic vocabulary. Both the Chinese government and its people see the term as relevant and useful. And not only the Chinese are reinterpreting this term to fit their needs. The coverage of China's rising soft power has appeared in non-Chinese media outlets, including the *New York Times*, the *Financial Times*, CNN, and the *Asahi Shimbun*, to name just a few. Mainstream media in the democratic world seem to despise China's suppressive political nature yet acknowledge the country's "softer" influences.

Nowhere is this awkward coexistence better illustrated than a 1996 *Newsweek* cover that portrays China as a young man forcefully pounding the globe underneath him. The man's left side presents an upbeat picture: a white-shirted professional with skyscrapers, planes, highways, trains, and satellite antennas in the background, all symbolizing China's roaring march toward modernization. The young man's right side, however, is all about threats: he is a soldier waving the Chinese flag, and the background is filled with missiles and fighter jets. The text reads, China: Culture, Economy, and Military Power—The New Giant Flexes Its Muscles.[26] The outside world knows of China's unpleasant political nature, but the country can still claim charm elsewhere. The world simultaneously adores and abhors China's ascendancy.

Being a democracy may be one wooing resource, but its place in international relations is not guaranteed and is not invariably prioritized. Values in the international realm must be differentiated from those cherished domestically. Moreover, as categories, both "democracy" and "nondemocracy" may have separate editions for international and domestic consumption. That is, a democracy can act arbitrarily in international politics and in so doing render its domestically cherished democratic values largely irrelevant. By the same token, an authoritarian state could woo diplomatically by posing as conciliatory and consensual, making its undesirable domestic policies irrelevant to foreign recipients.

This phenomenon might be considered the darker side of soft power. But given that the assumption itself is value-laden, "underexplored" or "unexpected" would be more accurate ways of describing this disconnect. Whatever adjective is used, scholars face the challenge of exposing this darker or unexpected dimension rather than making an implicit yet teleological arrow pointing from democracy to soft power. Otherwise, the gap between soft power in theory and in practice will be increasingly difficult to bridge.

Even for a democracy, the prodemocracy assumption creates problems. The established wisdom asserts that unlike hard power, with most of its resources controlled by the state, a charm game is much less coordinated. The role of the state, particularly a democratic one, is much more limited, as resources that constitute soft power come primarily from society rather than from government.[27] This point should not necessarily be viewed as a defect. Rather, this means that a vibrant and pluralistic culture can glow naturally (hence the "Cool Japan" thesis), and the state can help by becoming an artful salesman.

Two problems emerge from this kind of analyses. First, it leads to a vast exaggeration of the role of popular culture in international relations, even to the extent of equating soft power with popular culture; second, it confuses the issue of who possesses soft power. On the first issue, sensational coverage of popular fascination with cultural products (songs, movies, cuisines, literature, and the like) ignores a simple human capability: People can harbor conflicting messages. We can fall in love with all these foreign goods but still remain suspicious of foreign governments. In 2002, a year when 49.1 percent of Japanese felt unfriendly toward China, while only 45.6 percent said otherwise,[28] one Chinese-Japanese joint survey also showed that the Japanese public's top impression (chosen by 36 percent of respondents) about China was that it "has a unique culture and tradition." The second-most-popular answer was "No impression," at 15 percent. Answers with negative connotations (China being polarized and crime-ridden, self-centered, or bureaucratic) garnered percentages no higher than the low teens.[29] Combined these two polls reveal disconnectedness, as the positive "cultural-tradition" frame has apparently done little to soothe political hostility.

China is not unique, as contemplations of Japan's soft power also expose this problem. Hardly any discussion of Japan's soft power fails to mention the country's popular culture, with a few predictable commercial icons like Hello Kitty, Pokémon, and Doraemon. Hollywood blockbusters with Japanese themes, such as *The Last Samurai* or *Memoirs of a Geisha*, are also unsurprising references. Despite the immense popularity of such icons, questions remain: Do these cultural icons automatically become power, or are we just talking about popular culture for its own sake? What diplomatic goals has the global acclaim for Japan's coolness helped the country achieve? Here, a metamorphosis from culture to power is assumed rather than proved. But the coexistence of the popularity of these icons in China and South Korea and these two countries' deeply entrenched political suspicions toward Japan should serve as an intuitive warning: Commercial successes do not necessarily smooth over diplomatic hostilities. Japan's own researchers seem to realize this problem. Konno Shigemitsu laments that the Japanese preoccupation with soft power, with its single-minded focus on popular culture, is only "soft" without "power."[30] Beyond China and Japan, there are other victims of this Midas Touch–like assumption of iconic commodities' diplomatic impact. Mickey Mouse, rock and roll, McDonald's, and Coca-Cola are just a few examples abused in contemplations of U.S. soft power.[31] These products or brands, known for their Americanness, indeed enjoy high popularity around the globe, even among the young generations in the Islamic world.[32] Yet these well-liked icons apparently have done little to lessen suspicion or even hatred toward the United States as a government.

While the adjective *soft* may sound nonthreatening, the decisive component of the term is still *power*. Soft power, therefore, is instrumental, self-interested, calculating, and competitive, qualities that it shares with its harder cousin. Promoting a state's charm is not a political pageantry. We still need to examine what the goal is and whether it has been achieved through softer means.

This point leads to a further critique of the mainstream scholarship: Who possesses power? There would be little doubt about the answer if the question concerned hard elements such as the military. But in large part because of our fascination with popular culture, Mickey Mouse and Big

Macs seem to be able to claim soft power. Both are indeed popular, but neither Disney nor McDonald's is charged with the responsibility of making U.S. foreign policy. Popular culture and commercial successes may be treasure troves, but in and of themselves, they are only capabilities waiting to be transformed into power.

Bring the State Back In

Acknowledging the merits and limits of the conventional wisdom, I highlight the role of statist actors in creating soft power. The central question I examine is how governments and leaders seek to protect and enhance national interests through soft diplomatic mechanisms such as wooing, persuading, setting up examples, and the like. In other words, this book is not just one more cheerleader for soft power. Rather, I expose how mainstream scholarship has become an increasingly superficial part of the intellectual hoopla regarding cultural or commercial issues, overlooking players that really matter in using softer approaches to achieve diplomatic goals—governments and leaders. Coverage of cultural or commercial successes may be fun, but it may be irrelevant to power. After all, statist actors, not cultural icons or private enterprises, possess power both hard and soft. Furthermore, though approaches may be soft, the underlying concerns may be quite zero-sum-based and antagonistic. Unfortunately, popular discourses on soft power have become increasingly value-laden and morally suggestive, going so far as to equate soft power with "nice" power. This is wrong: Soft power can be as confrontational and competitive as its harder counterpart as long as they serve the same master of national interests.

Jointly, these two recognitions stress the connection that soft power literature carries with traditional power-based IR perspectives. Locating its intellectual roots will help us "harden" our understanding of soft power before it becomes too soft and irrelevant. Governments and leaders promote soft power through wooing essentially by using nonthreatening approaches to lessen foreign hostility, win international acceptance and consent, and secure other countries' cooperation on policy issues. Clarifying this concept leads to ideas for further research on the different shades along the spectrum of power and on the possibilities between softer and harder diplomatic approaches, recognizing the goal-oriented and state-led nature of both approaches.

An emphasis on the state is a logical consequence of identifying the three main sources of soft power: political values, legitimacy of foreign policy, and popular culture.[33] Scholars' extensive discussions of how these three factors shape a country's charm often overlook the fact that they are consequences rather than spontaneous entities and that important forces lead to their production.

The state's role in embodying values and making foreign policies is obvious. Political values such as freedom of expression and the right to vote would lose much of their meaning without being housed by formal institutions at the state level. When Chinese students took to the streets in 1989 to demand more freedom, they waved banners bearing stars and stripes. Tiananmen Square's Goddess of Democracy, a ten-meter-tall statue made of foam and papier-mâché, also bore a striking resemblance to the Statue of Liberty. All these gestures openly displayed Chinese students' admiration for the political values and democratic rights for which the United States was perceived to stand.

Similarly, the Cold War Soviet-U.S. rivalry had a major ideological angle involving communism versus capitalism. Though terms of choice varied, including *beacon of light* and *evil empire* depending on whether one spoke as an alliance member or an enemy, both superpowers were perceived by each other as well as by their junior partners as the leading force for a set of universal ideas and values. A nondemocracy's control of political values is even less disputable. The term *nondemocracy* in itself says a lot about the regime's very limited tolerance of noncompliant ideas. These states do not just have their officially sanctioned values and ideas. Rather, these ideas exist to the extent of disallowing contesting views.

Values in the international realm are even more subject to state initiatives. A democracy that upholds principles of human rights and fundamental freedom may choose not to abide by the same democratic ideals on the international scene. Conversely, a nondemocracy may not necessarily sound like a bully in international politics. Harry Harding has pointed out the irony that the United States sometimes handles its relations with other countries in a manner that differs little from the way the Chinese government controls its domestic subjects, with a common arsenal that includes intimidation and domination. China, by contrast, is learning to use the language of tolerance and democratization in international politics, as Beijing repeatedly emphasizes the need for "dialogue," "consensus," and "multilateral cooperation."[34] Such tactics seek to kill two birds with one stone—to legitimize China's authoritarianism and to weaken U.S. credibility.

The differentiation between domestic and international values also leads to the acknowledgment of the state's role in crafting foreign policy, an arena that states used to monopolize. Even with the ever-expanding presence of nongovernmental organizations and multinational corporations, states remain the most important actors in international relations, the only political organizations that can credibly claim legitimacy in speaking on behalf of the entire citizenry. Furthermore, nonstate actors in non-democracies would envy whatever limited progress their counterparts in democracies have achieved. In political environments where the right to assemble and freedom of speech are not respected in any meaningful way, nonstate actors have a much harder time gaining any input in the making of foreign policy.

Finally, few observers would deny that authoritarian regimes control popular culture. The degree of state penetration varies. North Korea, for example, stands at one extreme: The state dictates nearly every imaginable aspect of mass culture, even such trivial matters as the length of skirts or what styles of pants are deemed appropriate for women.[35] Chinese artists, however, seem much freer. However, the authoritarian tutelage means that if the Chinese government chooses to interfere, it can still exert massive influence beyond the wildest dreams of a democratic government. State interference may take the form of ordering TV stations to show only Chinese-made cartoons during peak times, banning the use of dialects in movies and TV dramas, ordering mandatory screening of "patriotic" movies, or limiting each TV station to one reality show per year. Some of these regulations have triggered widespread complaints from the industry and the public, but once the order comes out, they have no option but to follow. Hence, whatever cultural scene exists in China is there because of the government's encouragement or at least leniency. Pluralism is artificial, and vibrancy is nothing more than a facade.

A democratic state's role in popular culture is debatable, but historically, democratic states can be behind the promotion of national charm. During the Cold War, for example, the Central Intelligence Agency funded cultural exchange programs with the communist bloc in hopes that Soviet visitors would be impressed by Americans' "spectacular freedom to speak our minds" and would learn that "the free world was not just a political cant."[36] In the 1980s, a survey found that Voice of America (VOA), a broadcast agency under the State Department's jurisdiction, became the most credible source of information for Chinese college students.[37] VOA not only broadcast news but also carried programs that exposed Chinese listeners to literature, football, movies, and jazz, a whole new world full of fascinations.

The American government, of course, is not unique in promoting its country's allure abroad. In more recent years, South Korea has been one state that has effectively advertised its national charm. The "Korean wave" that has swept across East and Southeast Asia could not have maintained its momentum without the financial and organizational support of the South Korean government.[38] In 1998, countless Beijing residents became familiar with Korean President Kim Dae-jong, who greeted them every day before the 6:30 evening news with a warm invitation to visit his colorful country. The South Korean government has also hired both Korean and foreign celebrities as "cultural ambassadors" to entice tourists.[39] The South Korean case shows that a democratic state is by no means passive, even with regard to assuming a role in promoting society-based popular culture.

Three Sources, Three Images

How, then, do we assess the state's effectiveness in enhancing its soft power? Such assessments can come from observing interactions among three images corresponding to the three sources of soft power: state image based on values, diplomatic image based on the legitimacy of foreign policy, and popular image based on cultural and commercial products. Charm or lack thereof is the product of interactions among these images. These three images do not carry equal weight in making soft power. State and foreign policy images are most relevant to achieving diplomatic goals. A country's popular image, no matter how much buzz it generates, is least effective. Even when successful, popular image can become irrelevant if images in the other two arenas are seriously tainted.

Contextualization is the essence of power analysis. Here, I emphasize the notion of "recipient context." Conventional wisdom tends to treat the global audience as an abstract, unified entity, and the audience's scale may indeed be global. But its compositions and characters are always local. Different countries and regions have varied historical experiences that lead them to prioritize values differently. Such prioritization can change over time. Soft power analysis is thus as much a study about the target to be wooed as about the wooing source.

In Southeast Asia, for example, values of noninterference and equality outweigh the wooing country's democratic status. Thus, even though only 13 percent of Thais believe that China is democratic, more than 60 percent feel that China has played a positive role in constructing a new international order, and 86 percent support establishing "special relations" with China.[40] In Japan in the 1970s, conversely, popular outcries for meaningful independence and autonomy from America twisted into fantasies of China as a model of these desirable qualities, despite the country's highly interventionist foreign policy and barren popular culture. These cases reveal that the hierarchy of values is neither uniform nor static.

The more comprehensive a wooing source's charm across these three image areas, the more stable its soft power will be and more able it will be to solicit acceptance and cooperation from the target. But striving for such an encompassing charm may simply prove unrealistic. Differences in domestic values, for example, may be impossible to bridge. Effective wooing, however, is possible if a value-based common ground can be detected and if that common ground can be emphasized. If the effort of customizing values succeeds, local surrogates can propagate the wooing state's charm. The presence of these willing recipients is most crucial for achieving voluntary embrace of the wooing state.

Figure 1 illustrates this analysis. All three sources of soft power must be filtered by different recipient contexts. Two contextual factors influence which value(s) the targeted recipient prioritizes: the country or the region's historical experience and the wooing country's existing image (stereotype). Such recipient contexts subsequently shape the wooing party's consideration of what values will be prioritized and how to make new policies or frame existing ones to credibly reflect these values. Such strategies, if executed successfully, will enhance the wooing party's charm. The pattern between the wooing and the wooed thus becomes interactive.

In addition, diplomatic wooing does not unfold in a vacuum but is subject to the wooing country's domestic agendas. Successful wooing demands not only a firm grasp of what the recipient wants but also synchronization of the wooing country's domestic and diplomatic agendas. Lack of consistency between these two sets of agendas will hurt the credibility of wooing. For example, despite its promising start, the effect of China's "peace offensive" toward Japan was seriously compromised by Mao's increasingly erratic and radical domestic agenda.

Making charm relevant to power requires assessing the effect of such charm offensives. Doing so requires differentiating the targeted audience into elite and masses. For the former group, one can observe whether there is the emergence of local surrogates that will act as willing interpreters—that is, will voluntarily propagate the wooing country's charm within their home audience and will seek policy coordination with the wooing country (agenda sharing). For the latter group, polls are key barometers of whether the wooing country is perceived in a generally friendly, indifferent, or hostile manner.

A dotted line separates popular culture from the other two components of soft power, suggesting the uniqueness and possible irrelevance of popular culture in soft power. Songs, movies, fashion, and cuisine are but a few examples of products rich in cultural meaning. As commodities, they may

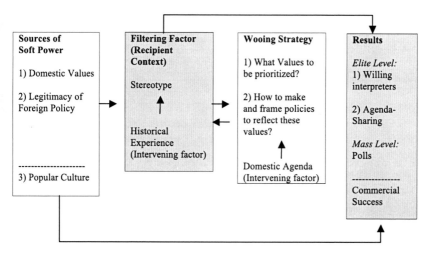

Fig. 1. Soft power—mechanisms and effects

bypass historical sensitivities and become admired even by a politically hostile audience. Such commercial successes, however, do not automatically turn into political leverage. A country's culture may be viewed as cool while its foreign polices or domestic values are despised. In this scenario, popular culture operates in a self-contained, commercialized universe. It is still soft but loses its connection with power.

Figure 1 also deconstructs Nye's concept of soft power into different components and presents its execution as a dynamic, ongoing process. In so doing, the figure clarifies what soft power is not—particularly how it differs from propaganda and public diplomacy, two closely associated but qualitatively different concepts.

To be sure, the three concepts overlap. Both soft power and propaganda seek to influence a given audience's perception of a targeted issue. The two questions raised in the "wooing strategy" box are common tasks for both soft power promotion and propaganda campaigns. However, the adjective *soft* dictates that soft power is about how to attract and soothe an audience, while propaganda serves more diverse purposes, including how to convincingly intimidate and menace. The two concepts also differ in tactics: To make a country's charm convincing requires value-based bonding, which in turn demands authenticity. In other words, the audience needs to be convinced that the values the wooing source preaches are the same values it faithfully practices—the power of setting up examples. Propaganda, conversely, may include cheating, fabricating, and coercing. Finally, in terms of conceptual scope, soft power is a diplomatic concept, whereas propaganda may also target domestic audiences. Soft power and public diplomacy differ in that the adjective *public* speaks volumes about the latter's target. Indeed, the U.S. Department of State's diplomatic handbook defines *public diplomacy* as "government-sponsored programs intended to inform or influence public opinion in other countries."[41] In practice, the term tends to emphasize exerting influence through cultural exchanges, television and radio programs, and movies.[42] But soft power is more comprehensive in that it aims to enhance its charm at both the elite and public levels and in that the mechanisms it employs are more diverse than relying on cultural mechanisms, whose utility for enhancing power should be viewed with a grain of salt.

Method

This project relies on a combination of archival research and interviews. The archival research spans English, Chinese, Japanese, and Korean resources, including declassified diplomatic files, politicians' memoirs, newspaper editorials, scholarly works, and polls. I conducted interviews with diplomats, lawmakers, members of nongovernmental organizations focusing on international exchanges, political scientists, and media professionals in China, Japan, the United States, Taiwan, and South Korea. My goal was to get data on both the intentions of the wooing parties and the reception of wooing efforts by their targets. The majority of the interviews were informal, usually in the form of private conversations. I found them more useful than formal ones, as people were more open in casual settings. These conversations helped me detect genuine attitudes behind public messages, such as the Othering China consideration behind Japan's charm offensives, that seldom appear in official documents.[43] Reflection on the shortcomings of the policies followed by interviewees' countries was another theme that often surfaced in these conversations. This point was particularly useful in the Chinese context, where public criticism of the government and living leaders remains largely taboo.

I also used polls to estimate the popularity of the wooing party among the receiving masses. Polls can be volatile, yet this characteristic serves the purpose of this research well. After all, contextualization requires understanding what value strikes a chord with the intended foreign audience. Moreover, a longitudinal analysis of polls can illustrate the trajectory of popular mood in the wooing country. In some cases, discrepancy between poll numbers and events may lead to intriguing questions. For example, recent polls show that the Japanese public cited "anti-Japan sentiment [*han'nichi kanjō*]" as a prime reason for China's declining popularity. Yet, a historical analysis reveals that there is nothing new about such Chinese views. The real question thus becomes why the sentiment now bothers the Japanese.

Analysis of soft power thus requires historicization. Although the concept is relatively recent, countries have long used softer means (attracting, convincing, persuading, and so forth) to achieve diplomatic goals. Empirical examinations of soft power, however, seem to focus on contemporary trends.[44] This is unfortunate, for scholars are thus competing with journalists to see who can most vividly describe events. The problem is that interesting and sensational stories that attract readers or viewers do not necessarily indicate power, a point made clear by the superficial acclaim popular culture has generated in our understanding of soft power.

Soft power is not omnipotent. It also does not replace hard power. Nye contends that soft power can be more useful in achieving "general" diplomatic goals rather than specific functional goals.[45] Therefore, by using archival research and interviews, I offer a trajectory-based analysis of the making and achieving of general goals through softer means.

Both China and Japan are powers with global impact, but I have less ambitious goals for this book. The scale of comparisons here is regional rather than worldwide. I am particularly interested in examining Japan and China's efforts to woo each other as well as adjacent countries such as South Korea and Taiwan. A grand comparison on a global scale is beyond my capabilities as a single researcher. Such an analysis would require broader linguistic skills and more time and money than I possess and thus must be undertaken by a team of researchers. This book, however, represents a first step toward a more comprehensive and collaborative project.

I do not examine the wooing of the United States, although both Beijing and Tokyo see their relations with Washington as key to their overall diplomatic agendas. Moreover, Russia, the European Union, Australia, Africa, and Latin America hold considerable weight in Chinese and Japanese diplomacy, but they too are omitted. Situational constraints aside, structural reasons also explain the book's regional focus. China and Japan may have increasingly long arms, but they are still first and foremost East Asian powers. Neither one has attained the level of comprehensive global political, economic, and military presence that the United States enjoys. China and Japan may indeed aim for global stardom, but to achieve this goal, they would still need East and Southeast Asia as a base as a consequence of the two countries' extensive human, material, and historical connections to this area. Unsurprisingly, both Beijing and Tokyo have repeatedly stressed that boosting their relations with neighbors is a top priority. From this perspective, a regional focus reflects diplomatic reality on the ground.

In the final chapter, I go beyond the regional context and demonstrate the wider implications of the key findings. For China and Japan to woo beyond their doorsteps would still require understanding the recipient context, knowing what the audience would value the most, and seeking the loudest value-based resonance or accepting the limits of wooing. Furthermore, these recognitions apply not only to China and Japan but also to other countries.

Chapter Overview

Chapter 1 examines the trajectory of charm in bilateral relations between China and Japan. This relationship can be divided into three phases, with each phase manifesting a unique pattern of diplomatic wooing. During the first phase, from the founding of the People's Republic to the end of the Cultural Revolution, China undertook an active yet inconsistent charm offensive toward Japan, while Japan's recipient context was characterized by the emergence of a cross-ideological audience that cherished values of independence and autonomy. China entered this picture as an exemplar of these two values. Media coverage in Japan, which had a tendency to chase public sentiment, presented China selectively by highlighting it as an independent, autonomous, and even morally superior country despite the fact that it was on the verge of collapse because of the Cultural Revolution. China's charm increasingly evolved into a Japanese fantasy rather than an intentional effort by China. In other words, such Japanese distortion implicitly served a domestic purpose, demonstrating what a strong, independent, and self-confident Japan could achieve if it let its ambition soar.

In the second phase, the "honeymoon era" of the 1980s, Japan not only continued to see China as charming but also began to charm China, which perceived Japan as a modernization teacher. Wooing at the elite level became more balanced, as characterized by the Hu Yaobang–Nakasone Yasuhiro bond. These cordial developments notwithstanding, the honeymoon framing is misleading, since the 1980s also witnessed rising anti-Japan sentiment among the Chinese masses, and this sentiment was implicitly encouraged by China's paramount leader, Deng Xiaoping, who showed a declining interest in wooing Japan.

Japan-China relations entered a new phase in the wake of the Tiananmen Massacre. Charm began to depart from bilateral relations at both elite and popular levels. Instead, an Othering consideration started to spill over into their respective efforts to woo others. Against this background, subsequent chapters examine the two countries' in-group bonding and mutual Othering elsewhere.

Chapter 2 examines China and Japan's efforts to woo countries in Southeast Asia, a strategically vital region. The defining feature in this recipient context is that norms of independence and equality are cherished more than others. A long history marred by interventions, invasions, and a condescending attitude means that both Chinese and Japanese efforts to woo would have to start as mending projects, turning around their legitimacy deficits. Until the mid-1970s, despite their drastically different post–World War II paths, neither China nor Japan fundamentally revamped its image in the region. Whereas China was seen as overly political and extremist, Japan was perceived as economically exploitative. Furthermore, Southeast Asian countries viewed both of these one-dimensional images as precursors to dominance of some kind over the region. There was little soft power to speak of.

The "awakening" of Japan's wooing strategy came in the form of the 1977 Fukuda Doctrine, which held that policies should stress and materialize the norm of equality. The doctrine was well timed, as local elites were desperately searching for non-Western alternatives and thus were eager to act as interpreters for Japanese charm. China's awakening came much later but quickly caught up. Lacking electoral constraints, Beijing became more efficient in making and framing policies to lure Southeast Asia. Southeast Asia thus has prospered by sitting on the fence, enjoying the benefits from its two northern neighbors' rivalry for affection and mutual Otherings.

Chapter 3 examines China and Japan's effort to woo South Korea. This case shows that recipient context not merely conditions the effectiveness of wooing but can be decisive. South Korea's history of ancient superiority and recent humiliation has created a much higher level of both elite and public audience sensitivity toward either Chinese or Japanese dominance. This factor has compromised the effectiveness of both countries' charm offensives toward South Korea.

Japan normalized relations with South Korea nearly thirty years before China did so. For this reason the chapter gives more weight to Japan's wooing efforts toward South Korea. Korean suspicions and Japanese condescension fed on each other, with the result that Japan served as a model without receiving credit for doing so. In other words, South Korea substantively copied yet openly disparaged Japan. Since soft power involves a follower's open acknowledgment of a model's charm, this coupling would constitute precisely the opposite of soft power. Furthermore, South Korea's democratization has not given rise to substantive value-based bonding. On the contrary, Japan's willingness to maintain good relations with South Korea's military regime has added new baggage to the already heavy burden of Japan's history. Many South Koreans see protesting Japan as a new way to celebrate their hard-won democracy. To further dim Japan's charm, the country's economic woes have cast doubt on the allure of its economic model. Japan-bashing is giving way to Japan-passing, hardly a successful story for Japan's soft power.

China's rise has probably contributed to the Japan-passing perception among South Koreans. Japan's failure to woo, however, has not brought South Korea closer to China. The Korean appreciation of China's importance is based almost entirely on security and material considerations, reflecting China's hard rather than soft power. Two factors have greatly compromised Beijing's efforts to woo South Korea. First, China is far from innocent in South Koreans' collective memory; instead, Korea has been the sole victim, and China forms part of the Other that contributes to the narrative of the Korean nation's heroic quest for independence. Second, Beijing has been squeezed by a conflict between domestic and diplomatic agendas. Driven by its persistent paranoia about ethnic tension, China would sacrifice soft diplomatic gestures toward South Korea to maintain internal ethnic stability. Third, stereotyping remains rampant among both the Chinese and the Koreans. Particularly on the Chinese side, there are signs that South Korea may have even surpassed Japan as the prime target of popular ridicule. These three obstacles have combined to make Beijing's wooing gestures largely ineffective.

Chapter 4 examines Taiwan as a wooing target for China and Japan. Unlike South Korea and the Southeast Asian countries, the issue of national identity still hangs in the Taiwanese air. Having ruled the island in the nineteenth century and for most of the first half of the twentieth, China and Japan are particularly important in shaping the Taiwanese political imagination regarding statehood and national identity. Indeed, they define the boundaries of such imagination: moving closer to one border means moving further away from the other. Hence, the Taiwanese case can reveal not only wooing but also Taiwan's own effort to distance itself from either China or Japan as it navigates its own destination.

While Beijing is more eager to win the hearts and minds of the Taiwanese people, China's charm has been severely abridged by a number of factors. First, a significant and growing portion of the Taiwanese public rejects the Chineseness as a national identity, the ultimate goal of Beijing's charm offensives. Second, even for those Taiwanese who acknowledge their Chinese roots, China's authoritarian nature creates deeply entrenched fear and distrust. In the Taiwanese eyes, political fiascos like the Great Leap Forward, the Cultural Revolution, and the 1989 Tiananmen Massacre are not only horrifying but also harbingers of what could happen if reunification were to occur. Third, the economic gap between Taiwan and China has created a sense of Taiwanese superiority toward mainlanders. Human and cultural exchanges have become regular, yet stereotypes are still rampant. Overall, China as a state holds few charms for the Taiwanese audience.

By contrast, particularly since the 1990s, Japan and Taiwan have engaged in a commingling process that has elevated their relations to quasi-official status. Three factors stand out in such mutual wooing: a positive interpretation of colonial experience, a new bond of democratic identity, and mutual cultural attractions with immense popular support. Jointly, these phenomena have created an upward spiral of bilateral relations. Taiwan has deepened its independence legitimacy among Japanese elites and public alike; in return, Japan has enhanced its diplomatic leverage vis-à-vis China. Notwithstanding its enlarging connections with China, Tokyo has become increasingly flexible in its execution of the One China policy in spite of Beijing's entrenched sensitivity and repeated warnings.

The conclusion discusses new trends in China's and Japan's wooing efforts and examines implications for diplomatic wooing that may apply to a wider context. Beijing's wooing campaign has taken a selectively hardening edge toward democracies in Europe and North America. Chinese leaders have realized that effectively connecting with "Western democracies"[46] in the political realm is virtually impossible (since doing so would require China to compromise on key issues such as Tibet, Taiwan, and freedom of the press). The Chinese government has launched a new campaign to fight with the West for the right to speak, as exemplified by Vice President Xi Jinping's unusually hard-line speech in 2009 in Mexico. China's quest for its right to speak also has wider implications. Such attitudinal hardening in the political realm may usher in a new round of diplomatic Othering by Beijing: By framing the right to speak as a representative of non-Western developing countries, China is abandoning courting the Western market on political issues as a means of enlarging its value-based resonance elsewhere. China's self-promoted charm may thus acquire a harder edge.

On the Japanese side, Prime Ministers Abe and Asō emphasized "value-oriented diplomacy [*kachikan gaikō*]." To convince both domestic and foreign audiences that the term is not just a slogan, such efforts took a broad geographic scope—"the Arc of Freedom and Prosperity" that lines the "outer rim of the Eurasian continent."[47] However, the concept remained a largely Japanese product with little foreign consumption and fell out of vogue soon after its inventors left office. The newly elected Democratic Party of Japan government, despite its initial efforts to warm up to China, witnessed a serious deterioration of bilateral relations and consequently reaffirmed its once strained alliance with the United States. The trajectory identified in chapter 1—soft power's thinning relevance in China-Japan relations—has become all the more apparent.

In addition to examining recent developments in China's and Japan's wooing efforts, the conclusion also summarizes this book's key themes: a critique of the conventional wisdom's questionable preoccupation with popular culture's impact on soft power, an emphasis on the need to analyze recipient context, and a call to place governments and leaders at the center of scholarly examinations of soft power. I also question the academic utility of a term currently in vogue, *smart power*. A dissection of its definition illustrates that there is nothing new in this concept, as scholars have persistently examined its goal (a winning strategy) and its means (how to achieve the proper doses of hard and soft power elements). The value-laden adjective *smart* also casts doubts on the term's intellectual utility. It has gained its popularity partly as a result of rising popular frustration with the Bush administration's foreign policies. This somewhat sensational framing may make the term useful for politicians and media pundits, but scholars of international relations must study the various contextualizing possibilities of power rather than seek to find a magical adjective.

ONE

A Short History of Charm in Japan-China Relations

Given the high level of distrust and antagonism between Japan and China to-day, it is hard to believe that charm has ever played a role in Sino-Japanese relations. Japan, however, was among the first noncommunist countries that the newly founded People's Republic sought to woo. In this process, China found an unexpected army of Japanese recipients, driven by either ideological affinity or commercial lure, willing to propagate or even fabri-cate charm. Given the presence of such fascination, either real or imagined, the two countries' recent attitudinal U-turn demands explanation: Despite extensive material and human connections, how has Japan metamorphosed from a prime target of attraction into the focus of nationwide hatred? How has the Japanese side responded to Beijing's changed approach?

This chapter examines charm's ever-dwindling role in China-Japan relations. The trajectory of bilateral relations can be divided into three phases, with each phase manifesting a unique pattern of diplomatic woo-ing. From the founding of the People's Republic to the end of the Cul-tural Revolution, Chinese leaders, particularly Chairman Mao Zedong and Premier Zhou Enlai, launched a "peace offensive [*heping gongshi*]" charac-terized by conciliatory gestures. These leaders also attempted to build a common identity with Japan by Othering the United States as the com-mon enemy. Such framings struck a cross-ideological chord among the Japanese, who were yearning for independence and autonomy. Beijing's effort to woo was intermittent at best, subject to domestic turbulence. Yet the Japanese popular desire to achieve meaningful independence from the United States by having a more autonomous China policy helped sideline

chaotic Chinese policies. The "charm offensive" was more of a Japan-fab-
ricated, self-serving homegrown phenomenon than a deliberate Chinese
strategy. From the Japanese end, both the continued fear of the spread of
communism and the public befuddlement at China's adolescent temper attest to the shallow nature of China's attraction.

The late 1970s and 1980s marks the second phase, the "honeymoon
era," when material and human exchanges between China and Japan grew
exponentially. Bonding at the top level became more balanced, as characterized by the near-brotherhood between Japanese prime minister Nakasone Yasuhiro and China's party chief Hu Yaobang. Despite such progress,
the label *honeymoon* is misleading, because anti-Japan sentiment began to
explode in China during the 1980s. Hu was eventually sacrificed on the altar of domestic infighting, with conservatives citing his pro-Japan stance as
his major fault. The real puzzle, therefore, is not the cordiality of the relations but why Japan's positive perception of China weathered such storms
at both elite and popular levels. Two factors at play in the first phase—elite
perception and popular discourses—continued the tradition of fabricating charm for China. The country became a unique communist state and,
more important, an eager student of Japan. The interplay between foreign
policy and state images now tilted toward China's progressive state image,
with its anti-Japan sentiment sidelined.

The 1989 Tiananmen Massacre marked the beginning of the end of
charm's role in Sino-Japanese relations. Japanese popular discourses regarding Chinese charm lost major ground as the bond of common values
proved illusive. Given China's rise and Japan's malaise, such fabrication
also no longer had much domestic demand. Leaders still matter, though in
a different direction, as fond feelings were replaced by open hostility. To
some extent, Jiang Zemin and Koizumi Jun'ichirō personified their respective countries' worsened images. The impact from the chilly Jiang-Koizumi
years has been enduring, as their successors are still coping with vengeful
nationalism. At the same time, willing interpreters of Chinese charm have
become few and far between in Japan, and vice versa.

Negative foreign policy and state images feed on each other and create
a downward spiral. Othering has persisted as a mentality and tactic, but
now China and Japan have turned on each other, appealing to third countries. The two countries have used in-group bonding and Othering in their
wooing efforts elsewhere.

Cultural exchanges have largely failed to exert meaningful influence on
diplomatic issues and thus have lost their connection with power. At some

moments, cultural exchanges were charged with political meanings, like the Peking Opera Diplomacy from the Chinese end and the Matsuyama Ballet from the Japanese side. Early in China's "reform and open" era, Japan also dazzled the Chinese public with its technical superiority through a series of exhibitions. A whole generation of Chinese children grew up watching Japanese animation and reading Japanese comic books. Cultural exchanges have become even more robust in recent years, with collaborations by iconic celebrities on a number of movie and television projects. Such cultural exchanges, however, have apparently failed to cushion popular resentment in the realm of higher politics. Unable to be transformed into political capital, such soft exchanges have been delinked from diplomacy, operating in their own commercialized world.

China's "Peace Offensive" against All Odds

The onset of the Cold War cast a huge shadow over Japan's relations with the newly founded People's Republic of China (PRC). At the time, Japan was still under the American occupation, whereas China leaned to the Soviet side. As junior partners in two confrontational camps, the two countries found their room for diplomatic maneuvering greatly restrained, and they had been at war with each other only four years earlier.

Under these structural limits and agonizing memories, one would anticipate that China's new leadership would take an assertive stance toward its former aggressor, now America's alliance partner. China's Japan policy, however, was far more flexible and cannot simply be dismissed as a subsystem of Sino-U.S. relations. Structural and emotional factors indeed constrain individuals, but leaders' personal incentives still matter, especially in the newly founded PRC, where revolutionary leaders like Mao Zedong and Zhou Enlai enjoyed paramount authority.

An example illustrates these leaders' dominant influence on shaping foreign policy direction. At the end of the civil war, American ambassador John Leighton Stuart (Chinese name Situ Leideng) decided to stay in Nanjing, the capital under siege, and attempted to make contact with the Chinese communists. His plan was bold: Even the Soviet ambassador was fleeing to Guangzhou with Chiang Kai-shek's nationalist government. Stuart's effort, however, was shattered by the publication of Mao's indictment of America's imperial control of China, which appeared under the the title, "Farewell, Leighton Stuart! [Bie le, Situleideng!]," adding a level of personal humiliation. A footnote described Stuart as "a loyal agent of

America's cultural aggression of China."[1] Chinese middle school students subsequently were required to memorize and recite the article, engraving the name Situleideng in generations of countless young minds as synonymous with American imperialism. Ironically, in November 2008, nearly sixty years after the publication of Mao's article and thirty years into the normalization of bilateral relations, Beijing staged a grand ceremony to welcome Stuart's ashes back to Hangzhou, the city where he grew up. The man who was once a living embodiment of American plot against China is now touted as a symbol of Sino-U.S. friendship.[2]

China's leadership took a noticeably different approach toward Japan. Beijing's purpose was still utilitarian: It wanted to create more breathing room for the new government among hostile neighbors. But its method was markedly softer. Its first statement on Sino-Japanese relations appeared in a short commentary published by the Xinhua News Agency on January 21, 1949, nearly nine months before the founding of the People's Republic. "Japan's Election and China [Riben de xuanju he Zhongguo]," called on "the two great nations of the Far East to construct a cordial friendship."[3] The *People's Daily*, the Communist Party's mouthpiece, also published a series of editorials in the early 1950s to stress the importance of normalizing relations between the two countries.[4]

In addition to official statements, Mao and Zhou personally invested in projecting a tolerant image to visiting Japanese guests. They launched what can be seen in retrospect as China's first charm offensive or what some Chinese scholars refer to as a "peace offensive [*heping gongshi*]" in an overall hostile political climate.[5] At a time when China's formal diplomatic relations were limited to countries in the communist bloc, Mao and Zhou met regularly with visiting Japanese delegations, attempting to court the guests by assuaging their concerns about war guilt and highlighting the bond between the two countries. As scholars of Sino-Japanese relations observed, an interesting pattern emerged: The Japanese delegations usually brought up the issue of war guilt, and Mao and Zhou would respond that there would be no need to apologize endlessly for the wrongdoings of someone else, the Japanese militarists.[6] In a typical speech, Mao told a group of Japanese diet members on October 15, 1955,

> Our ancestors quarreled and fought—So what? Let's forget all this! We should forget—What is the use of keeping unpleasant things in our minds? . . . It makes no sense to once again demand that you pay your old debts. After all, you have already apologized, and you cannot apologize every day, can you? It is not good for a nation to be bitter all the time. We understand this point.[7]

In another conversation with Nangō Saburō, chief representative of Japan's trade mission to China, Mao even jokingly thanked Japan's Imperial Army, whose invasion "educated the Chinese people, without which they wouldn't have woken up and united, and [the Chinese communists] would have remained inside mountains and could not make it to Beijing to watch the Peking Opera."[8]

Mao made these remarks in his typical style, framing serious issues in colloquial terms and poking fun at his own people and party. His dominant authority could allow him to do so without being questioned about his loyalty. But on a more regular basis, Premier Zhou best embodied China's effort to woo Japan. Zhou was a master at projecting a conciliatory image for China on diplomatic occasions, and he also had more meaningful connections with Japan, having studied sporadically in the country for two years in his early twenties. Zhou met with Japanese delegations more frequently than with any other foreign guests during his twenty-seven-year tenure as China's chief diplomat. China's diplomatic archive shows that from May 15, 1950, when Zhou made his first statement on Japan policy as premier, through June 12, 1975, when he met his last Japanese guest, Fujiyama Ai'ichirō, a former foreign minister, Zhou met Japanese guests a total of 287 times.[9] He received a total of approximately 610 Japanese delegations during these meetings.[10]

Like Mao, Zhou repeatedly dismissed the need for Japanese delegations to apologize. Whereas Mao did so in his characteristic half-joking way, Zhou bashed China itself. On one occasion, Zhou pointed out to the remorseful Japanese guests that a Chinese ethnic group, the Mongolians, had also attempted to invade Japan, though they failed.[11] Zhou's "self-criticism" probably offended Mongolians, for he was referring to the two attempted invasions by Kublai Khan in the late thirteenth century, when China was a part of the Mongol Empire. Such framing, however, renders his effort of posing as tolerant all the more obvious.

The Japanese politicians that Zhou wooed were not necessarily left-leaning. Takeiri Yoshikatsu, the then chief secretary of the quasi-Buddhist Clean Government Party and a messenger between the two governments, remembered with apparent admiration that at a July 1971 meeting, Zhou said that China would renounce its right to demand war reparations from Japan.

> I had thought [the Japanese side] would have to pay around $50 billion. Zhou's answer was totally not what I had anticipated, and my body began trembling. [Zhou told me that] China paid 250 million *liang* of silver for its loss to Japan in the 1894 war.[12] To pay for this, heavy taxes were imposed, and the Chinese people suffered. How cruel it was! We

do not intend to do the same to the Japanese people, as they should not be responsible for the war and made to carry the reparation burden.[13]

Another politician enchanted by Zhou was Nakasone Yasuhiro, a conservative hawk who later became a dominant figure in Japanese politics in the 1980s. Zhou's wife later revealed that the premier sensed that Nakasone was likely to become Japanese prime minister in the future and consequently met with him three times in one day in 1973, with the last meeting ending at 1:30 in the morning. At these meetings, Zhou surprised Nakasone by criticizing Japanese socialists for being "unrealistic" in opposing Japan's right to self-defense.[14] Zhou ultimately saw Nakasone to the door and helped him put on the coat, impressing the young minister so much that a quarter of a century later, he still remembered the episode admiringly: "What a great statesman," Nakasone wrote; "a premier would accompany a [trade] minister to the door and put on a coat for him. It was a learning experience that helped me grow."[15] Such personal esteem did not prevent friction from arising in China-Japan relations during the Nakasone era, but Nakasone's esteem for Zhou was a precursor to the Japanese leader's later bonding effort with his Chinese counterparts, and such top-level bonding could act as a cushion at crucial diplomatic moments. Genuine friendship with Hu Yaobang and the desire to avoid hurting him were a decisive factor in convincing Nakasone to abandon another visit to the controversial Yasukuni Shrine.

As China's revolutionary legends sought to win the hearts and minds of the Japanese audience, their main resistance arose from within China. Yet their authority could allow them to quell such concerns without having their prestige questioned. In one case, Zhou commuted death penalties for Japanese war criminals locked in Chinese prisons. When lower-level prosecutors complained, Zhou explained that the sentence reductions were a means of accelerating reconciliation and that "twenty years from now you will come to appreciate that I made a correct decision."[16] Sai'onji Kazuteru, a reporter for the *Asahi Shimbun*, also revealed that Zhou would send advance teams to places where Japanese guests were to visit. Such teams were charged with explaining to the Chinese hosts that the Japanese visitors were China's "important friends" and must be welcomed warmly and that normalizing relations with Japan was a necessity.[17]

Assessing the Peace Offensive

China's peace offensive, however, was not completely successful. Two factors compromised the effort: first, an incongruity existed between the calm and tolerant image its leaders attempted to project and their increasingly unpredictable domestic agenda; second, Chinese leaders used Othering tactics that at least in the short run justified the Japanese conservatives' concern that China was interventionist and was attempting to export revolution to Japan.

Had China's domestic reality been open and stable, Mao and Zhou's tolerant gestures would have been more convincing. But Mao proved erratic, and a series of mass mobilization movements ensued. As a result, the Japan-targeted peace offensive was interrupted and even derailed by internal political turbulence.

The most serious setback to bilateral relations occurred in 1958 and was triggered on May 2, when a Japanese right-winger removed China's national flag at a stamp exhibition in Nagasaki. The Japanese police quickly released the man on the grounds that Japan did not recognize the People's Republic, so he faced only a misdemeanor damage charge and the episode did not constitute a diplomatic incident. Nine days later, Beijing issued a furious statement and cut off all economic and cultural connections with Japan. No visitors from the PRC set foot in Japan for the next two years, and bilateral trade dropped to almost nothing in 1959.[18]

The same Mao who had been espousing tolerance and understanding was also behind this out-of-proportion diplomatic jolt. China was experiencing his Great Leap Forward, and he had sidelined Zhou and other moderates. The Nagasaki incident occurred as the Chinese Communist Party was convening for the second plenary session of the Eighth Party Congress. As the party archive reveals, at this meeting Zhou's "self-criticism," thus far largely confined to domestic policies, began to spill over into foreign policy. One of his mistakes, Zhou confessed, was not paying enough attention to the chairman's warning that Chinese leaders must remain alert to Japan's "hidden imperialist elements."[19] Zhou's self-bashing may or may not have been genuine: he also privately told his subordinates "not to seal all the windows [with Japan] and not to say things excessively [to the Japanese side]."[20] Yet Mao's eccentric behavior, coupled with his insurmountable authority, compelled Zhou to shelve his peace offensive in favor of political survival.

Another factor that hindered Mao and Zhou's efforts was a Japanese counterpart who at best could be described as lukewarm. Yoshida Shigeru, the architect of Japan's postwar political order, was strongly anticommunist. He explicitly stated that the Japanese government under his leadership had no interest in pursuing political relations with communist China.[21] Hatoyama Ichirō, a prime minister known for pushing for "autonomous diplomacy [*jishu gaikō*]," refused to normalize relations with China if do-ing so meant sacrificing Japan's ties with Taiwan.[22] Conservative Kishi Nobusuke was a leading member of the "Taiwan faction [*Taiwan ha*]" of the Liberal Democratic Party and personally befriended Chiang. Kishi's much less combative successor, Ikeda Hayato, learned from his predeces-sor's forced departure, emphasizing the "politics of patience and tolerance [*hanashiai no seiji*][23] and avoiding risky waters such as dealings with China. Instead, Ikeda focused on improving economic welfare, a realm that could garner public consensus. In short, inhospitable domestic political weather and a wary Japanese counterpart rendered Beijing's wooing intermittent and one-sided. From soft power's perspective, at least at the official level, willing recipients of China's charm were few and far between.

Japan's ruling conservatives' fear of communist China was not pure paranoia. The Othering tactic employed by the Chinese leaders was par-ticularly alarming. Othering was not new to Mao and Zhou; in fact, the strategy would simply require them to replicate the United Front [*tong yi zhan xian*] policy they had used to bond with various social sectors dis-gruntled with Chiang's Kuomintang (KMT) government yet suspicious of the communists. Mao and his lieutenants called for these disparate groups to unite with the goal of overthrowing the KMT, dismissing the groups' differences as minor.[24] Transplanting this approach to Sino-Japanese rela-tions, Chinese leaders sought to recruit enthusiastic Japanese interpreters of Beijing's charm by Othering the United States and Othering Japanese conservatives. Mao's July 1964 speech to a group of Japanese lawmakers clearly illustrates his effort to build a common identity with his Japanese audience based on anti-U.S. grievances.

> Our two countries have a common problem: There is one country standing above our heads. You would think that China is an indepen-dent country, but are we really? The answer is no. We are not yet com-pletely independent. Your situation in Japan is the same. Your Japan is also not completely independent. This is our common point. . . . This is OUR region, and people should control their own countries. Hence we demand America to take its hands off. . . . We are the Japanese people's friends, and we think you understand Chinese people well.[25]

Mao gave many such speeches to various Japanese guests over the years. Likewise, Zhou told Japanese visitors that as a proud country with a long history, Japan "should work hard to surpass America" in normalizing rela-tions with China.[26] Mao's framing of China and Japan as "not completely independent," however, must also be seen in the context of the Sino-Soviet split: Warm up to China would distance Japan not only from the United States but also from the Soviet Union, which coveted Japan's abundant oil and fertile fishing grounds. Thus, courting Japan seemed to Chinese leaders a natural outgrowth of the larger economic and geopolitical forces. Indeed, soon after the normalization of relations with China, the Japanese business community began to secure China as a new provider of oil.

On the surface level, such Othering inevitably brought the two governments on a collision course. Chinese leaders frequently criticized their Japanese counterparts, particularly the governments under Yoshida and Kishi, as "American puppets" intentionally delaying the normalization process.[27] For its part, Tokyo remained suspicious of Beijing's Othering tactics. A confidential file "On the Chinese Communist Party's Foreign Involvement and Domestic Situation," compiled by the Japanese Ministry of Foreign Affairs in March 1955, warned Japanese bureaucrats and politicians that China was attempting to intervene in Japan's domestic politics in the name of a "peace offensive [*heiwa kōsei*]," and that China might try to intervene on a wide range of issues from constitutional revision to elections.[28]

Common-Value Community in the Making: Another Look at Othering

It is easy to notice this confrontational dimension, but a trajectory approach offers new insight into the silver lining of China's Othering tactic. Open hostility notwithstanding, Mao and Zhou's words struck a deeper chord with the Japanese audience. The Chinese leaders were sharp to sense that grievances regarding the United States were not confined to the Japanese Left. Indeed, some conservatives were among the loudest voices arguing that Japan needed to regain its independence from America. Conservatives were also more likely to evoke the common cultural trait that Japan shared with its Asian neighbors, though with an assumption that Japan was Asia's natural leader.[29]

Yoshida admitted that he was torn between the pressure exerted by his U.S. counterpart, John Foster Dulles, to isolate China and his personal desire to recognize the country.[30] Though deeply anticommunist, Yoshida believed that one diplomatic priority was to distance China from the Soviet Union.[31] Indeed, Yoshida felt so strongly about China's "noncommunist" nature that he tried to persuade Dulles to allow Japan to "counterinfiltrate" China through trade activities and wean the Chinese government from the Soviet bloc.[32]

Othering thus is not a uniquely Chinese tactic. Yoshida saw Japan as more capable than the United States of talking to China; he believed that the Japanese (and the British) best understood the Chinese way of thinking, which never embraced communism, as Americans mistakenly believed.[33] In retrospect, however, Yoshida apparently failed to anticipate that a nationalistic China could be just as if not more threatening to Japan as a communist China.

Katō Kō'ichi, a diplomat who later became a Liberal Democratic Party heavyweight in the 1990s, corroborates Yoshida's hidden desire to engage China. When Katō joined the Ministry of Foreign Affairs in 1963, Yoshida made a rare appearance before a joint gathering by participants in different area-study workshops at which the young Katō was the lone China specialist. Yoshida declared that China was the country that "I would like you folks to study the most."[34]

This nuance, though buried at the time by an official war of words, is revealing in retrospect: when Tanaka Kakuei finally set out to normalize relations with China after the Nixon shock, his support crossed the ideological spectrum. Beijing's "United States as common enemy" bonding did not immediately propel Sino-Japanese relations in their desired direction. However, beginning with Yoshida, conservatives commonly perceived Japan as ill-treated by a United States that did not really understand Asia. Frustrations stemming from this grievance would later resonate with Mao and Zhou's Othering after conditions ripened. In a sense, a warmer current with its stress on a common Asianist identity always flowed underneath the icy surface of intergovernmental hostility.

Both Chinese diplomacy under Mao and Japanese Yoshida Doctrine diplomacy thus acquire duality. The former was constantly torn between the independence and noninterference discourse, on the one hand, and the zeal to spread revolution, on the other. As early as in 1950, Mao criticized the Japanese Communist Party (JCP) for being too timid to follow the "armed struggle" course.[35] A schism resulted on the Japanese Left, as Tokuda Kyū'ichi, the then JCP's chair and an open admirer of Mao, fled to Beijing, where he began to give radio speeches promoting violent revolution until his death in 1953. Following Josef Stalin's death, rising tensions with the Soviet Union further convinced Mao that China had become the only guardian of the communist ideal and that he was the rightful leader of this global cause. As China intensified its effort to recruit JCP into its "anti-Soviet revisionism" camp, JCP leaders became increasingly frustrated and suspicious, leading to an open rupture with the Chinese Communist Party (CCP) in 1966. After his failed meeting with Mao, chair Miyamoto Kenji cut off the party's connections with the CCP.[36] In August 1968, after beaten and humiliated by China's Red Guards, the last two members of the JCP left a Beijing engulfed by the fever of the Cultural Revolution.[37] The two parties would not be on speaking terms with each other for the next thirty years.

The JCP had no reasonable hope of becoming a governing force and could thus afford to talk the talk—that is, to stick to its all-out confrontational stance toward China. But the world of Japan's governing elites was much more practical, as politicians and businessmen had to constantly and awkwardly balance the lure of China with an acceptance of the United States as Japan's diplomatic boundary-setter. In this process, a quest for independence from a greater power became increasingly visible as a shared Chinese and Japanese desire. At the same time, the prospect of transforming China once again into an outlet for Japanese goods as well as a provider of raw materials, especially petroleum, remained as alluring as ever. This profit-driven calculation was reflected in Japan's national newspapers' stories on importing Chinese oil to support Japan's continued economic growth.[38] At the time, the scenario of China and Japan locked in a head-to-head competition for resources seemed light-years away. In fact, editors at the *Yomiuri Shimbun* went so far as to imagine Japan helping China explore the oil potential in Siberia should China's economic growth someday create greater demands.[39] All in all, despite Japan's formal adherence to its alliance with the United States, an undercurrent of Japanese grievances, coupled with commercial allure of China's market and resources, was gathering strength.

Against this background, Nixon's blitzkrieg-style 1972 visit to China greatly embarrassed Japan but also offered it a blessing in disguise.[40] Driven by a sense of betrayal and a fear of being left behind, the long-fermented Japanese disgruntlement with the United States exploded. Japan rapidly transformed itself from a passive observer to an active participant in the international momentum of recognizing the PRC. Public discourse exaggerated the shared desire for independence to the point of neglecting China's chaos. Japan-China relations entered a bizarre era. Driven by a package of domestic desires, willing Japanese recipients began to manufacture charm for a China that actually possessed little of it.

The best place to observe such "China fever" is Japan's highly influential national newspapers. Scholars have long noted Japanese newspapers' chasing rather than agenda-setting tendency. This risk-averse habit makes good business sense in Japan's white-hot print media market.[41] What journalists choose to say exemplifies their efforts to mirror popular mood. Not only the left-leaning *Asahi Shimbun* but also the more neutral *Yomiuri Shimbun* and *Nikkei Shimbun* constructed a positive image of China as independent and morally superior despite the fact that the country shut itself to the outside world and was still in the midst of the Cultural Revolution.[42] On January 1, 1973, for example, a *Yomiuri Shimbun* editorial passionately paid tribute to Mao's China and reminded Japanese readers that they had been morally left behind by the Chinese:

> Right now in China, everyone is working hard for the people. As a result, Chinese society's improvement has become a self-fulfilling process. ... In Japan, although it would be unreasonable to expect everyone to work hard for the benefit of the common society, at least people should learn to become more considerate toward one another.[43]

The venue was as important as the message itself. This piece was not an ordinary editorial but a *shin'nen shasetsu* (New Year's editorial). Major newspapers tend to use these pieces to offer a general evaluation of Japan's situation in the past year and suggestions for its direction in the coming year. According to one press veteran, under the forward-looking facade, New Year's editorials are chasing pieces that reflect the Japanese press's attempt to mirror rather than to challenge the public mood.[44] Hence, both the content and the timing of the message reveal the intensity of Japan's China fever. Even the conservative *Sankei Shimbun*, which was known for its pro-Taiwan stance, described China as "our independent neighbor."[45] For its part, the business community was eager to transform China into an outlet for Japanese goods as well as a provider of raw materials, especially petroleum.[46] The pro-China frenzy was thus both emotional and substantive, spanning the ideological spectrum.

Were such positive views of China confined to Japan during this period? After all, leftist forces in North America and Western Europe also perceived Mao as an iconic figure, and the Cultural Revolution inspired massive political mobilizations beyond China's doorstep. Even acknowledging the global scale of the ideological fervor stirred up by Mao, some factors unique to Japan were at work. A useful comparison is to see the mainstream American media outlets' coverage of China prior to Nixon's February 1972 visit. *Time* ran a special report, "A Guide to Nixon's China Journey," in which journalists examined various aspects of the country. Despite the magazine's approving tone regarding Nixon's visit, it cast China in a much less idealistic fashion. In describing the history of Sino-U.S. relations, the editor wrote,

> In a historic tumble of events, the [American] missionary movement was swept by a larger, more militant native movement, which combined

raw terror with a renascent Chinese nationalism. In the process, China has been transformed into a new society whose ideology and structure would defy reconciliation with the U.S.—unless the U.S. too became a Maoist-style revolutionary society.[47]

The report also suggested that the real reasons that the two powers had approached each other were Chinese fear of the Soviet Union and the U.S. legacy of friendship with China, plus "a large measure of Yankee curiosity."[48] Nowhere in the coverage was China framed as an inspiration for the United States. Such a comparison of two allegedly neutral media outlets suggests that bilateral factors made the Japanese press markedly more positive with regard to China.

Strictly speaking, this was not a new round of Beijing's charm offensive, as China was at the edge of total collapse. Rather, the Japanese media were doing China's job for an ultimately self-serving purpose: As influential interpreters, the media were fantasizing China's charm not to appease Beijing but to confront Japan's own status as an underachiever in global diplomacy. China's stress on "independence" presented a hint of what a much stronger Japan could achieve if it let its confidence soar.

Japan's mainstream media also voiced concerns about a perceived moral decay and rise of egoism and consumerism, unfortunate by-products of rapid economic development. But even with regard to this darker side of the Japanese miracle, China could offer clues: The Cultural Revolution, with its utopian zeal of building an altruistic society free of materialistic sins, looked morally inspiring. Seen from this perspective, the *Yomiuri Shimbun*'s construction of a moral contrast between Japan and China no longer seems incomprehensible. But although the editors pleaded with the Japanese to learn from their Chinese counterparts, there were never any calls for readers to copy what the Chinese were doing and to start a Japanese Cultural Revolution. And on some occasions, Japanese correspondents expressed their bewilderment at the unpredictability and fervency associated with the Chinese movement.[49] Japanese journalists apparently were content to keep "learning from China" as only a slogan. Although the desire for independence and autonomy was widely shared, so too were the fear of communism and the consensus of relying on the United States for protection. In this sense, despite their extravagant praise, few Japanese took seriously China's charm.

China's Othering tactic did not change the unilateral and often chaotic rhythm of its peace offensive. It was also subject to Mao's ever-changing domestic agendas. But the tactic did highlight a value cherished by the

Japanese recipients regardless of their ideological standing and thus laid the psychological ground for the normalization process. Tanaka went to Beijing after only two months as prime minister, but the Japanese media did not perceive his trip as at all hasty. Rather, it was justified and, if anything, unnecessarily delayed by U.S. manipulation.[50] China's charm as a diplomatic opportunity to showcase Japan's ascendancy proved too strong to resist. The allure of a foreign country, just like its nemesis, fear, can be conjured up for domestic consumption.

The Honeymoon Facade

The 1980s is popularly referred to as the "honeymoon era" of relations between Japan and China. Looking back on those good old days, mainstream scholarship tends to dismiss such friendliness as a result of two countries embracing each other after many years of separation. The passion was genuine yet superficial and bound to be transient. From this perspective, the cooling down of this emotion beginning in the 1990s hints at more "normal" relations.[51]

This "happy reunion" argument has its validity. But by dismissing this period as an "abnormal" phase of Sino-Japanese relations, this approach glides over the content of each country's charm (or its absence) as perceived by the other. First, the honeymoon era had a darker side: The 1980s was not all about handshakes, toasts, and hugs. A series of disputes surfaced between the two governments, with those involving historical matters becoming increasingly acrimonious. In the mid-1980s, massive anti-Japan protests broke out in major Chinese cities. As Allen S. Whiting points out, the Chinese public had a less-than-desirable view of Japan's foreign policy. With minor exceptions, China's popular feelings toward Japan unmistakably tilted in a negative direction.[52]

As Whiting's book reveals, the 1980s marked the beginning of a reduction in Beijing's efforts to court Japan. From this perspective, the usage of the term *honeymoon* becomes misleading, as it neglects the fact that anti-Japan sentiment was a constant component of Chinese popular emotion of Japan. Poll data can offer insights into this affection gap: the Chinese became more wary of the Japanese than vice versa. A 1988 Sino-Japanese survey shows that 18 percent of Chinese respondents saw Japan as the biggest threat to peace, trailing only Vietnam (with which China fought an intermittent war in the 1980s) and the Soviet Union (with which China had yet to normalize relations). In contrast, less than 5 percent of the Japanese respondents chose China, making the country less threatening than the

Soviet Union, North Korea, the United States, and South Korea.[53] More Japanese thus felt threatened by two formal allies (the United States and South Korea) than by communist China.

Although suspicion of Japan was a constant feature of Chinese popular sentiment, Mao and Zhou could quash this negative sentiment with their paramount authority. Deng, by contrast, felt a greater need to sacrifice Japan to appease conservatives. June Teufel Dreyer characterizes Chinese politics in the 1980s as "loosening" versus "tightening" between conservatives and reformers. Japan policy certainly attests to such a tug-of-war.[54]

The real puzzle thus becomes why the Japanese continued to perceive China as charming much of the 1980s despite rising Chinese resentment? Based on Whiting's findings but making a step beyond his unilateral framework, I analyze wooing from an interactive perspective. Leaders' personal perceptions carried as much if not more weight. Fond feelings at the very top level pushed Japan's China policy toward the softer end, a phenomenon best exemplified by the genuine friendship between Prime Minister Nakasone Yasuhiro and General Secretary Hu Yaobang. Second, popular discourses in Japan continued the tradition of manufacturing charm for China. Not only politicians but also the media were willing to sound conciliatory. The tension between China's state and foreign policy images continued, but elite bonds and popular emotions jointly tipped the balance toward China's progressive state image, thereby sidelining the anti-Japan component of foreign policy.

Nakasone genuinely believed that China was converging with Japan on core values of market economy and open society.[55] Such Japanese optimism led to a greater willingness to be conciliatory to assist reformers in Beijing. Chinese leaders' personal enchantment continued to exist, with a kind of "brotherhood" bond between Nakasone and the reform-minded Hu. Nakasone's memoir offers profuse praise for Hu, calling the Chinese leader a "hero" with "great tolerance and broad vision."[56] Hu was the first Chinese politician to receive the honor of addressing a joint session of the Japanese Diet, and Nakasone made no secret of the fact that he extended this unprecedented invitation to signify his support for Hu's reforms. As proof of their personal bond, Nakasone invited Hu to a family dinner during a 1983 visit. Hu returned the favor by having Nakasone as his family guest the following year. Through such encounters, their sons also became friends.

It took a diplomatic crisis, however, to fully reveal the power of such feelings. After his 1985 visit to the Yasukuni Shrine triggered anti-Japan protests in China, Nakasone sent Inayama Yoshihiro, chair of the New Japan Steel, to China to assess the damage to Japan's image. Vice premiers Gu Mu and Wan Li told Inayama in a secret meeting that Nakasone's visit could weaken Hu's position. The desire to protect Hu, Nakasone admitted, was the key reason that he stopped visiting the shrine.[57]

Despite Nakasone's good intentions, his not-so-subtle friendship with Hu hurt the communist leader, and Conservatives forced him to resign in 1987. An official CCP document listed six reasons. The first four were domestic, as Hu was accused of organizing his inner circle, antagonizing ethnic relations in Tibet, exaggerating the severity of corruption cases, and forcing senior party cadres into retirement. The remaining two involved diplomacy with Japan: Hu was criticized for inviting Nakasone despite his lack of apology for Japan's wartime sins and for causing a "messy situation" by inviting three thousand young Japanese to China.[58]

Two years later, the ousted reformer died of a heart attack, triggering the massive prodemocracy movement that eventually resulted in the Tiananmen Massacre. Nakasone's affection for Hu survived not only his political demise but also his death. After the crackdown, the Chinese government forbade any public mention of Hu. Nevertheless, Nakasone asked the new Chinese leaders for permission to meet with Hu's widow and to bow to Hu's tomb, rare gestures that clearly went beyond the official etiquette. China's new leaders denied both requests.[59]

Nakasone relied more than his brotherly relationship with Hu to support optimism about China. During his 1984 visit, Nakasone received a welcome he described as "unprecedented." In the city of Wuhan, where the two countries had fought a bloody battle nearly fifty years earlier, two million people took to the streets to catch a glimpse of the visiting Japanese prime minister. The CCP was certainly a master at staging massive welcoming ceremonies. But in Nakasone's eyes, the zeal exuded by the Chinese bystanders was unexpected yet genuine, with some people cheering from the rooftops. Nakasone wrote: "I felt so enthused that I decided to get off the car to shake hands with the crowd. But I was quickly surrounded and almost could not breathe. It took the Chinese police and bodyguards so much effort to pull me out of the crowd."[60] Nakasone's optimism was further bolstered by his second visit two years later, when leaders jointly declared "no war ever again" between the two countries. His speech at the Peking University, where students had protested strongly against his Yasukuni visit, met with loud applause, and Hu was in attendance.

Nakasone was not the only high-level Japanese politician to harbor a positive perception of an open and tolerant China, and this perception translated into policy. Japanese foreign minister Ōkita Saburō implied to the press that China's tolerant gesture of renouncing reparation requests played a role in the Japanese government's decision to offer China official development assistance (ODA).[61] Inayama, Nakasone's messenger and the chair of Japan's powerful economic lobbying group, Keidanren, was more explicit: He claimed that given China's tolerance, offering aid to the country became Japan's moral responsibility. To Inayama, ODA would symbolize the reconciliation between two former enemies.[62]

However, the ODA to at least some extent constituted reparations in disguise. China's forbearance was by no means unprecedented. Chiang Kai-shek had officially waived reparations right after the war, and Mao did so again in 1972. Backpedaling by Beijing on such promises would thus have achieved little other than hurting its diplomatic credibility and infuriating the Japanese right wing, and Inayama and Okita must have realized that a failure to provide ODA would have damaged Japan's relationship with China. But by taking the emotional route and framing China as unusually forgiving, their choice reveals the existence of a Japanese audience receptive to such marketing: Japanese eyes would see such a positive image of China as convincing.

Indeed, elite optimism regarding China was echoed at the popular level. According to a senior Japanese diplomat, "Deng's new market orientation was favorably received by the Japanese people, who perhaps had never felt comfortable with China's earlier revolutionary zeal. The new orientation, however, was one with which the Japanese were quite familiar. Throughout the 1980s, it looked as though China's political system also was headed down toward a certain degree of democratization."[63]

The faith that China was eagerly following in Japan's footsteps also supported the encouraging tone of the country's media coverage. Even the left-leaning *Asahi Shimbun* was no longer shy about exposing the political gap between Japan and China, seeing not only Japan's economy but also its democracy as what made the country ahead of China.[64] The *Yomiuri Shimbun*, which had become the country's largest newspaper, urged the Japanese government not to hesitate to give China a hand in its quest for modernization. The paper also praised bilateral relations as "at their best" even in the wake of China's anti-Japan protests.[65] After the 1989 Tiananmen Massacre, the paper's editors reflected remorsefully, "It is after all an illusion that because of Deng's modernization policy, China will share our language of democracy."[66] Paradoxically, the *Yomiuri Shimbun*'s disillusionment revealed the continued practice of fabricating China's allure, a practice implicitly driven by Japanese good feelings about their own country. In essence, it is a natural extension from hailing the Cultural Revolution and pondering what a stronger and more confident Japan could achieve. If there is any difference, it is that the Japanese superiority vis-à-vis China became more comprehensive.

To be fair, other countries joined Japan in viewing Beijing with high expectations. *Time*, for example, illustrated American enthusiasm for China during this period, twice choosing Deng as its Man of the Year. Japanese optimism should also not be written off as simply being superficial or naive, for political developments in China did offer reason for hope. China's liberal-minded intellectuals often write nostalgically about the good old days of the 1980s, particularly the years under Hu, as the most open period they ever experienced.[67]

Yet the 1980s also witnessed the rise of a series of acrimonious disputes between the Chinese and Japanese governments. In 1982, Beijing protested loudly about a new Japanese history textbook that allegedly toned down the country's World War II atrocities. Inside China, a two-month media campaign was waged to remind people "not to forget the bloody history" and to "be aware of the revival of Japanese militarism."[68] Three years later, Chinese college students took to the streets of major cities to protest Nakasone's visit to the Yasukuni Shrine. They also condemned the influx of Japanese goods as constituting a new round of "economic invasion."

Deng showed two faces. On one hand, he offered profuse praise for Japan. During his visit to Nissan's headquarters, for example, Deng wrote, "Learn from the great, diligent, brave, and wise Japanese people. We salute you."[69] He also humbly insisted, "China is not a beauty and should not insist on being referred to as one. . . . We particularly need to learn from Japan"[70] and "to go to Japan to look for elixir of life."[71]

But Deng could also sound like a condescending teacher. Unlike his mentor, Zhou, Deng reprimanded Japan for the wounds it had historically inflicted on China. On one occasion, he bluntly reminded his Japanese guests from the Clean Government Party that "in the entire world, Japan is the country that owes the most to China."[72] Deng also chose to disgrace Japan when meeting with dignitaries from other countries. On April 6, 1987, for example, Deng told visiting Swedish prime minister Gösta Ingvar Carlsson that "on betraying and persecuting the people of China, Japan is No. 1."[73] Two years later, Deng repeated his "Japan owes China the most" remark to Soviet leader Mikhail Gorbachev.[74]

Resentment from China's paramount leader did not go unnoticed on the Japanese side. Yanagitani Kensuke, a senior official at the Ministry of Foreign Affairs, complained to Japanese reporters that Deng had become "someone above the clouds [*kumo no ue no hito*]." Deng took Yanagitani's comments as implying that the Chinese leader was "old and confused" and openly showed his displeasure to a visiting Japanese delegation.[75]

The Japanese responses are more revealing than the Chinese initiations. Such bureaucratic frustration, though reported by the media, largely failed to tarnish the positive perception of China as a progressive socialist state and an eager student of Japan. The view of Japan as so far in the lead implicitly supported perceptions of China as open, eager, and harmless. As one senior Japanese diplomat later admitted, despite China's huge size, Japan perceived China as a "small country" that posed no danger to Japan's leading position in Asia and saw China as possessing the traditional innocence that Japan had lost in its hasty pursuit of wealth.[76] Japan was willing to act in a conciliatory manner toward a much weaker yet idolized counterpart.

Japan's sense of superiority inadvertently enhanced the soft power of a much weaker rival. Governments and the public, just like individuals, can be more tolerant and agreeable when they feel secure and proud. A willingness to listen and to apologize was thus a sign of Japan's strength and self-confidence. From the official to the popular realms, the Japanese willingness to show moderation and concession was evident: Suzuki Zenkō's government conceded to the Chinese request by agreeing to revise the problematic textbook. The *Yomiuri Shimbun* criticized Tokyo's clumsy diplomacy for failing to provide a timely and clear response to China's concerns.[77] The *Asahi Shimbun* went further, explaining that Beijing merely wanted "to see the facts as they were" and "to urge the Japanese people to reflect on Japan's past wrongs."[78] Neither press giant described China's bashing as using history as a card that could gain benefits from Japan, a frame that would become popular in the 1990s. Deng's increased references to historical wounds also did not stop Nakasone from singing the Chinese leader's praises: Deng impressed Nakasone with his "candor on China's internal problems and cordiality."[79] Finally, Yanagitani paid a steep price for venting his dissatisfaction: After Deng became angry, the Japanese diplomat was forced into early retirement.[80]

Throughout the decade, the Japanese public perception of China remained immune to these acrimonious diplomatic disputes. As the annual poll conducted by the Japanese Cabinet Office shows (figure 2), China's image stayed positive, with those who said they were "feeling friendly toward China" remaining between 60 and 70 percent during the 1980s. These polls also illustrate that Japanese public sentiment toward China operated independently from Japan's views about its other major diplomatic partners, South Korea and the United States. The Japanese people have consistently viewed the United States in a very friendly manner, particularly since Barack Obama assumed the U.S. presidency. Positive views of South Korea have moved steadily upward since the late 1990s. In contrast, China was perceived much more negatively after the 1989 Tiananmen Massacre and after massive anti-Japan riots occurred in a number of major Chinese cities in 2004. In 2010, the two countries' bitter quarrel over a disputed island sent the negative number to an all-time high of 77.8 percent.

In the 1980s, however, China was topped in popularity only by the United States and was far more popular than South Korea. This popularity did not mean that the Japanese public cared little about anti-Japan feelings. During the 1970s, anti-Japan protests in Thailand and Indonesia shocked Tokyo and triggered a major charm offensive. Moreover, in 2005, when those who chose the same "feeling friendly toward China" answer dropped to 32 percent, "anti-Japan" feeling was cited as the top reason (by 76 percent) by those who said they felt unfriendly (see figure 2 and table 1). Intensity of the anti-Japan sentiment aside, other reasons must account for the lessening of Japanese perceptions of China's charm.

From Affinity to Animosity

The Tiananmen Massacre in 1989 would be one such apparent reason for the decline of China's charm among the Japanese public. According to the annual Cabinet Office poll, China's popularity fell to the 50 percent threshold in the fall of 1989, a 20 percent drop from the previous year (figure 2). Another poll of 344 Japanese college students one month after the massacre also revealed a significant worsening of China's image, with its "undemocratic" perception rising from 56 percent to 93 percent and those who felt China "untrustworthy" increasing from a mere 17 percent to 53 percent.[81] Indeed, how could any foreign audience link the word *charm* with gory images of the government's violent crackdown? If anything, the high expectations China had generated prior to the catastrophe only deepened the frustration. Almost overnight, China was demoted from a model student to a pariah. Shock, disillusionment, and a sense of self-inflicted betrayal all contributed to the collapse of industrialized democracies' perceptions of China's charm.

The country's image among the Japanese public has never recovered. Even Emperor Akihito's unprecedented 1992 visit, hailed by both governments as a success, did little to improve popular perception. China's popularity recently has further declined to the 20 percent threshold. However, such declines should not be attributed simply to the lingering effects of the

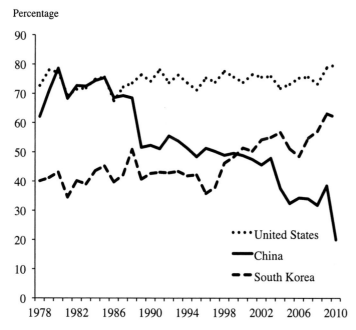

Fig. 2. Japanese public's responses to how friendly they feel toward the United States, China, and South Korea (1978–2010). (Data from annual surveys by Japanese Cabinet Office, http://www8.cao.go.jp/survey/h21/h21-gaiko/2-1.html.)

Tiananmen Square: Only 17.4 percent of those who said they did not like China in 2005 attributed their feelings to China's status as a communist, nondemocratic country. Instead, emotional and strategic reasons dominate the list (see table 1).

Anti-Japan sentiment among the Chinese was already visible during the 1980s but was less important to the Japanese public than is now the case. This inconsistency is revealing: As China's muscle-based hard power has grown, its charm-based soft power vis-à-vis Japan has dwindled. Japan has become much less willing to appear conciliatory toward an ever-stronger China. The Tiananmen incident's more enduring legacy, in retrospect, is to remove a filter that muted or moderated the assertive dimension of China's foreign policy. With China's progressive state image devastated, its anti-Japan side has become not only exposed but highlighted.

Real changes also took place in the Chinese government's diplomatic calculations. Foreign and domestic affairs are always closely intertwined, in China as elsewhere. With its communist ideology going up in flames, the post-Tiananmen CCP had to search for a new base to justify its continued control. The answer was to enhance patriotism and to depict the party as the sole qualified guardian of the Chinese nation. Doing so would inevitably require reconstructing history and setting up external enemies against which the party could claim to fight heroically. Japan's past invasion renders it the easiest target.[82] Among the "one hundred patriotic movies [*baibu aiguo dianying*]" that the Chinese government recommends to students, eighteen have themes related to fighting foreign invaders, and thirteen are about resisting the Japanese invasion.[83] Among the one hundred "main sites for patriotic education [*aiguo zhuyi jiaoyu jidi*]," twenty-one are related to the theme of resisting foreign invaders and fourteen are about fighting the Japanese. Thus, Japan far outweighs other foreign evils in the government-manufactured public memory. In this sense, Japan has been sacrificed on the altar of China's domestic politics.

Whether courting or shunning, individual leaders still matter. China-Japan relations have remained very personal, but the generational shift in leadership transformed that personal attitude from affinity to animosity. Any analysis of the worsening of mutual perceptions during this period would be incomplete without examining the personal preferences of Chinese president Jiang Zenmin. Unlike Zhou Enlai, who enchanted Japanese politicians with different ideological colors even in difficult times, Jiang

TABLE 1.   Reasons Identified by the Japanese Public for Why They Dislike China (2005)

Rank	Reason	Percentage
1	Strong anti-Japan sentiment	76
2	Different views on history	44.4
3	Territorial dispute	34.4
4	Crimes by Chinese living in Japan	30.1
5	Different views on politics and security	17.5
6	One-party Communist state with no freedom	17.4
7	China's expansionist military policy	10
8	Economic competition	5.8
9	Experience of using Chinese products	2.9
10	Experience of traveling to China	1.5
11	Sports competition	0.8
12	Other	4.6

Source: Data from a joint survey by Japan Research Center and Institute of Journalism and Communication, Chinese Academy of Social Sciences, 2005. For a discussion on the survey, see Yō'ichi Itō and Takeshi Kōno, eds., *Nyūsūhōdō to shimin no taigaikoku'ishiki* (News coverage and citizens' perception of foreign countries) (Tokyo: Keiō University Press, 2008), 8.

rubbed salt into old wounds. His 1998 state visit to Japan, hailed by China's official media as "historic," indeed became so, but for the wrong reasons: It ended as a diplomatic disaster. As it became clear that Jiang was not going to get a written apology from his Japanese counterpart, Obuchi Keizō, for Japan's "wrongful history," the Chinese leader grew visibly frustrated, lecturing a wide range of Japanese audiences from the emperor to college students on the dangers of "sticking to the wrong view on history." He also refused to sign the joint statement on forming a strategic partnership between the two countries, thereby openly displaying his displeasure.

The Japanese media made plain their frustration. One cartoon published by the *Yomiuri Shimbun*, "Why Don't You Have a Correct View of History?," portrayed Jiang as a domineering guest, standing on a chair and pointing down at Obuchi, while saying "past," "invasion," "dissatisfaction," and "view on history." The bowing Obuchi was murmuring "reflection," "apology," and "the future."[84]

The visit became so tense that even clothing was interpreted as signifying China's displeasure: Jiang attended the emperor's dinner in a Mao suit. However, he wore the same attire to Bill Clinton's state dinner. Moreover, the Chinese foreign ministry claimed that his garb had been selected prior to the visit. Such details no longer mattered, however, and the mood was ruined. Jiang's much-anticipated visit ended as such a failure that he largely came to personify a new yet unpleasant image of China in Japan's popular discourses.

To many Japanese, the visit cemented Jiang's reputation as a hawkish if not boorish guest. But Jiang had already developed a habit of bashing Japan. The diplomatic debacle was thus a disaster years in the making. Jiang explicitly stated that the issue of Japan's history of aggression "should not just be kept on the table but needs to be stressed permanently."[85] Realizing the presence of alternative voices, he openly challenged the moderates: "On the history issue and the Taiwan issue, some comrades think we have dwelled on them for too long. But I think the more we confront these two issues, the better it is for the development of China-Japan relations."[86] At another meeting, Jiang reminded high-ranking Chinese diplomats that Japan still had militarists and that China "must keep the warning siren blowing all the time."[87]

In addition to criticizing Japan before domestic audiences, Jiang also made his point on international occasions. During Jiang's November 1993 visit to South Korea, he bluntly expressed his displeasure toward Japan to his counterpart, Kim Young-sam, who shared the disdain:

Every time I met with leaders from Japan, I have always emphasized that history should not be denied. The only proper solution is to admit one's mistake humbly. The reason why there have been repeated speeches on denying the invasion and defending militarism from Japan is because of the Japanese government's ambivalence. It has not told historical facts to its citizens and the younger generations.[88]

Japanese scholars speculated about why Jiang so disliked their country, with some citing the death of his adoptive father, Jiang Shangqing, at the hands of the Japanese military as a key factor.[89] On the Chinese side, criticizing top leaders who are still living carries tremendous political risks. To this day, mainstream Chinese scholarship on Jiang's failed visit, including moderate voices, remains largely subdued.[90] A few chose to blame the Japanese side.[91] But some scholars and media professionals have privately admitted that Jiang mishandled the visit.[92]

To make matters worse, the dislike at the elite level has become more symmetrical. In my multiple interviews with Japanese reporters, academics, and diplomats, the eccentricity of Prime Minister Koizumi Jun'ichirō often came up. His decision to visit the Yasukuni Shrine annually throughout his tenure not only hampered Japan's foreign policy image but left some of Japan's own diplomats confused and discouraged, at least privately. Such views represented a significant change from the 1980s, when Nakasone and other politicians attempted to curb bureaucratic frustration. With bold and bitter politicians unconstrained, bureaucrats proved powerless to conduct effective damage control.

Jiang and Koizumi were not simply extreme individuals. Rather, their rise signaled a structural change in bilateral relations: early moderating voices, or the "bridge-builder" generation (*jue jing ren* in Chinese, literally "well-digger"), faded from the political stage. Newer leaders on both sides were more nationalistic. Jiang and Koizumi stood out but were by no means outliers.

These leaders also confronted a narrowing gap between Japanese and Chinese capabilities, an even bigger structural change, and the resultant changed public sentiments on both sides. Consecutive joint surveys have demonstrated a nearly perfect contrast of public mood in Japan and China. Figure 3 compares how the Chinese and Japanese anticipated their futures in 1997 and 2002. While a majority of the Chinese respondents expected their lives to be "better" or even "much better" in both polls, a majority of the Japanese respondents anticipated either stagnation or a change for the worse. Material changes, when coupled with such a contrasting shift in

Percentage

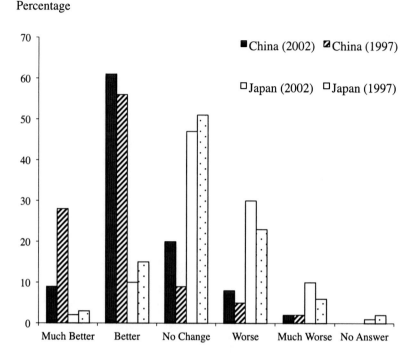

Fig. 3. Optimistic China vs. pessimistic Japan: Chinese and Japanese answers to the question "predict your life five years from now" (1997, 2002). (Data from joint surveys by *Asahi Shimbun* and Chinese Academy of Social Sciences in 1997 and 2002; data available from *Asahi Shimbun*, September 27, 2002.)

popular sentiment, increased the possibility that one's ambition would collide with another's sensitivity.

With help from Koizumi, Jiang and his cohort have left at least two legacies that continue to haunt Sino-Japanese relations. First, anti-Japan sentiments converged at the elite and public levels. As a vibrant democracy, Japan found its state image largely blocked, whereas its foreign policy image remained cast in a historical-traumatic mold that shaped any effort toward becoming a "normal" country as a sign of a rebirth of militarism.[93] More than fifty years after World War II, history has remained Japan's dominating frame for the Chinese public.

Table 2 makes this pattern clear: In 1997 and 2002, the Chinese public's top ten images of Japan expose how history still dominated shortcut references to Japanese identity. The table also shows that popular culture may be irrelevant to lessening political hostility: Five Japanese celebrities made Chinese respondents' top ten list in 2002, but these soft "good guys" apparently helped little in eliminating Chinese anger toward Japan triggered by Koizumi and wartime Japanese military generals.

Actions speak louder than words. Beijing apparently realized that it had gone overboard. Its leaders, including Jiang, significantly toned down their criticism when Obuchi visited China in 1999, and during his visit to Japan the following year, Chinese premier Zhu Rongji made a number of conciliatory gestures, including appearing on a TV talk show and claiming that China never intended to force Japan to apologize. The "Fourth Generation" leaders demonstrated an even less confrontational posture in their first few years: Jiang's successor, the usually emotionless president, Hu Jintao, was photographed playing ping-pong against Japanese player Fukuhara Ai, and Premier Wen Jiabao did his morning jogging in a Tokyo park and chatted with curious bystanders.

Yet the damage has proved persistent. Figure 2 shows that China's popularity has continued to dive. Minor improvements in 2009 were wiped out as approval levels dropped to an all-time low of 20 percent the following year. Second, as a number of scholars point out, virulent anti-Japan

TABLE 2.   Identify the First Name That Would Come to Your Mind When You Hear the Word "Chinese" (for Japanese respondents) or "Japanese" (for Chinese respondents) (2002)

Japanese Answers	Chinese Answers
1. Mao Zedong (1[a], political)[b]	Koizumi Jun'ichiro (—, political)
2. Jiang Zemin (4, political)	Tanaka Kakuei (3, political)
3. Zhou Enlai (3, political)	Yamaguchi Momoe (2, cultural)
4. Deng Xiaoping (2, political)	Tojo Hideki (1, political, World War II)
5. Confucius (7, historical)	Yamaguchi Isoroku (5, political, World War II)
6. Chiang Kai-shek (5, political)	Nakada Hidetoshi (—, sports)
7. Jacky Chan (10, cultural)	Sakai Noriko (9, cultural)
8. Kong Ming (8, historical)	Takakura Ken (7, cultural)
9. Sun Yat-sen (9, political)	Miura Tomokazu (14, cultural)
10. Zhu Rongji (—, political)	Okamura Yasuji (6, political, World War II)
Consort Yang (10, political)	

Source: Asahi Shimbun, September 27, 2002; survey jointly conducted by the Chinese Academy of Social Science and Asahi Shimbun.

[a]Numbers in parentheses indicate rankings in 1997 in the same poll; — indicates that the person did not appear in the "Top 15" list in 1997.

[b]Name in box indicates that the person had already passed away when the survey was conducted.

sentiment squeezed Chinese leaders into a corner, constantly balancing between bolstering patriotism for survival and placating vengeful nationalism for growth.[94] More simply, shouting anti-Japan slogans offered the Chinese masses a rare taste of freedom of expression, partly explaining why anti-Japan protests often had a carnival atmosphere, with protesters amusing one another and even the police laughing. Venting anger toward Japan not only was politically safe but could be fun. Thus, there is little reason to envision that anti-Japan sentiment will disappear from popular discourse, though its intensity will wax and wane depending on events in Tokyo and how Beijing conveys such events to its people. In short, the relationship between Chinese leaders and anti-Japan sentiment has followed a pattern (table 3).

Japanese sensitivity to gains and losses vis-à-vis China, substantive or symbolic, has become elevated. For example, in December 2009, Japanese media outlets recently worked themselves into a lather over the question of whether Japan went too far in pleasing China by agreeing to a ceremonial meeting between Emperor Akihito and the visiting Chinese vice president, Xi Jinping, on short notice. One Japanese legal scholar dismissed the popular notion that the Japanese government had violated the constitution by not informing the emperor one month in advance for such meetings, yet Japanese nationalists' anger was real, and coverage of the dispute dominated the airwaves for days.[95]

Another haunting legacy of the Jiang era is that Chinese experts on Japan were forced into silence or into refuting their true beliefs. Mainstream scholarship has not sufficiently addressed this dimension, yet it is crucial to our understanding of diplomatic wooing. Some Chinese scholars vehemently defended Jiang's position and attacked the few moderate voices as traitors. However, several Japan specialists told me that although they took such positions publicly, their private views were more moderate. Some of China's most authoritative Japan experts led a loud campaign to denounce Ma Licheng's article that proposed putting history to rest in China-Japan relations, a piece that triggered a storm of public anger.[96] Moderates had

TABLE 3.   Transition in Four Generations' Time: How Chinese Leaders Dealt with Popular Anti-Japan Feelings

Mao	Deng	Jiang	Hu
Diverted and suppressed	Tolerated and utilized	Revitalized, re-created, and exaggerated	Seeks to contain but increasingly cornered

to employ "curved writing" (a Chinese phrase for indirect criticism) to su-perficially praise Jiang's Japan policy while criticizing its extremist nature.[97] Without directly challenging Jiang, such moderate voices argued that Chi-na's diplomacy should pay attention to "the feelings of ordinary people" in other countries and that "China-Japan relations have acquired a momen-tum that can no longer be dictated by personalities of particular leaders."[98]

This legacy is important for understanding wooing, showing that the chilly Jiang and Koizumi years deprived Japan of "willing recipients and interpreters" of the country's charm among the Chinese. Those who re-ally understood Japan (*chi'nichiha*) could not be counted on to promote the country's accomplishments. From Japan's end, the fact that Chinese scholars would sound more moderate if not positive in private only added to the frustration. As one Japanese diplomat told me, when his government offered a visiting China Central Television crew opportunities to interview Japanese nongovernmental organizations, a famous anchorman leading the team turned them down and confessed that any reports on "nonof-ficial" and particularly "religious" organizations would bring trouble back home.[99] An open and democratic Japan was thus blocked entry into mil-lions of Chinese households.

People-to-People Confrontation: Learning to Love Sushi but Hate Koizumi

Mutual dislike has now acquired a popular base in both countries. Cultural exchanges are numerous, but such activities are less effective at counteract-ing their countries' worsening state and foreign policy images. Though often referred to as a tool for fostering understanding, cultural exchanges have become commercial rather than political activities. As a result, al-though they may generate big money, these activities have been operating more and more in a self-contained manner, bearing no close associations with high politics issues that are the main sources of deteriorating percep-tions. In layman's terms, people in these two countries have no problem with enjoying each other's cuisine, arts, songs, and movies without lower-ing their guard about noncultural issues. Insofar as their bilateral relations are concerned, there is no shortage of soft exchanges, but they have a neg-ligible impact on hard issues.

Such was not always the case. When Mao and Zhou launched their peace offensive, China and Japan had no formal, state-to-state connections. In such a context, cultural exchanges became a crucial mechanism for making contacts. Realizing that anti-Japan sentiment was common among Chinese artists, Zhou persuaded Mei Lanfang, a Peking Opera legend, to serve as the head of a 1956 cultural delegation, a significant achievement because Mei had refused to sing for Japanese authorities throughout the war. Zhou told Mei that the Japanese people were also victims and that his trip would facilitate reconciliation between the two nations. Mei's two-month visit to Japan was a huge success. His troupe put on thirty-two shows in a dozen Japanese cities, with audience chanting political slogans in support of normalizing relations with China.[100]

Mei was only one of the many cultural messengers charged with political missions. Indeed, visiting Japanese artists were prime targets of Chinese leaders' appeals. Members of the Matsuyama Ballet Troupe, for example, were regular guests of Mao, Zhou, and subsequent leaders. Its performance of *White-Haired Girl*, based on a well-known Chinese revolutionary drama, made the troupe a household name among Chinese audiences. In 2008, China's chief diplomat, Tang Jiaxuan, claimed that ballet diplomacy with Japan was as important as ping-pong diplomacy with the United States. Tang also declared that China would not forget the Matsuyama dancers' contributions. The troupe responded by staging a new show for its Chinese guests, *Ode to the Yellow River*, which pays tribute to Chinese patriots fighting Japanese invaders.[101]

As the Chinese leaders sought to use cultural exchanges as a diplomatic tool, one natural advantage was the existence of willing Japanese participants, most of whom were left-leaning and driven by a sense of war guilt and consequently were willing to pass on messages from the PRC government to the Japanese public. In 1950, the first national congress of the Japan-China Friendship Association was convened, with 180 participants from unions, parties, business groups, academia, and cultural groups. According to its charter, the association sought to "deeply reflect the wrong view of China held by Japanese citizens" and to "foster cultural exchanges to promote better understanding."[102] To fulfill these goals, the association organized activities such as picture exhibitions about China and information exchanges between Chinese and Japanese academic institutions and published a regular newspaper, *Japan and China*.

Such groups faced two sets of constraints, those from a deeply suspicious Japanese government and those from the unpredictable Chinese government. But as J. Victor Koschmann points out, they kept the pro-China flame burning even during difficult times.[103] The subsequent explosion in such sentiment hence did not appear out of nowhere but had historical links. These repentant statements by Japanese people added credibility to Chinese leaders' claim that blame for the invasion should go to Japanese militarists rather than ordinary people.

Furthermore, both political barriers were removed after the end of the Cultural Revolution, ushering in a period of vibrant cultural exchange. A series of industrial exhibitions and television programs elevated Japan's state image to new heights. A 1979 exhibition, *Japan Today*, drew huge crowds. Most of the pictures showed not scenes of nature but robots on assembly lines at factories, automated agricultural machines, and electronic household appliances. One corner of the exhibition hall featured a big screen displaying modern street scenes. As one scholar recalled it, the Chinese audience was "stunned" to realize how far behind China had fallen and how urgent the need to modernize had become.[104] To show viewers that a character was about to join China's quest to modernize, a 1979 hit Chinese comedy, *What a Family* [Qiao zhe yi jia zi], showed him reading a book titled *Scientific Japanese*. Japan became a symbol of modernization, China's new national goal.

Japanese actors also came to dominate Chinese screens during this period. The first foreign movie that China imported was a Japanese crime thriller, *For You! I Wade the Angry River* [Kimiyo! Fundo no kawa wo watare]. For Chinese viewers accustomed to seeing only "revolutionary" movies, the Japanese film's shooting and kissing offered a sensory feast. The star, Takakura Ken, became China's first iconic celebrity, and inspired by his masculinity, young Chinese women began asking. "What's wrong with Chinese men?"

The Chinese government supported Japan's cultural penetration during this period. Political sensitivity was ostensibly low. China's most-watched television program, *Joint News Broadcast* [Xinwen lianbo], was preceded by commercials for such Japanese brands as Casio and Seiko. Joint production of movies also commenced, with one on reconciliation (*An Unfinished Go Game*) and *Panda Story* becoming major hits.

Although China-Japan relations have subsequently worsened, cultural exchanges have remained lively. Culture has acquired a life of its own, and since the mid-1980s, cultural exchanges have gradually departed from formal diplomacy. The issue now is not a lack of cultural exchanges but their failure to improve each country's images of the other. Prime Minister Asō Tarō was correct—Chinese youngsters have proved no stronger than their counterparts elsewhere at resisting the temptation of Japanese animation. Japanese fashion trends and cuisine are also closely followed in China. Cultural exchanges have become more symmetrical: celebrities from both countries, some with global stardom, have collaborated on movies. A few such productions, including *Memoirs of a Geisha* and *Red Cliff,* have been immensely popular. In 2008, NHK, Japan's national broadcaster, dedicated December as China Month, broadcasting documentaries about the country's natural beauty and about ordinary people's lives in prime time slots on high-definition channels. Yet these softer touches have done little to soothe tensions elsewhere. Both the Chinese and Japanese publics seem to have learned to enjoy each other's cultural products without liking their governments, policies, or even people.

A New Round of Othering

Table 4 summarizes the departure of charm from mutual relations in the 1990s. Animosity at the top and people-to-people antagonism at the base joined forces, not only destroying the two countries' views of each other but also render Othering inevitable as China and Japan reached out to different countries. In a highly symbolic move, Jiang Zemin chose Honolulu as the first stop on his 1997 state visit to the United States. After laying a wreath at the USS *Arizona* Memorial, Jiang reminded his American audience of the days "when China and the United States were fighting side by side against fascism."[105] China's foreign minister, Li Zhaoxing, was even more straightforward. In the widely viewed live broadcast of his March 2006 press conference, Li invoked a string of comparisons to criticize Japanese leaders' lack of repentance:

TABLE 4.   Deconstruction of China's and Japan's Worsened Mutual Images

	State Image	Foreign Policy Image	Cultural Image
China in Japan's eyes	Nondemocratic dimension exposed	Anti-Japan sentiment exposed and highlighted	"History and tradition" still as dominating frames but popular culture becoming more accepted; no strong impact on lessening hostility
Japan in China's eyes	Democratic dimension blocked	Efforts to achieve "normal" status cast as threatening	Popular culture highly commercialized and with vast numbers of followers; no strong impact on lessening hostility

A German official once told me that the Germans cannot understand why Japanese leaders would do such things [as visit the Yasukuni Shrine]. Such acts are stupid and immoral. This is what the Germans said. . . . [A]n American official told me that the Americans will never forget what happened on December 7, 1941. A Malaysian friend told me that on the same day as the Pearl Harbor attack, the Japanese launched an air raid against Malacca and wounded a lot of innocent people. Cases like these are numerous, and even three hours would not suffice for me to cover them all.

Li's remarks drew ire from Tokyo. Cabinet secretary Abe Shinzō denounced Li as lacking basic diplomatic manners for using the words *stupid* and *immoral*. Abe also stated that he had "never heard of any German official" making such comments and challenged Li to name the German who had done so.[106] Being defensive is no longer sufficient for Tokyo, as Japan expands its reach to Southeast Asia, India, and the South Pacific. In-group bonding has remained an active diplomatic practice for both China and Japan, but the two governments have now begun to cast other countries as members of the in-group and each other as nonmembers.

TWO

Southeast Asia: Learning to Treat Neighbors as Peers

In this chapter, I examine China and Japan's efforts to woo Southeast Asia.[1] Given its resources and location, Southeast Asia's strategic importance is obvious. A long history of interactions also means that neither China nor Japan is a stranger to the region. Familiarity, however, can breed both admiration and suspicion. Juxtaposing Japan and China's reputations in Southeast Asia with soft power's three sources (foreign policy, political values, and cultural exchange) results in a rather gloomy picture. An extended history imbued with domination has created a "legitimacy deficit" for China and Japan in the region. In times of both war and peace, their foreign policies long reinforced their threatening images in the eyes of Southeast Asian countries. Their towering presence helped in-group bonding among Southeast Asian countries, with noninterference and equality prioritized.

As a consequence of such largely negative historical experiences, any Chinese or Japanese effort to allure must start as a mending project to soothe suspicions. The advent of wooing efforts was accompanied by diplomatic campaigns to stress noninterventionist and equal rhetoric, even offering to permit the Association of Southeast Asian Nations (ASEAN) to dictate the pace of regional integration.

Furthermore, rising hostility between Japan and China has added an Othering component to their charm offensives toward Southeast Asia. China has been trying to appear positive partly by constructing an unhelpful and hesitant Japan. Japan has attempted to ostracize China by portraying it as threatening, nondemocratic, and destabilizing. Luring Southeast Asia away from the embrace of the Other has become a part of diplomatic rivalry between China and Japan. Southeast Asia has been the winner in this courting game, and polls indicate a regional consensus in favor of sitting on the fence—that is, accommodating one power's ambition only to the extent that doing so does not endanger ties with the other. Both powers are respected. Neither is trusted.

Some variation exists within Southeast Asian countries' attitudes toward China and Japan. A recent poll conducted by the Japanese Foreign Ministry shows that the people in six key ASEAN countries (Singapore, Thailand, Malaysia, Vietnam, the Philippines, and Indonesia) are almost evenly divided: People in the first three countries see China as the most important partner and believe that it will remain so, whereas people in the last three countries see Japan as the most important partner and believe that it too will remain dominant.[2] The chapter's conclusion offers a more detailed discussion of such variance using a package of trade, demographic, and survey data. But such intragroup difference does not clash with treating the region as a unitary entity, because these countries uniformly cherish the values of noninterference and equality in their relations with their two powerful northern neighbors. Effective wooing, therefore, requires China and Japan to pose as equals despite their structurally unequal relationships with the ASEAN countries. Furthermore, although they have different attitudinal preferences toward China and Japan, none of these Southeast Asian countries has shown a tendency to come closer to one of the two powers at the expense of antagonizing the other. So the argument regarding fence-sitting still applies.

Southeast Asia's Strategic Importance

Southeast Asia has extensive connections with both Japan and China. Trade volume is a most useful indicator: In 2006, Japan was the biggest trading partner with ASEAN, the flagship organization that includes ten Southeast Asian countries.[3] Totaling approximately $162 billion, trade with Japan accounted for 11.5 percent of ASEAN's total external trade. China ranked fourth, following the United States and the EU-25, but its share of ASEAN's total trade was only 1.5 percent less than Japan's. In 1993, China's trade volume with ASEAN was only one-tenth of the Japanese level. In 2006, it was almost on a par with Japan's (figure 4). In 2007, China overtook Japan as ASEAN's top trading partner. ASEAN has been both Japan and China's fourth-biggest trading partner since the late 1990s.[4]

China and Japan's human connections with Southeast Asia are also vast. In 2010, more than 5.4 million Chinese and 3.3 million Japanese visited

Unit: US $ Million

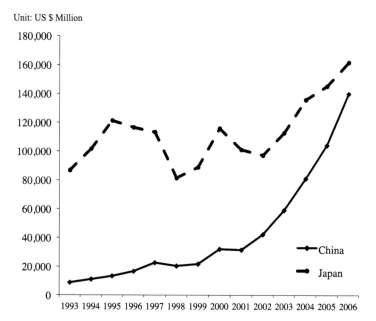

Fig. 4. ASEAN's trade with Japan and China (1993–2006). (Data from *ASEAN Statistical Yearbook 2006*, http://www.aseansec.org/13100.htm [accessed April 10, 2008].)

Unit: 1,000 Persons

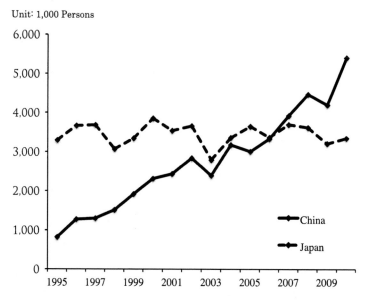

Fig. 5. Numbers of Chinese and Japanese tourists visiting ASEAN countries (1995–2010). (Data for 1995–2005 obtained from *ASEAN Statistical Yearbook 2006*, http://www.asean.org/13100.htm; data for 2006–10 obtained from ASEAN Tourism Statistics, http://www.aseansec.org/stat/Table.pdf.)

the region, making those two countries the top two sources of tourists in the region. As figure 5 illustrates, whereas the number of Japanese tourists has hovered around 3 million since the turn of the twenty-first century, the number of Chinese tourists has more than quadrupled, surpassing the Japanese total in 2007.[5]

Southeast Asia is also a choke point for energy-dependent China and Japan. According to the U.S. Department of Energy, fifty thousand vessels per year pass through the Strait of Malacca, only 1.7 miles at its narrowest point.[6] Most of the fifteen million barrels of oil shipped daily through the strait go to the Northeast Asian markets, with Japan and China two of the major destinations. If vessels had to detour around the strait, they would have to travel an extra one thousand miles through Indonesia's Lombok Strait further south, considerably raising oil prices. With China's and Japan's growing energy demands, the volume of oil shipments through the Strait of Malacca will only increase further and with it the region's strategic importance.

Starting from Below Zero—China's and Japan's Reputational Debt in the Region

China and Japan's material and human connections with Southeast Asia are not only extensive but also enduring. However, history has also haunted relations between Southeast Asian and its two powerful northern neighbors. Chinese and Japanese invasions, exploitations, and interventions have deeply wounded the Southeast Asian countries, and the unbalanced nature of the relationship has led to an uneasy coupling of familiarity and suspicion.

Indeed, the history of communication between China and Japan on the one hand and Southeast Asia on the other is permeated by the word *inequality.* Traditional Sinocentric viewpoints held that the further south one moved from the northern center of civilization, the more uncivilized people became. Under this philosophy, China's remote southern provinces were primary destinations for exiles, and Southeast Asia, even further south than the "barbarian" southern provinces, lay at the periphery of the Middle Kingdom's imperial scope.

As a symbol of submission, maritime kingdoms and principalities in Southeast Asia began to pay tributes to the Chinese imperial court as early as the eighth century. In return, the court would largely refrain from using force to take over the region. In fact, the court even offered occasional protections to kingdoms against threats imposed by others. In 1408, for example, Ming emperor Yong Le offered protection to Brunei against the Java's demand for tributes.[7] The Chinese imperial court would tout junior kingdoms' submission as a symbol of China's moral superiority, a claim that bears kinship with soft power. However, China was not the only power to which the region's maritime kingdoms paid tributes: Similar exchanges occurred with Arabs, Indians, Persians, and Japanese at various points.[8] More important, the imperial court's self-proclaimed moral superiority was overlaid on a sense of condescension toward Southeast Asia. Such arrogance was present in official documents. The Chinese terms *fan ren* and *nan man*, both meaning "barbarians to the south," were used to describe indigenous people living in what is now known as Southeast Asia.

China's rapid nineteenth-century decline did little to boost Southeast Asia's status as Japan—another northern maritime power—simply replaced the Middle Kingdom as the region's overlord. Like China, Japan possessed an entrenched sense of condescension toward the region. When Fukuzawa Yukichi, a prominent Meiji era intellectual, raised his "Leave Asia, Join Europe" thesis, Southeast Asia was not even on his mind. Fukuzawa conceived of backward "Asia" as primarily Northeast Asia, especially the moribund China and Korea. Southeast Asia did not even qualify to join this inferior league. Similarly, the official Iwakura Mission made a global tour and reported that the region was rich in resources yet populated by indolent people.[9]

The Japanese state formally entered the region after World War I. The empire set up the Nanyōchō (South Pacific Mandate) to administer formerly German-controlled Southeast Asian islets, which were transferred to Japanese control as a result of Germany's defeat. During the interwar years and through World War II, the Japanese empire grouped Southeast Asia with China, Korea, and Taiwan into the Greater East Asia Co-Prosperity Sphere.

Such institutional assimilation, however, hardly marked a step forward from Fukuzawa's discrimination. The Japanese condescension not only persisted but became more overt: the dominance of the Japanese race over other Asian races was taken for granted, and Southeast Asian peoples were seen as the most inferior of the dominated races. Japanese Southeast Asian specialist Gotō Kō'ichi has observed that as Japan became increasingly influential in Dutch-controlled Indonesia, instead of abandoning the Dutch-imposed three-tiered racial categorization of "Europeans, Asian foreigners, and aboriginals," the Japanese foreign ministry forced Dutch authorities to elevate Japanese nationals out of the "Asian foreigners" category into a separate group on par with "Europeans."[10] The derogatory term *dojin* (dirt people) remained common in public discourse to describe indigenous people of Southeast Asia, who remained at the bottom of this racial hierarchy.

China and Japan embarked on new paths after the end of World War II. In China, a brief yet bloody civil war resulted in the nationalist government's flight to Taiwan and the founding of the People's Republic on the mainland. In Japan, the American occupation transformed the country into a constitutional monarchy with a "no-war" pacifist constitution. Despite the two countries' much-altered political landscapes, they continued to share one commonality—they failed to improve their reputations in Southeast Asia. Instead, China's reputation plunged to new depths, and Beijing became a prime target against which Southeast Asian countries rallied. Japan gained a new but not complimentary nickname, "economic animal." The anti-Japan sentiment reached its climax in January 1974, when thousands took to the streets in Bangkok and Jakarta to protest Japan's "economic invasion" at a time when the country's prime minister, Tanaka Kakuei, was in the region for a goodwill visit.

What accounts for such spectacular failures? Any effective diplomatic wooing must echo the values of recipient countries. As a consequence of Southeast Asia's historical experience of domination by bigger powers from Northeast Asia, Western Europe, and America, the region's leaders prioritized nationalism, noninterference, and equality. However, neither China nor Japan built viable bonds with the region on these foundations. Their "outsider" image was not only threatening but also one-dimensional: China's involved revolutionary infiltration, while Japan's involved economic exploitation.

Bankruptcy of China's Reputation

Leaders in China or Japan tried their best. On the Chinese side, inconsistency, which also jolted its peace offensive toward Japan, was the major problem. In the first few years after the founding of the People's Republic, the Chinese government hardly viewed Southeast Asia as a regional bloc. For Beijing, the standard for categorizing countries was ideological rather than geographical. In one of the new country's first foreign policy statements, Vice President Liu Shaoqi loosely grouped countries in the region, together with Japan, India, and the Korean Peninsula, as "colonies and semicolonies" where "revolutionary forces are rapidly surging" and "people are aspiring to the Chinese path."[11]

Burma and Indonesia were among the first nonsocialist countries to establish diplomatic relations with China. Yet even for them, suspicions would not easily fade away. Cheng Ruisheng, Mao's translator, recalled that Burmese prime minister U Nu once said that prior to meeting Mao, he thought of the Chinese leader as a "Hitler-like" figure.[12] U Nu was concerned about Chinese dominance and evidence that the Chinese Communist Party had funded insurgent groups working against the Burmese government. Yet he also sought to avoid upsetting the neighboring giant. His effort to walk this tightrope was revealed during his first encounter with Mao in 1954.[13]

> U: I am very happy that I have this opportunity to salute to the great leader of the People's Republic of China. We have heard Chairman Mao's name for a long time. The chairman's name has always been a source of inspiration for young people in Burma who are fighting for freedom.
>
> Mao: Thank you. . . . [T]he Chinese people are also pleased, because our two countries are neighbors and have been friendly to each other for years. In history, has China fought any war with Burma? Not many times, right?
>
> U: Twice: Once with Kublai Khan during the Yuan Dynasty; another time during the Qing Dynasty. But we have never fought with the Chinese.
>
> Mao: On both wars, we Chinese were wrong. China invaded you. Historically speaking, Korea and Vietnam were bullied the most by China. Burma was less so. From now on we should get along peacefully.
>
> U: Frankly speaking, we are always afraid of big powers. But Premier Zhou's visit to Burma greatly diminished our fear.

U carefully mentioned that he did not see the invaders as truly Chinese, a point Mao shrugged off. U's profuse praise for Mao and indirect hint at Burma's concerns regarding Chinese domination pointed to a unique interaction between Burma and China: The former would accord the latter the status of *pawk pauh* (sibling) while keeping a comfortable distance from this elder brother, a balancing effort that Martin Stuart-Fox has termed the "Burmese approach" and that other Southeast Asian countries have more or less copied.[14]

China's relations with Indonesia were also plagued by suspicion. Despite the establishment of formal diplomatic relations in April 1950, Jakarta did not send an ambassador to Beijing until October 1953. China's first ambassador to Indonesia, Wang Renshu, reported to his post soon after the announcement, but no one from the Indonesian government welcomed him at the airport, and officials refused to admit some junior Chinese diplomats for fear that they would try to spread communism to Indonesia.[15]

Ambassador Wang, a renowned poet, apparently did not help the situation. In fact, he created the first image disaster for the new China. On October 1, 1951, as the official banquet to celebrate the founding of the People's Republic came to an end, the half-drunk ambassador took off all his clothes from waist up, thinking that all the guests had left, and called on his comrades to finish off the remaining bottles. The next day's Indonesian newspapers ran a photo of the topless and boozing Chinese ambassador.[16] A humiliated Beijing soon stripped Wang of his post, but the damage was done.

Initial setbacks notwithstanding, Beijing soon became aware of postcolonial countries' desire for national independence and noninterference and attempted to build in-group bonding by echoing such appeals. It touted its joint invention with India of the "Five Principles of Peaceful Coexistence," which highlighted noninterference, nonaggression, and equality. Soothing newly independent countries' suspicion proved difficult, however, as demonstrated by the initial responses to China's participation at the first Asian-African Conference in Bandung, Indonesia, in 1955. The Chinese delegation soon realized its dire reputation among attendees: Countries as diverse as Iraq, Ceylon, the Philippines, and Thailand condemned China for spreading communism. The barrage against Beijing became so strong that Zhou Enlai, the head of the Chinese delegation, had to abandon his original speech and improvise a talk in which he stated, "The Chinese delegation is here not for a fight but for unity, not to highlight our differences but to stress our commonalities."[17]

Beyond formal conference sessions, Zhou sought to meet with delegations that remained openly hostile to China. Zhou attempted to reassure the Thai foreign minister that Beijing did not seek allegiance from Chinese living in Thailand and that he would be welcomed in China, including Yun'nan Province, which had a sizable Thai population.[18] Zhou's moderate and conciliatory posture transformed him into a central figure at the conference, and its final declaration reiterated the noninterference principle developed by Zhou and Jawaharlal Nehru. In the particular context of Southeast Asia, Zhou's performance earned him the personal friendship of the Indonesian president, Sukarno. And although the Thai government turned down Zhou's invitation to visit, it lifted the ban on Thais visiting China and resumed trade connections.[19] The Thai foreign ministry also claimed that "according to international principles, China's communist government is the real legitimate government of China."[20] In the wake of the Bandung Conference, China not only set up formal relations with Ceylon, Cambodia, and Nepal but also commenced its official aid with a focus on South and Southeast Asian countries.[21] Chinese leaders were apparently encouraged by this climax of amity. During an April 1960 visit to Burma, Zhou and foreign minister Chen Yi donned Burmese costumes and jumped into the crowd celebrating Sangkran (the traditional Burmese New Year), getting soaked.[22]

The success of Zhou's effort, termed "smile diplomacy [*weixiao waijiao*]" by China's media,[23] should be viewed with two qualifications. First, Zhou's charm offensive was not geared particularly toward Southeast Asia: His "peaceful coexistence" principle was first iterated in 1953 with Nehru. At the Bandung Conference, the Chinese delegation was ready to meet with anyone. Zhou also showed his willingness to reach out to the United States, China's top enemy, two years earlier at the Geneva Peace Conference. Although it is widely believed that U.S. secretary of state John Foster Dulles refused to shake hands with Zhou at that conference, Zhou contended that the incident never happened. He contended that his soft gesture of asking for a handshake involved undersecretary of state Walter B. Smith, who was caught completely off guard.[24] Fearing that shaking Zhou's hand would violate Dulles's policy of refusing to shake hands with the Chinese, the panicky Smith grabbed a coffee cup in his right hand and used his left to pat Zhou's arm.[25] Zhou's efforts at these two conferences represent Chinese leaders' attempts to construct the image of a reasonable China willing to work with other countries.

Emphasizing nonintervention does not mean that Chinese leaders abandoned their conviction that global wars were inevitable. On the contrary, faith in the temporary nature of peace means that value-based bonding was superficial and volatile, prone to become victim to China's agenda, an ultimately destabilizing factor. In the wake of the successful launch of Sputnik, Mao made a speech, "East Wind over West Wind," hailing socialism's global surge. As Chinese scholars admitted, efforts to reach out to communist insurgents and encourage "armed struggles" intensified.[26] Disappointed at the Soviet Union for becoming hopelessly appeasing, Mao projected China as the real savior of communist ideals. In practice, this self-aggrandizement translated into a hierarchical perception of relations between China and the countries to be saved—little different from the moral superiority that China's imperial court assumed. This viewpoint was a blatant betrayal of the ideas of equality and noninterference that Mao had advertised not long before. Mao behaved much in the same way as the Mongol and Manchu emperors that he had condemned.

Southeast Asia's geographical proximity and the large Chinese population rendered the region vulnerable to Beijing's changed agenda. Thailand, for example, saw its thawing relations with China frozen again as China began openly to support the Thai Communist Party's insurgent activities in the country's northeast. The *People's Daily* made no secret of China's intervention efforts, announcing that China had a "righteous and irrefutable responsibility [*yiburongci*]" to assist the Thai people's armed struggle "against American imperialism and its tail-wagging Thai dogs."[27] In 1962, Beijing set up an underground radio station, the Voice of the People of Thailand, in Kunming to push for a "people's war" inside Thailand. Beijing also set up similar radio bases to offer propaganda assistance to communist insurgents in Burma and Malaysia. The Chinese Communist Party also cultivated its ties with the Indonesian Communist Party and the Philippine Communist Party.[28]

The intensity of Beijing's intervention varied among countries but was particularly intense in Indonesia and Thailand.[29] Beijing's influence also was immense in Cambodia, but the Cambodians were actively seeking a protector in the face of threats from Thailand and Vietnam. In Malaysia, Singapore, and the Philippines, Beijing-backed communist insurgents were more of a security annoyance, and the ethnic Chinese populations in both Singapore and the Philippines had more Taiwan-leaning sympathizers.[30] Beijing's intervention was the weakest in Burma.

Despite such variances, the scope of Beijing's intervention was indeed sweeping. A 1968 map in the *People's Daily* illustrated China's revolutionary ambitions. The "Illustration of the World's Splendid Situation [*Shi jie da hao xing shi tu*]" depicts Burma, Thailand, the Philippines, Laos, Vietnam, Malaysia, and Indonesia as engulfed by "armed" and "anti-imperialist" struggles.[31]

Reality pointed in a different direction however. Chinese diplomacy had experienced a huge debacle three years earlier when a coup in Indonesia eliminated the country's communist party and resulted in a massacre of Chinese residents. A country with which China had come close to forming an alliance had turned into an anticommunist bastion. Indeed, fear of China prompted ASEAN's formation in 1967 by Indonesia, Malaysia, the Philippines, Singapore, and Thailand, and Beijing quickly denounced the organization as "an imperialist tool."[32] At the same time, China largely botched its peace offensive toward Japan. Ironically, however, China's official connections with some Southeast Asian governments and the region's large and economically dominant Chinese population made the human cost of China's wooing failure there much higher. Local Chinese paid the dearest price for the bankruptcy of China's reputation.

Japan's Failure to Repair Its Image

Unlike China, Japan did not have an army of expatriates in Southeast Asia. Furthermore, the Japanese government shared an anticommunist stance with the majority of the countries in the region. Under these conditions, Japan would seem to have been in a better position to repair its reputation. But Japan's image-repair effort cannot be considered a success.

Different political paths notwithstanding, the lessons of Japan's failure bear striking similarities to those of China's. Like China, Japan failed to transform the one-dimensional nature of its image. Whereas China was seen as overly political and extremist, Japan was perceived as economic and exploitative. Furthermore, Southeast Asian countries viewed both one-dimensional images as precursors to dominance of some kind over the region. Also like China, leaders' judgments matter, and Japan's long-held beliefs in its own superiority continued to influence judgments in Southeast Asia. Southeast Asia never went beyond being an auxiliary component of Japanese foreign policy, attached by default to a larger agenda of helping Japan manage relations with bigger powers. These factors challenged Southeast Asian countries' values such as national independence, equality, and neutralism. With little value-based bonding, Japan's ever-deepening material connections exacerbated Southeast Asia's fears.

Japan's postwar reentry into Southeast Asia came with a dose of reluctance. The loss of the huge Chinese market compelled Japan to go south in search of markets and raw materials.[33] The Japanese government's concept of Southeast Asia was rather vague. A 1953 document prepared by the Asian Bureau of the Ministry of Foreign Affairs defined "Southeast Asia" as including "the area from the Philippines to Pakistan." In this bloated view, the economic importance of South Asian countries, especially India, Ceylon, and Pakistan, was higher than that of Indonesia, Malaysia, and the Philippines, which would be part of contemporary definitions of Southeast Asia. As Hatano Sumio and Satō Suzumu point out, with relatively stable political situations and no war reparation issues, South Asia looked more attractive to Tokyo.[34] Not surprisingly, then, Japan chose India to be the first recipient of official development aid in 1957.

However, starting from the mid-1950s economies in South Asia went increasingly stale. To maintain Japan's economic recovery process, a deeper engagement with countries in the narrower Southeast Asia became unavoidable. Yet to open their doors demanded addressing the issue of war reparations. The bilateral negotiation processes were gruesome, but U.S. intervention meant that Japan ultimately paid much less than had originally been anticipated.[35] As payment for wrongful policies, the money Japan offered certainly carried political meaning. But prime minister Yoshida Shigeru believed that no money should be paid simply to put the past to rest. Meeting with Dulles in 1954, Yoshida made it clear that reparations must be future-oriented and executed as investment to boost Japan's economic recovery.[36] In keeping with Yoshida's vision, a process turning a political arrangement into an economic arrangement was under way.

Southeast Asia's auxiliary status in Japan's foreign policy calculations remained unchanged. That is, the region did not stand on its own but was perceived as an instrument to help Japan manage relations with bigger others. Yoshida stated that helping Southeast Asia develop constituted a "link" in the United States–Japan alliance and that Japan stood as a bridge between Southeast Asia and America, turning raw materials provided by the former into products for the latter.[37]

Diplomacy with the United States was not the sole agenda to which Southeast Asia was bound. A policy paper prepared by the Economic Research Bureau under the Hatoyama administration identified stopping rising Chinese influence as the reason for more active Japanese economic development assistance in Southeast Asia.[38] For countries craving recognition and equal treatment, this continued subordinate status was hardly pleasing. And Yoshida did not seem to care, justifying his contempt for Southeast Asia by arguing, "You have to trade with rich men; you can't trade with beggars."[39]

Though Yoshida had set the precedent, the prime minister who best exemplified this condescending view was Kishi Nobusuke. On the surface, Kishi seemed to value Southeast Asia's place in Japanese foreign policy more than his predecessors. Instead of choosing the United States as the destination for his first official trip, Kishi went south to Burma, India, Pakistan, Ceylon, Thailand, and Taiwan. Although some of these countries would not fit contemporary definitions of Southeast Asia, both official and media discourses referred to the trip as a "tour of Southeast Asia [tō'nan ajia rekihō]." During the trip, Kishi explained the "three principles" of postwar Japanese diplomacy: the country was focused on the United Nations and saw itself as a member of the Free World and of Asia. The third point was most relevant to Southeast Asia: By including Southeast Asia, Taiwan, and

South Korea but rejecting China, Kishi's "Asia" was an ideological rather than a geographical notion. During the Meiji era, Fukuzawa had excluded Southeast Asia from the already inferior Asian league. Now Kishi chose to do the opposite by excluding China.[40]

Such a U-turn, however, hardly elevated Southeast Asia's supplementary status in Japanese foreign policy. Indeed, the only difference was that Kishi was not shy about stating his utilitarian purpose. Years later, he recalled, "I wanted to enhance Japan's status in Asia—that is, I wanted to make Japan the center of Asia. I also wanted to increase Japan's leverage in my meeting with [U.S. president Dwight Eisenhower] and make Japan-America relations equal."[41]

Such a self-assigned sense of historic mission was not limited to people inside the government. The members of the Research Group on Asian Problems (Ajia Mondai Kenkyūkai), a think tank that advised Kishi on Asian affairs, harbored a similar Japan-centered Asianist view. Fujisaki Nobuyoshi, a professor at Keiō University and a founding member of the group, claimed that although conditions no longer allowed Japan to be the alliance leader (*meishu*) of Asia. Japan's responsibility as Asia's elder brother (*chōkei*) remained.[42]

With Japan displaying such condescension, it is not surprising that Southeast Asia failed to fully embrace Tokyo. Indeed, despite Kishi's gestures and the warm official welcomes he received, substantive accomplishments at restoring Japan's elder-brother leadership were scant. Kishi's proposal to establish the Southeast Asian Development Fund was turned down twice by his Southeast Asian hosts, who feared that the effort would lead Japan to dominate regional cooperation.[43] Suspicions continued to stand in the way of Japan's attempts to gain political capital.

Japan missed one more opportunity to strike a chord with Southeast Asian countries. Fear of China was a major motivation for the founding of ASEAN, yet Japan did not grasp this chance to enhance in-group bonding. In fact, at an internal meeting of ambassadors to Southeast Asian countries in March 1973, Japan's senior diplomats dismissed the organization as "somewhat emotional" and a mere statement of the region's neutralism.[44] Only one month later, ASEAN issued a joint statement criticizing Japan for dumping synthetic rubber. In July, Malaysia sent its top economic official to Tokyo to deliver another warning on behalf of ASEAN that Japan must curb exports of synthetic rubber. Realizing that ASEAN was not all about emotions or about China and that its members could speak with one voice, Japanese prime minister Miki Takeo expressed his wish to attend the organization's summit in 1976. But Japan received another humiliation when ASEAN announced that it had no intention of inviting him. Tokyo's initial dismissal of ASEAN might have been a simple misjudgment, but the result certainly hindered rather than enhanced bonding.

In short, Japan's material and human connections with Southeast Asia increased markedly beginning with Yoshida. Yet Southeast Asia's auxiliary position in Japan's foreign policy, together with Tokyo's preoccupation with enhancing its economic presence and a condescending view, created an unpleasant image of Japan as an economic animal.

Japanese prime minister Tanaka Kakuei felt the heat of the region's anti-Japan sentiment. On a 1974 "goodwill" visit to Southeast Asia, he was engulfed by angry protests in Bangkok and could not leave his Jakarta hotel because of rioting. Yet Tanaka quickly dismissed what he saw as protesters using Japan as a scapegoat for their anger at domestic problems.[45] This Japan-as-scapegoat thesis resurfaced three decades later, when massive numbers of Chinese took to the street to protest Japan. In both cases, the argument had some validity—domestic and international politics are invariably intertwined. Particularly for citizens of authoritarian countries, Japan has provided a safe outlet for anger. Yet this thesis alone does not suffice. Why has Japan become a default choice for scapegoating? To blame an authoritarian host is easy, but to deny that Japan's negative image has a huge market is hard.

The Fukuda Doctrine—New Rhetoric, New Policies

Mainstream scholarship, particularly in the Japanese language, views the birth of the Fukuda Doctrine in February 1977 as a turning point in Japan's Southeast Asian policy.[46] The term refers to the concluding speech that Prime Minister Fukuda Takeo delivered to the Filipino Congress in Manila, the last stop on his tour of six Southeast Asian countries. Subsequent Japanese prime ministers have invariably referred to this speech and vowed to follow its spirit.

The defining part of the speech was a three-point outline. First, Japan, a nation committed to peace, rejected the role of a military power and on that basis resolved to contribute to the peace and prosperity of Southeast Asia and the world community. Second, Japan would construct a new relationship with Southeast Asia based not solely on material bonds but also on cultural and social exchanges. Japan would regard Southeast Asia as a true and trustworthy friend. Third, Japan would strengthen its connections with ASEAN members as an equal partner.[47]

Starting with Fukuda, Japanese officials accorded great significance to the speech, proclaiming that it marked the first time that Tokyo established a vision for postwar Japan–Southeast Asia relations.[48] A sense of buoyancy was apparent in the prime minister's autobiography, in which he recalled, "As my speech came to an end, the hall was engulfed by deafening applause. I said to myself, 'With this [speech], haven't we opened the future of Asia?'"[49]

Fukuda was not the first postwar prime minister to attempt to put Japan–Southeast Asia relations on a new path, but his speech did signal changes in Japan's Southeast Asia policy. A new rhetoric that stressed equality replaced the old assumptions about Japan's natural leadership. Japan as elder brother was to be replaced by Japan as equal partner. The new prime minister apparently realized that a dose of humbleness would better serve Japan's interests.

Diplomatic speeches by Japanese prime ministers rarely become emotional. But Fukuda's speech was an exception. Admitting suspicions and hostilities on the ground, Fukuda expressed Japan's desire for a "heart-to-heart" relationship with Southeast Asia and Japan's willingness to mobilize all diplomatic resources—political, social, and cultural as well as economic—to achieve this goal.

The doctrine was also preceded and followed by concrete policy changes. As foreign minister in 1972, Fukuda had realized that Japan's policy toward Southeast Asia was seriously skewered toward economy. Having studied the British Council and West Germany's Goethe Institute, he was a key proponent of the creation of the Japan Foundation, a quasi-governmental organization charged with fostering cultural, social, and academic exchanges. Unsurprisingly, Southeast Asia was a major recipient of foundation funding.[50] His 1977 trip also saw the founding of the ASEAN Cultural Fund, an organization to which Japan offered five billion yen to foster cultural exchanges within ASEAN members as well as between ASEAN and the rest of the world.[51] The ASEAN Cultural Fund signaled a new mode of "embedded initiative" diplomacy: Japan would embed its initiatives within a multilateral framework and present them as collective wisdom. It was even willing to allow ASEAN to sit in the driver's seat, with full jurisdiction over the fund's operation.

Good Timing and Willing Interpreters: The Other Side of Japan's Awakening

Has the Fukuda Doctrine indeed turned Japan–Southeast Asia relations to a whole new page? Japan's official discourses seem to say yes. Subsequent Japanese prime ministers have repeatedly used Fukuda's catchphrases, "heart-to-heart" and "equal partners." In a 2002 speech, "Japan and ASEAN in East Asia: A Sincere and Open Partnership," delivered to Singapore's Institute of Southeast Asian Studies, Prime Minister Koizumi Jun'ichirō paid tribute to the Fukuda Doctrine:

> Twenty-five years ago, in 1977, Prime Minister Takeo Fukuda made a speech in Manila, citing "equal partnership" and "heart-to-heart understanding" between Japan and ASEAN. Based on the fundamental concepts of the "Fukuda Speech," Japan's ASEAN policies have been passed on from that time to each subsequent cabinet. I, too, am eager to promote such policies.[52]

Surveys conducted by the Ministry of Foreign Affairs in Indonesia, Malaysia, Thailand, Singapore, and the Philippines starting in 1978 reveal solid improvements in Japan's image.[53] The percentage of those who felt that Japan's war atrocities should never be forgotten fell from more than 30 percent in 1978 to 20 percent in 2008. By contrast, those who felt that the past should be put to rest rose from 37 percent to 68 percent. While history continues to haunt Japan's relations with China and South Korea, it has largely disappeared as an obstacle in its relations with Southeast Asia. In addition, the vast majority of respondents described their countries' relations with Japan as "good" or "generally good." Roughly the same percentage of respondents agreed that Japan could be "trusted" or "generally trusted."[54] Japan's image improvement was solid enough to embolden Prime Minister Takeshita Noboru to call the region Japan's "power base [senkyo]."[55]

However, to attribute all these improvements to the Fukuda Doctrine would be exaggerating its effect. In fact, the improvement of Japan's image in Southeast Asia was as much internally driven as externally elicited. The Fukuda Doctrine was well timed. The late 1970s and the 1980s witnessed accelerating economic growth rates among Southeast Asian countries. As a result, Japanese commodities known for their quality and design became more affordable to mass consumers.[56] More important, pro-Japan local surrogates in the political and economic realms voluntarily propagated Japan's attraction to the masses. Local elites used "Learn from Japan" movements to serve their quest for non-Western development alternatives. A charm offensive is most effective when its goal meshes with local aspirations. Kishi's dream became reality as Japan became the undisputed leader of the "Asian way" without arousing local suspicion.

One example of local surrogates propagating Japan's charm to serve their own agendas took place in Malaysia under Mahathir bin Mohamad. Mahathir's fascination with Japan started at a young age. As he argued in *The Ma-*

lay Dilemma, the Japanese occupation convinced him and many other Malays that the West was not invincible vis-à-vis Asian countries.[57] As a rising Malay nationalist during the 1950s and 1960s, Mahathir grew increasingly disillusioned with senior leaders such as Tunku Abdul Rahman, whom Mahathir saw as kowtowing to the British and enlarging the inequality between the rich Chinese minority and the impoverished Malay majority.

Mahathir's various ministerial stints in the 1970s allowed him ample opportunities to travel the world and search for non-Western alternatives to development. He felt naturally drawn to the Japanese model, with its emphasis on the state's role in guiding industrialization.[58] As the education minister, he began to promote Japan as a new destination for Malaysian students. Mahathir's fascination with Japan grew so strong that some analysts described it as an "infatuation" or "obsession."[59] When he assumed the premiership, he formally launched the Look East policy in 1982 to supplement his earlier Buy British Last initiative. According to Mahathir, the Japanese model's significance was larger than Japan itself, for it symbolized the Asian way of development that should bind together Japan, Malaysia, and other Asian countries.

Mahathir became a popular figure among Japan's political elites. According to Shiokawa Masajūrō, former chief secretary to the Fukuda Cabinet, the Look East policy helped boost Japan's popularity. Fukuda also expressed delight at the fact that "a politician from Southeast Asia would have such a high respect for Japan."[60] Japanese conservative celebrity Ishihara Shintarō joined Mahathir to produce a book, *The Asia That Can Say "No,"* taking a page from Ishihara's earlier book, *The Japan That Can Say "No."* An elite-level ideological alliance was emerging.

This alliance served different purposes, providing a non-Western alternative for Malaysia and a leadership role for Japan in the eyes of Ishihara and those who shared his views. But the two forces interacted in a symbiotic manner. Since Japanese superiority convinced Mahathir and other local elites of the viability of an "Asian way," Fukuda's charm offensive acquired a new layer of significance as an economic liberation movement. Mahathir was not the only convert, nor was his Malaysian government the only one awed by the Japanese model: Singapore, the Philippines, and Thailand launched versions of the Learn from Japan campaign.[61]

Limits of Japan's Courting: Image Remains One-Dimensional

The Fukuda Doctrine did not resolve all of Japan's problems. Despite local elites' vigor, Look East and Learn from Japan campaigns soon ran into local resistance, and suspicions began to arise about whether copying the Japanese experience was feasible given Southeast Asia's very different cultural and demographic realities. Despite the high marks the Japanese accorded to Mahathir, Japanese investment in Malaysia increased little. The amount of Japanese official development aid grew only slightly during the 1980s, and Japan refused to ease Malaysia's debt burden.[62] In addition, no discernible changes occurred in Malays' work ethic despite Mahathir's vigorous urgings that they be more like their Japanese counterparts.[63] Hence, the Look East policy had unimpressive material impact.

Furthermore, these campaigns brought Japan only scant political capital. While Japanese prime ministers after Fukuda continued to uphold his doctrine, the moment they attempted to step out of the Southeast Asian regional frame, they saw their initiatives resented and resisted by countries in the region. Prime Minister Ōhira Masayoshi's Pan-Pacific Ocean Cooperation Concept (Kantaiheiyō Rentai Kōsō), for example, was aborted largely as a consequence of Southeast Asian countries' fear that by including the United States and South Pacific powers such as Australia and New Zealand, the idea would diminish Southeast Asia's collective power.[64] Ōhira's failure reveals that Learn from Japan campaigns did not eliminate a Southeast Asian countries' entrenched fear of being marginalized or sidelined by bigger powers.

And although Japan's popular image has become less threatening, it has remained one-dimensional as an economic power. An analysis of editorials of three major English-language newspapers in Singapore, Thailand, and Indonesia over a twenty-year period reveals that even during the heyday of the 1980s, the local desire to see Japan turn its economic might into political capital was lukewarm.[65] Japan was indeed better perceived, but Southeast Asia was by no means becoming Japan's power base. Tokyo's assessment of how it was perceived by others seemed to remain one step ahead of reality. A turning point was imagined rather than real.

In 2008, a survey sponsored by the Japanese Ministry of Foreign Affairs showed that people in Indonesia, the Philippines, Vietnam, Singapore, Thailand, and Malaysia were most interested in Japan's "science and technology" (54 percent) and "economy" (54 percent). Interest in Japan's politics and foreign policies ranked ninth among the eleven categories, at 17 percent. Economic and technological cooperation was also the top area in which respondents wanted to see Japan become more active, with 66 percent choosing this category. Whereas recent Japanese governments have actively pursued greater political and military roles, only 6 percent of the ASEAN respondents wanted to see Japan enhance its military presence even in the name of peacekeeping, the last area in which the public would like to see a stronger Japan.[66] The gap persists between Japan's perception of its political potential and recipient assessments.

Because of its one-dimensional nature, Japan's image is closely tied to the country's economic performance. The economic malaise that troubled Japan for the entire 1990s led to a loss of self-confidence, triggering Japanese media and scholars to ponder whether the country was still a model worth following.[67] Worse still, Japan's economic stagnation unfolded in sharp contrast to China's rapid economic ascendancy. All of a sudden, a new alternative was surfacing from a country that Japan increasingly saw in a hostile manner.

The Path to China's Charm Offensive

China's effort to save its reputation came much later than Japan's. Beijing normalized relations with Thailand, Malaysia, and the Philippines in the wake of the Nixon shock. China also shared ASEAN's concerns regarding Vietnam's military presence in Cambodia. But Beijing's wooing was in a very rudimentary stage. In fact, it would be more accurate to describe the normalization period as a time when China came to have a vivid sense of the depth of its "debt of fear" in the region. For example, Singapore's prime minister, Lee Kuan Yew, went to China in 1976 but expressed no interest in normalizing relations with his host country. Lee spoke more about the differences between Singapore and China than about friendship. He also urged China to abide by its promise of noninterference.[68] Lee again displayed his ultrasensitivity in November 1978, when Deng Xiaoping visited Singapore after stops in Thailand and Malaysia. Lee prohibited any spontaneous welcoming activities for the Chinese delegation, and at the banquet, he belabored Singapore's differences from China. Deng was apparently annoyed by Lee's rhetoric: Reporters noticed that Chinese delegation members had crossed out the word *friendly* from a sentence that originally read, "his excellency the prime minister's friendly speech."[69]

Lee's Chinese ethnic background might have contributed to his extremely high level of sensitivity, yet he was by no means an exception. As a chief diplomat in charge of China's Southeast Asia policy recalled, making Beijing's noninterference stance convincing was a major task in the normalization talks with Malaysia, Thailand, and the Philippines.[70] Although China normalized political ties with these countries, it also found a thick emotional wall hard to penetrate.

China's subsequent Open Door Policy shifted the country's preoccupation to learning from industrialized countries in Western Europe, Japan, and North America. Admitted one Chinese diplomat, one problem in Beijing's foreign policy during this era was "neglecting our old friends in the developing part of the world."[71] Southeast Asia was probably never China's friend, but it nonetheless belonged to the world this diplomat identified. Trade data support this lament: Although the amount of China-ASEAN trade increased in absolute terms, their mutual importance was meager compared with other trading partners. In 1990, the total trade volume between China and ASEAN members was six billion dollars, less than one-third the level of trade between China and Japan alone.[72] For the entire 1980s, China's share oscillated between 1 and 2 percent of ASEAN's total foreign trade, whereas ASEAN's share of China's international trade never topped 4 percent; Japan accounted for nearly 30 percent.[73] Moreover, two major Southeast Asian powers, Indonesia and Singapore, had yet to normalize relations with China. Though much smaller in influence, Brunei was not prepared to recognize Beijing.

Beijing reached out to Southeast Asia in the wake of the Tiananmen Massacre, when China was shunned by the West. Emphasizing noninterventionism as a common value, China normalized relations with Singapore and Indonesia in 1990 and Brunei in 1991. Yet this campaign was hardly targeted specifically toward Southeast Asia. Rather, as an international pariah, the Chinese government was willing to talk to anyone who would listen. In addition to Southeast Asia, Chinese leaders were resuming old friendships in Africa and Latin America.[74] It was more of a diplomatic move out of desperation than ambition.

As the international sanctions began to loosen, Beijing's policies toward Southeast Asia revealed their utilitarian purpose. In 1992, China's National Congress passed the Territorial Sea and Contiguous Zones Law, making legal claims on all disputed maritime territories, including the Diaoyu/Senkaku Islands, which were under Japanese sovereign control, and all the islands in the Spratly region, many of which were claimed and controlled by Vietnam, the Philippines, Malaysia, Brunei, or Taiwan. In 1995, the Chinese navy destroyed Filipino military structures on the Mischief Reef and set up Chinese markers, nullifying a 1992 ASEAN declaration, endorsed by China at the time, that stipulated that disputes over the Spratly Islands must be solved by peaceful means. China's provocative measures, together with its 1995 nuclear tests and its 1996 military exercises against Taiwan, stimulated the rise of a "China as a Threat" thesis in the region. China had not just failed to transform its threatening political image but had reinforced it. One consequence was the strengthening of security ties between

Southeast Asia and the United States, precisely the opposite of what China desired. The possibility of facing a full encirclement compelled Beijing to change tactics. Its educational campaign to stir up nationalism continued, but its scope narrowed. As Joshua Kurlantzick has written, China is once again willing to appear conciliatory except toward Japan and Taiwan.[75]

Turning Economic Crisis into Wooing Opportunity

The Chinese word *crisis* consists of the characters for "danger" and "opportunity." The 1997 Asian financial crisis, which hit Southeast Asian economies particularly hard, could not have been better timed to provide an opportunity for Beijing to create its own "Fukuda moment." Beijing's subsequent efforts to repair its image have been remarkable. China realized the importance of reputation much later than did Japan but quickly caught up.

Beijing's post-1997 charm offensive stressed the common values most cherished by the recipients—equality, noninterference, and multilaterialism—and substantiated them with solid policies. Chinese scholars have often touted Beijing's response to the Asian financial crisis as the first time that China took seriously its reputation.[76] To convince its Southeast Asian neighbors of the sincerity of Chinese words on equality from Premier Zhu Rongji down to party-controlled media outlets, official rhetoric at all levels framed the government's decision not to devalue the renminbi as a "self-sacrificing" move to serve the better public good—the economic stability of the whole region—and argued that China's self-sacrifice should be viewed as evidence of the country's status as a responsible power. A press statement prepared by the Chinese Ministry of Foreign Affairs stated,

> The Chinese Government, with a high sense of responsibility, decided not to devalue its renminbi in the overall interest of maintaining stability and development in the region. It did so under huge pressure and at a big price. But it contributed considerably to the financial and economic stability and to the development of Asia in particular and the world at large.[77]

Beijing was certainly not altruistic—Hong Kong's pegged exchange rate would have crumbled had the renminbi been devalued, and a devalued Chinese currency would likely have triggered a new round of devaluation of local currencies in Southeast Asia, leaving everyone, including China, at the same starting point with even dimmer economic prospects. But insofar as image is concerned, a policy's perception could be more important than its conception. Although in real terms, Japan's contribution of forty-four billion dollars did far more than China's actions to stabilize the financial chaos, China received louder applause.

Despite the money contributed, Tokyo failed to alleviate U.S. criticism that Japan should bear some responsibility for causing the financial chaos, that Tokyo's monetary offer was merely a delaying strategy to shield the country from painful yet necessary structural reforms, and that immobility and indecision were hampering Japan's development as a regional leader. By contrast, Bill Clinton praised China for its "disciplined and wise policy" of resisting the temptation to devalue its currency to boost exports and hard-currency earnings.[78] Clinton further upset Tokyo by satisfying the Chinese demand that he bypass Japan on his trip back to the United States, breaking with a long-established tradition. At the same time, U.S. opposition short-circuited Tokyo's initiative to establish the Asian Monetary Fund.

Clinton's decision triggered the birth of a quite literal term, "Japan passing," in the Japanese media. The Chinese response to the crisis gave rise to a diplomatic strategy that can be termed "minimum-maximum"—obtaining maximum diplomatic gains through minimum contributions by linking such contributions to the image of a rising, benevolent, and self-sacrificing Chinese power. China replicated this strategy in its response to the 2004 tsunami. Its official media outlet claimed that "once again, China is constructing the image of a responsible power through concrete actions."[79] The article ended with a strong sense of self-righteousness: "The 'China as a Threat' thesis is totally unfounded. The 'China as an Opportunity' thesis is an indisputable fact."[80]

China may also be enjoying the benefits of being a newcomer to the game of international donation. As Yamamoto Nobuto and Takagi Yūsuke discovered in their analysis of the *Jarkata Post*'s portrayal of Japan, despite the massive amount of money Japan poured in after the tsunami, local appreciation was scant. Instead, as a "donating power [*enjo taikoku*]," Japan was expected to contribute a lot. The two researchers concluded that the Japanese self-perception of being a political power had yet to make inroads among Indonesians. The image of an economic power (and thus donating power) remains deeply entrenched, even in a seemingly friendly country.[81]

Honoring the noninterference norm would be a natural choice for Beijing. To be sure, noninterference is in the eyes of the beholder, and complaints have periodically arisen about Chinese interfering in other countries' affairs in Southeast Asia as well as in other parts of the world. But China's leaders certainly attempted to revitalize this old concept in the wake of the Tiananmen Massacre, an understandable approach given the frequent international criticism, particularly from industrialized democracies, of China's human rights record. Chinese officials resurrected memories of Zhou Enlai at the Bandung Conference, praising the norm as a piece of "joint wisdom" long honored by China and Southeast Asia.[82] Never mind that China terrified the whole region with its revolutionary fervor during the 1960s. In the official discourse, such dissonance hardly ever existed.

In addition to creatively reimagining history, China also attempted to stick to the noninterference with regard to current issues. It remained quiet in the wake of the 1998 Indonesian riots even though Chinese communities were major victims and nationalists at home called for a stronger response.[83] Beijing's effort to silence domestic criticism on the Indonesian riot paradoxically proves that the anti-Japan sentiment has been encouraged and that Japan has been singled out for ostracization as China courts the rest of the world.

Japan on the Defensive

Beginning in the 1990s, China's and Japan's courting efforts toward Southeast Asia became intertwined, although they pointed in opposite directions. Japan has attempted to harden its ties with the region by stressing joint security concerns and the resultant necessity for cooperation. The Japanese government is also no longer shy about showcasing its democracy and labeling it as a common bond with the region. The hardening transition started with the 1996 Hashimoto Doctrine, the first major speech by a Japanese prime minister that did not mention history in discussing Japan–Southeast Asia relations. Under Koizumi, the 2003 Tokyo Declaration further stressed the two sides' "common respect for human rights and freedom" and vowed to establish a "dynamic and enduring partnership."[84]

But Japan did not abandon soft gestures. Rather, sensing that history is no longer a haunting factor between Japan and Southeast Asia and that Japan-targeted hostility is low, Tokyo is poised to receive security perks from its much-recovered reputation. This process implies an effort to elevate Japan's presence in the region to a beyond Fukuda phase: Two decades of soft gestures have begun to aim explicitly at fulfilling hard-power goals.

On both security and value-based issues, joint statements by Japan and ASEAN carefully avoided explicit mention of China, but Beijing nevertheless connected the dots: Tokyo's enhanced efforts to strengthen ties with Southeast Asia; the Japanese government's repeated concerns about

China's defense budget; the new United States–Japan Security Guideline, which did not exclude Taiwan from their defensive parameter; Japan's peacekeeping presence in Cambodia; and China's territorial disputes with both Southeast Asia and Japan. The overall picture, in the words of China's state news agency, is that Japan is actively recruiting Southeast Asia to endorse its "China threat" thesis.[85]

Different Japanese prime ministers have accorded China different weight in their calculations about embedding security in their Southeast Asia policies, and terrorism has become a more urgent security concern since 2001. But even moderate prime ministers have given China undeniable weight in reshaping Southeast Asia policy. After Fukuda Yasuo, a moderate prime minister and the son of Fukuda Takeo, finished a trip to Singapore in November 2007, he told a Japanese audience that China's ascendancy had totally changed Asia and that it was now time to rethink his father's legendary doctrine, though he was vague about specific changes.[86]

China is on a different path, as it has been attempting to soften its image by convincing its permanently suspicious neighbors that it is generous, reliable, and willing to sacrifice for the greater public good. To achieve this goal, China has actively embraced multilateralism. Othering has become most visible between China and Japan in this area. China's 1997 decision not to devalue its currency helped the country gain acclaim. Abandoning its accustomed bilateral diplomacy, China has also signed an assortment of regional integration agreements, most notably the partnership statement with ASEAN in 1997, the Treaty of Amity and Cooperation in Southeast Asia in 2003, and the China-ASEAN Free Trade Agreement in 2001. Its Early Harvest programs opened China's domestic agricultural market to ASEAN members and drew a sharp contrast with Japan, which remains vehemently protective of its farmers.

Japan is feeling the heat. In books as well as in private conversation, Japanese diplomats have expressed concern and frustration that Japan is being left behind by China in this bidding war of initiatives. Referring to the apparent absence of a free-trade agreement between ASEAN and Japan, one diplomat complained that "the game with China is not fair—we are a democracy, and our feet and hands are bound by politicians who have to listen to farmers."[87] Tanaka Hitoshi, a former administrative vice minister at the Ministry of Foreign Affairs, also admits that Japan signed its first bilateral free-trade agreement with Singapore because as a city-state, it would have few issues that conflicted with the interests of Japan's well-protected farmers.[88] Unlike the Japanese diplomat who criticized China's

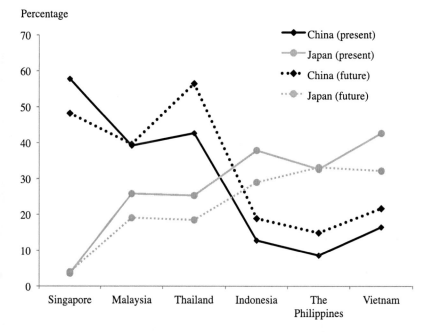

Percentage

Fig. 6. Perfect divide—percentages of people in six ASEAN countries choosing Japan or China as "the most important" present (2008) and future partner. (Data from Japanese Ministry of Foreign Affairs, *Surveys on Southeast Asian Countries' Public Attitude Toward Japan*, http://www.mofa.go.jp/mofaj/area/asean/pdfs/yorono8_02.pdf [accessed December 20, 2009].)

use of its nondemocratic status, Tanaka contends that Japan's problem is internal, as long overdue structural reforms are hurting Japan's international competition.[89] Despite their different explanations, the concern remains the same: an active China versus an immobilist Japan.

Another trend from the Japanese point of view is that China's popularity is on the rise. The Ministry of Foreign Affairs poll that demonstrated positive perceptions of Japan also showed that at a collective level, ASEAN citizens viewed China and Japan as nearly equally important: 29.7 percent chose China as ASEAN's most important partner, versus 28 percent for Japan. The United States was third, at 23 percent. However, crucial intragroup variance occurred. As figure 6 shows, people in Singapore, Malaysia, and Thailand (the China Group) already see China as the most important partner and believe that it will remain so. In contrast, people in Indonesia, the Philippines, and Vietnam (the Japan Group) see Japan as being and continuing to be the most important partner.

Trade may not explain the differences between the two groups. Both China and Japan are important export and import markets for all six countries (table 5). However, the percentage of ethnic Chinese in total population is much higher for the countries in the China Group than for those in the Japan Group (table 5). Also China has had hard power clashes with two of the three countries in the Japan Group (with the Philippines over the Mischief Reef in 1995 and with Vietnam from the late 1970s to mid-1980s), and its relationship with Indonesia has been highly acrimonious. This is not to say that the China Group perceived China's past as clean; rather, the members of the Japan Group are more fearful as a result of demographics, less smooth ethnic assimilation, territorial disputes, and more recent violence.

The problem for Japan, figure 6 shows, is that its future importance declines across the board. A "no change" rating from the Philippines and Singapore on its current and future importance is the best result Japan can secure. China's future importance, by contrast, increases in five of the six countries (including all the Japan Group members, which implies that it is catching up to Japan in influence). Its importance declines in Singapore. But in this case, China is still viewed as the most important future partner, and its loss comes as a result of India's growth (from less than 2 percent who perceived it as the most important present partner to 24 percent who

TABLE 5.   China's and Japan's Ranks as Trading Partners to Six ASEAN Members (2006) and Percentages of Ethnic Chinese Population in These Countries

Country	Rank as Export Market		Rank as Import Market		Percentage of Chinese in Total Population
	China	Japan	China	Japan	
Singapore	4	n/a[a]	3	4	75.60%
Malaysia	4	3	3	1	26%
Thailand	3	2	2	1	14%
Indonesia	4	1	2	3	3.30%
The Philippines	4	2	4	2	1.30%
Vietnam	3	2	1	3	1.13%

Source: Trade data from *Data Book of the World: 2009*, vol. 21 (Tokyo: Ninomiya Shoten, 2009). Percentages of ethnic Chinese population in Singapore, Indonesia, and Thailand from *Data Book of the World: 2009*, vol. 21, and represent levels in 2005. Percentages of ethnic Chinese population in Indonesia, the Philippines, and Vietnam are based on statistics provided by the Overseas Compatriot Affairs Commission, Republic of China, http://www.ocac.gov.tw/public/public_print.asp?selno=943&level=B&no=943 (accessed December 10, 2009).
[a]Japan was not on the list of top five exporting markets for Singapore in 2006.

believe it will be the most important future partner). At merely 4 percent, Japan has negligible importance for Singaporeans. The perceptions are moving in China's favor: For all the Japan Group members, China is catching up in significance, while for all the China Group members, Japan's importance is either stagnating or declining. The "Japan passing" thesis is not pure Japanese paranoia. The drift toward dwindling relevance is real.

In addition, China's status as a nondemocracy does not seem to bother ASEAN respondents. This finding runs contrary to Japan's goals with its "value-based diplomacy [*kachikan gaikō*]," a new direction charted by recent Japanese prime ministers.[90] A 2007 survey of 450 Thais conducted by Beijing University showed that whereas only 13 percent thought China was democratic and 50 percent thought otherwise, 57 percent agreed that "China's political system fits China," while only 9 percent disagreed. Nearly 60 percent of the respondents felt that the "leadership of the Chinese Communist Party is effective," and 86 percent supported "special relations" between Thailand and China.[91] The message is clear: The Thai public acknowledged that China was nondemocratic but felt that the system has worked for China and that how China governs itself should not impede the two countries' relations. Such tolerance of China's undemocratic nature is not exceptional. Since 2002, the Pew Research Center's annual surveys have consistently shown that more than 60 percent of Indonesians have a positive perception of China. Another 2004 BBC survey showed that 70 percent of Filipinos and 68 percent of Indonesians viewed China's international role in a positive way.[92]

Overall, Southeast Asia is apparently balancing between China and Japan, but the momentum is on China's side. Such views explain why despite high levels of regional public support for Japan's effort to become a permanent member of the United Nations Security Council, official Southeast Asian governments' support has been lukewarm at best. One Chinese scholar close to the government proudly pointed to backroom Chinese pressure as contributing to the "cooling down" of Southeast Asian support for Japan's UN dream.[93] Japan was also disheartened when ASEAN hijacked Japan's initiative to hold an ASEAN-Japan Summit by insisting on adding two new members, China and South Korea, thus transforming the occasion into ASEAN + 3 and watering down Japan's leadership.[94] As China's importance grows both in popular perception (figure 6) and in material terms (figure 7), Japan is increasingly unlikely to persuade Southeast Asia to join in containing China on hard power issues.

History has largely become a nonfactor in relations between Japan and

Percentage

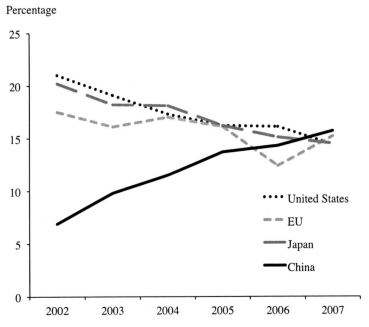

Fig. 7. China's unmistakable rise: Major trading partners ranked by their percentage shares in ASEAN's total foreign trade (2002–7). (Data from *Japanese Diplomatic Blue Book,* Ministry of Foreign Affairs, http://www .mofa.go.jp/Mofaj/gaiko/bluebook/index.html.)

Southeast Asia. In fact, its departure and the resultant low level of Southeast Asian hostility toward Japan have allowed some Japanese politicians and media pundits to cast China and South Korea as two outliers, exceptionally bitter and stubborn in not letting bygones be bygones. But it is too early to conclude that history has thus become a positive card for Southeast Asia–Japan relations. Instead, Japan still receives mild criticism from the region's politicians and media for unnecessarily poking China's sensitive nerves.[95] Singapore's Lee Kuan Yew apparently failed to persuade Koizumi to abandon his annual ritual of visiting the controversial Yasukuni Shrine. Lee had for long shrugged off any personal concern that Japan would indeed remilitarize, dismissing such assessments as paranoia.[96] But Lee was also concerned about the unfolding antagonism between China and Japan, the two Asian giants. Lee tortured answer when asked about his meeting with Koizumi betrayed his ambivalence and that of Southeast Asia more generally: "You know, Mr. Koizumi is a very strong man, very strong willed. He knows what the world thinks. He knows what I think. He will do what Mr. Koizumi thinks is good for Japan."[97] For his part, Koizumi remained defiant, telling reporters that Lee agreed that China was the troublemaker, a claim that Lee neither confirmed nor denied.

China and Japan face one common challenge in their future courting efforts. Structural relations between Southeast Asia and its two powerful neighbors are anything but equal. In this scenario, effective wooing means acting as an "indirect protector, enhancer, and promoter of regional integration," as two Southeast Asia scholars have written.[98] "Equal" treatment is actually special treatment that demands bigger powers' constant sensitivity to the region's counterdominance mentality—they must take recipient context into consideration. Both China and Japan thus must portray themselves as nonthreatening team members and as benevolent and generous neighbors in times of crisis. In policy terms, therefore, both countries need to embed their initiatives in a multilateral framework. They also need to let ASEAN hold the reins, dictating the pace of integration as a way of quelling uneasiness about either Chinese or Japanese dominance.

These two Asian powers also have disparate problems: China still has disputes with countries in the region over hard power issues, most notably the Spratly Islands. Beijing to date has sought to replace its predominantly political image with one that includes economic aspects. But its belligerent past will not easily fade away. In fact, Beijing's claim to the resource-rich Spratly Islands grew markedly aggressive in 2011. Despite high marks for the Chinese economy and leadership, no poll has indicated majority public support from ASEAN members for a greater Chinese military presence. Chinese scholars have admitted that such deeply entrenched suspicion poses a major challenge to China's diplomacy in the region.[99] The quality of products made in China may also become political—the goodwill generated by Beijing's much-touted tsunami aid to Indonesia was compromised by the disclosure that some of the food was past its expiration date.[100]

Japan is following a different path, seeking to turn its economic success into political capital. Doing so will require the Japanese state to fight not only a proactive China but also a static domestic electorate. It is therefore no surprise that vice foreign minister Tanaka Hitoshi has vented his frustration at being squeezed by these dual pressures. The Japanese model, which lost much of its luster in the 1990s, may dim further as the country's economy continues to struggle. If it falls short as an economic model and is not fully embraced in the political realm, what image can Japan offer

Percentage

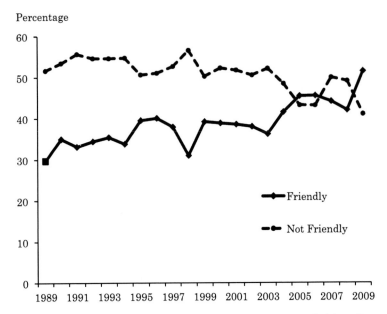

Fig. 8. Japanese public's responses to the question "Do you feel friendly toward Southeast Asian countries?" (1989–2009). (Data from Japanese Cabinet Office, *Sōrifu yoron chōsa* [Polls by the Cabinet Office], http://www8.cao.go.jp/survey/h21-gaiko/images/z20.gif.)

to justify itself as an exemplar? Furthermore, the Japanese public remains somewhat negative in its perception of Southeast Asians on a personal level. A twenty-year study of Japanese attitudes toward "Southeast Asian countries [*Tōnan'ajia shokoku*]" reveals that in all but three years, more people described themselves as harboring negative attitudes ("not feeling friendly") than the opposite (figure 8). To be sure, Southeast Asian countries registered a visible popularity rise in 2009, when 51.4 percent of the Japanese respondents said they felt "friendly" toward Southeast Asia, more than 10 percent higher than those who felt otherwise. But the sustainability of such popular goodwill to Southeast Asia remains to be seen. After all, the same report reveals that among young people in Japan (defined as those between 20 to 29), 50 percent still chose the negative answer of "not feeling friendly" toward Southeast Asia, whereas 48.7 percent chose the positive one. Such an unenthusiastic public perception makes one wonder whether even after thirty years, Fukuda's dream of a "heart-to-heart" connection remains little more than an aspiration.

To date, Southeast Asia has been the clear winner in the courting game between China and Japan, and these countries see no reason to abandon their balancing act, which constitutes a familiar and increasingly effective tactic. Remarks by elites and poll numbers also indicate a consensus in favor of sitting on the fence between China and Japan—both are respected, neither is trusted. Southeast Asia has historically taken this approach, and the region's interests may dictate its continuation.

THREE

South Korea: A Suspicious Power Resistant to Charm

This chapter examines China and Japan's efforts to woo South Korea. Though geographically a small country, South Korea is a global economic powerhouse, boasting the fifteenth-biggest GDP in the world in 2010. The country is an immediate neighbor and a major trading partner with both Japan and China. Cultural exchanges among the three are also vibrant. Located on the Thirty-Eighth Parallel, South Korea bears vital security importance to the whole region. Wooing this vital neighbor, however, turns out to be exceedingly difficult for China and Japan.

One factor distinguishes South Korea as a recipient context: A history of combined ancient superiority and recent humiliation has created a high level of South Korean sensitivity to dominance by a bigger power. This factor has limited the effectiveness of any charm offensive by its neighbors. Neither China nor Japan has much credibility in striking a common value chord with the South Korean public, which remains intuitively suspicious of any hint at being dwarfed. Pride, sensitivity, and ambition join together to create an emotionally closed South Korea, with bigger powers persistently suspected and frequently bashed. Indeed, the South Korean case may reveal the limits of charm offensives when recipients instinctively reject the wooing for the sake of protecting national character.

China and Japan do not share the same starting line on developing relations with South Korea. As North Korea's most important ally, China did not normalize relations with South Korea until 1992, long after Japan did so in 1965. This chapter thus offers a more detailed treatment of Japan–South Korea relations. An immediate impression is that a longer history of formal relations has not greatly helped Japan. Despite security and formal political connections, postwar Korea's rejection of Japan was comprehensive. Denied access to the Korean society, Japan could not construct its own image but remained at the mercy of the South Korean governing elites. These elites, authoritarian or democratic, often found incentives to heed rather than to transcend popular hatred of Japan. In such a context, Japanese government mistakes (often stemming from the elites' neglect of Korean sensitivities) would justify their country's lack of repentance, whereas Japan's improvements were dismissed or rendered irrelevant. The consequence is that Japan was being modeled in substantive terms without receiving acknowledgment. This is the opposite of soft power, leading Japanese observers to lament that the country became a sheep wearing wolf's clothing.[1]

Recent cultural exchanges between Japan and South Korea have created much media sensation but have done little to enhance Japan's political capital. Taking one step beyond the colorful world of cuisine, fashion, and TV dramas, there is scant evidence that either the "Korean wave" or the "Japanese wind" has led to mutual support for key issues like Japan's bid for a permanent seat on the United Nations Security Council or how to deal with North Korea's nuclear weapons. These exchanges have also done surprisingly little to improve Japan's image among Korean citizens, a situation Tokyo finds frustrating: Neither a "cool Japan" nor a shared democratic identity has pulled South Korea significantly closer. In fact, as one Korean scholar suggests, the lowering of Korean hostility toward Japan has resulted partly from Japan's relative decline.[2] The trend from "Japanbashing" to "Japan-passing" can hardly be called a victory of soft power.

China also has not effectively wooed South Korea and has succeeded largely in material terms alone. Like Japan, China has yet to win Korean hearts and minds. Three reasons explain the lack of success of Beijing's charm offensive. First, China is far from innocent in the Korean collective memory. As China's leaders attempt to use history as a bond to build a Japan-targeted "grievance alliance" with South Korea, they soon realize that history can backfire and that Korean anger will soon turn to China. In other words, China has simply been another Other on which the Korean nation relies to stress its heroic quest for independence. Second, Beijing has been squeezed by a conflict between domestic and diplomatic agendas. Driven by a persistent fear of ethnic tension, China has sacrificed soft diplomatic gestures to maintain stability in the domestic realm, as in the Goguryeo dispute with South Korea. Third, stereotyping remains rampant on both the Chinese and Korean sides. In particular, signs indicate that South Korea may have surpassed Japan as a prime target of Chinese popular ridicule.

This chapter concludes with an assessment of the consequences of the lack of soft power among China, Japan, and South Korea. With sensitivities repeatedly poked, leaders of these three countries remain haunted by abstract yet tangible "national feeling," and they are often reluctant to lend support to each other's diplomatic priorities. Furthermore, a zero-sum mentality embedded in a trilateral setting creates a tendency for governments to perceive that hostility in one set of relations often presents itself as a good opportunity to boost cordiality elsewhere. Wooing has become a confrontational mechanism, since it aims to create discord elsewhere and gaining benefits. Overall, high emotional barriers have rendered these three Northeast Asian powers underachievers in regional integration.

Historical Context: Korea as the Absolute Good and Japan as the Other

Korea is much closer to China than is either Southeast Asia or Japan. Lack of daunting physical barriers also made the country an ideal land bridge for passing on Chinese culture and advanced knowledge, including Buddhism, Chinese characters, medicines, and architecture. Proximity to the region's civilization center and its role as a messenger helped the rise of Korea's "little China mentality [*xiao zhong hua yi shi*]"—a sense of superiority to the world beyond China.[3]

This mentality clearly influenced Korean perceptions of Japan, a major recipient of Chinese knowledge through the Korean channel. As Kim Young-jak points out, whereas historical documents and literature written in Japan frequently refer to the Korean Peninsula, Korean historical records offer scant references to Japan.[4] Underneath this low level of attention was condescension. The few Korean writings that mentioned Japan generally used the term *wo*, which carried connotation of dwarfs. Other derogatory terms included *do'i* (barbarian islanders) and *i'teki* (barbarian aliens).[5] As a result of damage caused by seaborne Japanese marauders, people living in Japan were also called *waegu* (dwarf bandits), a derogatory term that appeared in Chinese historical records (*wokou*) as well. Ancient Korea shared China's view of Japan as backwater inhabited by uncultured people.

Japan's image worsened after Toyotomi Hideyoshi's two invasions of Korea in the 1590s. Both incursions eventually failed after Ming China sent in troops to fight on the Korean side. Yet during the war, Toyotomi's army occupied large parts of Korea, including Seoul and Pyongyang, and crushed the Korean economy. Official Korean documents claimed that arable land dropped to two-thirds of its prewar levels.[6] Famines ensued, along with losses of cultural assets such as archives and skilled artisans.[7] Paradoxically, Korea's weak response justified the impression of Japanese barbarism. If anything, Japan now acquired a new layer of wickedness, as it was not only uncivilized but also hostile. Korea's contacts with the Japanese Bakufu government resumed a decade later, but a mixture of condescension and humiliation still haunted Korean perceptions of Japan.[8]

The little China mentality did not affect only Korean's perception of lesser powers such as Japan. In fact, this superiority complex later turned on China, particularly after it was conquered by the Manchus. Mainstream scholarship contends that consecutive Korean dynasties regarded Confucianism, especially Song scholar Zhu Xi's interpretation of it, as the essence of Chinese civilization.[9] Under this assumption, a delinking of Chineseness (a cultural concept) from China (a physical concept) occurred, thereby guaranteeing that China's decline would not hurt Korean faith in the superiority of the Chinese civilization. In fact, China's domination by a non-Chinese ethnic group and consequent weakening only strengthened a sense that Korea had become the genuine embodiment of the Chinese civilization. Where this civilization first emerged no longer mattered as much as who had become its savior. Japanese scholar Ogura Kizō neatly summarizes this transformation as a series of equivalences: Korea = Zhu Xi's strand of Confucianism = Chineseness = Civilization.[10]

This faith in Korea as the protector of a more advanced civilization helped the country's governing conservatives weather the storm of the late nineteenth century. Neither China's humiliating defeat by Britain nor Japan's opening fundamentally toppled Korea's conviction of the superiority of Korean culture-cum-civilization. Although in 1881 the Korean government sent a high-ranking delegation to the newly opened Japan to study its modernizing experiences, some members were apparently unimpressed, waving aside Japan's changes and questioning the necessity of exchanges with such an inferior country.[11]

An even bigger frustration came from those who initially viewed Japan with awe and inspiration but later felt betrayed by the country's policies. The contrast between Meiji Japan and Qing China—the former successfully confronting challenges from the West and the latter in hopeless decline—convinced some Korean intellectuals that a new model was on the rise to their east and that Japan would assist Korea on its quest for modernization. Kim Okgyun, a leading Korean intellectual, envisioned Asia's future unfolding with Japan as Asia's Britain and Korea as the region's France.[12]

It was a one-sided love. Mainstream Japanese intellectuals such as Fukuzawa viewed Korea, along with China, as Japan's *akuyū* (bad friends) and believed that "nothing could be more stupid than to expect anything from China and Korea."[13] *Jiji Shimpo*, Fukuzawa's newspaper, was even blunter: "For the sake of the Korean people, we are wishing for the death of their country."[14] Although such Japanese disparagement seemed to target the inept Korean government, such editorial comments backed a larger plan for a superior Japan to lead the way in modernizing the rest of inferior Asia in accordance with a Western model. In practice, the 1876 Treaty of Ganghwa, whose first clause read, "Korea, as an independent country, enjoys the same rights as Japan does," proved only the first step toward Japan's eventual domination over Korea.

As Korea became a Japanese colony in 1910, the betrayal became complete. Brutal Japanization policies sought to eliminate every trace of the Korean culture, including the language and national costumes. One unintended consequence of such suppressions (or "cultural genocide")[15] is that Korean conservatives' outdated conviction in Korean superiority was vindicated rather than nullified, and the country remained the "absolute good."[16] Modern Korean nationalism hence sought to "restore" the country's superior uniqueness that had been ruthlessly trounced by Japanese colonizers. Japan became the Other against which Korea's tragic yet heroic nationalist myth was constructed.

Japan's Image during the Rhee Years: Deepening of Suspicion and Disregard

The first generation of South Korean leaders was staunchly nationalistic. President Syngman Rhee gained a reputation as a patriot for his long struggle against Japanese rule. Rhee saw little sense in embracing a country that had just traumatized his homeland for nearly half a century. Indeed, Rhee tried his best to avoid talking to Japan in a bilateral setting. Only when the United States turned down his request to have South Korea become a signatory of the San Francisco Treaty did bilateral contact with Japan become unavoidable.[17] Yet with the shadow of suspicion looming large, Koreans would have great difficulty finding the postwar Japanese state attractive.

The Japanese did not ease the situation, devoting little attention to Korean sensitivities. On the contrary, leading Japanese politicians repeatedly made remarks that exacerbated Korean suspicions. During the Korean War, for example, the Yoshida administration dispatched Japanese marines to assist the United States in naval minesweeping operations. When questioned about whether this act would violate Japan's pacifist constitution, Yoshida argued that waters surrounding Korea constituted Japan's "traditional maritime jurisdiction," so dispatching troops there was a domestic rather than international issue, a stance the Rhee government vehemently protested.[18] Yoshida again hit a Korean nerve when it responded to a Korean request for Japanese reparations for colonialism by proposing that any payments should be mutual, since Japan also deserved compensation for assisting Korea's modernization.[19]

Japan's dismissiveness and Korea's suspicion fed on each other and sent bilateral relations to the bottom. Three months after Japan made its "reversed reparation request [*gyaku seikyūken*]," on January 18, 1952, Rhee abruptly announced South Korea's sovereign control over between fifty and sixty nautical miles of nearby waters, declaring that Korean boats would have exclusive fishing right in this area. After the statement, commonly referred to as the Syngman Rhee Line, Korean troops opened fire on Japanese ships and arrested Japanese fishermen. According to Japanese estimates, by the time the two countries normalized relations in 1965, the statement and its ensuing policies had led to the arrests of nearly 4,000 Japanese, seizures of 328 Japanese boats, and 44 casualties. Financial losses totaled nearly nine billion yen.[20] While avoiding a direct military showdown, Japanese politicians continued to disregard Korean sensitivities. Kubota Kan'ichirō, chief negotiator for normalization talks, stated that "Japan's colonial control benefited Korea," leading the furious Koreans to cancel the talks.[21]

In short, a string of acrimonious incidents attested to the low level of trust between the two countries. The lack of Japanese efforts to redress past grievances aggravated Koreans' existing suspicions. A U.S.-led alliance was the lone factor binding Korea and Japan, and virtually no wooing took place during this period.

Japan, Made in Korea

Japan–South Korea relations improved significantly following Rhee's forced departure in 1960. Chang Myon, the prime minister and South Korea's de facto leader, set resuming normalization talks with Japan as his top diplomatic priority. Resisting popular protests, Chang liberated Park Heung-sik, an influential entrepreneur purged by Rhee as a consequence of his ties with the Japanese during colonial years, and used him as a personal messenger with Tokyo. On the Japanese side, the pro–South Korea faction (*chinkan ha*) was also on the rise within the ruling Liberal Demo-

cratic Party. The faction's leader, Yagi Nobuo, was a former colonial administrator and had extensive connections with key political and economic
figures on both sides.[22]

Such personal pipelines were undisturbed by South Korea's jolt into
a military dictatorship. In fact, Park Chung-hee, the new authoritarian
leader, was known for his deep roots in Japan. A graduate of a Japanese
military academy, Park achieved the rank of lieutenant while fighting with
the Japanese military and adopted the Japanese name Takaki Masao. Park's
familiarity with Japan was further reinforced by his selection of pro-Japan
figures, most notably Professor Yi Yong-hui from Seoul University and law-
maker Park Cheol-on, to continue the tradition of personal diplomacy.[23]

In spite of the visible improvements, normalization had its limits: The
process did not involve the two sides reaching a consensus on the past. The
Japanese chose to evade rather than to tackle an issue that was tremendously emotionally charged for many Koreans. For its part, the Park government, driven by the desire to speed up economic development and by
U.S. pressure, agreed to bypass history rather than to confront Japan.[24] On
the most contentious topic—whether the 1910 Japan-Korea Annexation
Treaty was legitimate at the time of its signing—the final wording of the
normalization statement could not have been more vague: The two sides
"confirmed that all treaties or agreements concluded between the Empire
of Japan and the Empire of Korea on or before August 22, 1910, are already
null and void." The ambivalence of *already* allowed both sides to interpret
the meaning as they saw fit: Whereas the Japanese insisted that *already*
meant that the treaty was legitimate at the time, the Korean government
told its discontented people that *already* meant "from day one."[25]

These bifurcated explanations attest to the hasty nature of the normalization talks. Expediency might help the two sides officially recognize each
other, but it carried a political price. Japan set up an embassy in Seoul
and poured in capital, but the effort did little to alleviate Korean popular
disdain for Japan. With no attempt to redress Korean grievances, Japan
gained little political capital in return. In fact, its reputation deficit deepened because it normalized ties with a military regime. The South Korean public did not believe that history had finally been put to rest; on the
contrary, a new grievance was born, as many Koreans perceived the Park
government as treasonously reaching out to a former enemy at the cost of
burying history.[26] With emotional wounds left untreated, the past would
inevitably boomerang back to disrupt the present.

Furthermore, Japan remained generally blocked from Korean society.
Japan's image remained at the mercy of the Korean governing elites, who

would winnow or frame certain aspects of Japan to fit their own agendas. Park's Japanese roots ran deep, yet even he could not remain totally deaf to the public disgruntlement regarding normalization, and he still needed to speak like a staunch nationalist. In justifying the need to reach out to Japan, Park admitted his purely utilitarian purpose of preventing the spread of communism. Right after the normalization treaty was signed, Park told the nation that he realized that the negotiating process with South Korea's "hatred-filled" enemy had caused much pain and that he understood the suffering of the six hundred thousand Koreans still residing in Japan. Nevertheless, Park argued, he must let go of the bitter emotions of the past to best serve Korea's future.[27]

The Chang-Park era saw a slight loosening of cultural exchanges between Japan and South Korea. The Seoul University of Foreign Languages began offering a Japanese language major in 1961, and book exchanges among schools commenced from 1965. However, Park largely sustained Rhee's closure of South Korea to Japanese cultural influences, rejecting or postponing a number of Japanese soft initiatives, including proposals to open a cultural office and to establish a joint cultural exchange committee.[28] Park took a heavy-handed approach to limiting the inflow of Japanese cultural products, launching nationwide campaigns to ban and confiscate Japanese records and movies. Japanese popular books and magazines were rejected on the grounds that they were being violent, sexist, and in poor taste.[29]

South Korea, however, faced a dilemma: Modernizing would render inevitable some kinds of learning from Japan. As Nam Ki-jeong points out, whereas the double quests for autonomy and modernization work in synergy for many newly industrializing countries, the two were on a collision course in the Korean context, as modernization evoked painful memories of the loss of Korea's independence to Japan.[30] To keep both endeavors on track would thus require some balancing mechanisms.

South Korean students were dispatched to Japan, where most of them would major in natural sciences and engineering. But attention to such substantive learning was more than offset by denunciations of the purported low quality of Japan's popular culture. Moreover, interest in Japan's social sciences was low, as mainstream Korean intellectuals continued to disregard Japanese achievements in these areas as nothing more than translating Western knowledge and thus not "genuine," an attitude that constituted a natural extension of Korea's deeply entrenched sense of cultural superiority vis-à-vis Japan.[31]

All these trends worked to the detriment of Japan's goal of enhancing its political capital. Japan became a model in actual terms without being acknowledged, let alone embraced. Even in the censored realm of popular culture, learning was happening, as large numbers of Japanese songs were readapted into the Korean language and became quite popular. Novels and animations were also translated informally or re-created as Korean works. The Korean public obviously found little tension between concealed learning from and open rejection of Japan. The Japanese showed little interest in wooing South Korea, in partly because the Korean regime blocked massive anti-Japan protests like those Tanaka Kakuei experienced in Thailand and Indonesia. Trade and investment proceeded largely undisturbed in spite of political antipathy.

In addition, Japan's left-leaning forces were never big fans of South Korea. Even for the public in the middle, discrimination against Koreans as "third-ranking nationals [santō kokumin]" remained deeply entrenched. The stereotype of Koreans as unlawful and violent was somehow "justified" by a series of violent incidents in the 1970s, most notably the kidnapping of Kim Dae-jung in 1973 and the assassination of Yuk Young-soo, wife of Park Chung-hee, in 1974. Kim's kidnapping was carried out by South Korean secret agents on Japanese soil, a blatant breach of Japan's sovereignty. And although Yuk was killed in Seoul, the assassin, Mun Seg-wang, was a Japan-born Korean. Media coverage of these incidents caused Japanese perceptions of both South Korea as a state and its people plummeted.[32] Unlike the "China frenzy" during roughly the same period, popular enthusiasm for warming up to South Korea was scant.

The "Japan made in Korea" phenomenon continued into the final phase of authoritarian rule by Chun Doo-hwan in the 1980s. Unlike Park, Chun and his supporting military officers belonged to the postcolonial Hangeul generation. Though they lacked personal grievances caused by Japanese colonial control, patriotic upbringing and a military background made Chun and his army cohort firm nationalists. To justify the legitimacy of his coup, Chun purged people with close connections with the Park regime, including those personal pipelines between South Korea and Japan. Japanese prime minister Nakasone Yasuhiro attempted to build a personal rapport with Chun much as he did with China's Hu Yaobang. Nakasone chose South Korea for his first official visit, and in 1984, Chun in return became the first South Korean head of state to set foot on Japanese soil. During Chun's visit, Emperor Hirohito expressed his "genuine regret" over the "unfortunate past" and vowed not to repeat it, a remark that Korea interpreted as a major attitudinal improvement.[33] Interactions between Nakasone and Chun, along with U.S. president Ronald Reagan's staunch support for both, led to a popular perception of a Reagan-Nakasone-Chun triangle.[34]

However, Japan's reputational recovery was hardly noticeable. Unlike Hu in China, Chun was deeply unpopular inside South Korea. Any personal courting thus ended up doing little to improve Japan's popular image among ordinary Koreans. Furthermore, South Korea under Chun remained closed to Japanese cultural penetration. Into the early 1990s, intellectuals continued to bash pop culture as an "invasion waged by Japanese cultural imperialism" and an "intentional act to exert a bad influence on the Korean youth."[35] Two rounds of disputes regarding history textbooks in the 1980s led South Korea to form a protest alliance with China, a country South Korea had not officially recognized, to denounce Japan's alleged attempts to revive militarism. Though no longer bound by the humiliation complex, Chun also brought up the reparation issue, not in the name of putting history to rest but in the name of South Korea acting as a defensive shield for a pacifist Japan: Japan should pay for that service.[36]

Thus, during South Korea's authoritarian years, material connections with Japan strengthened markedly in terms of politics, security, and economics. However, Japan made little progress in winning acceptance from the Korean public. Being emulated without being credited is the precise opposite of soft power. By gliding over history in the normalization treaty, Japan seemed to offer only a lukewarm response to many Koreans' deepest grievance.

Japan also seemed to care little about Korean perceptions. In fact, as long as economic activities remained undisturbed, consecutive Japanese governments remained quiet about South Korea's discriminating policies against Japanese cultural influence. In retrospect, neither this "image subcontracting" nor Tokyo's tolerance helped Japan gain appreciation from the Korean public. As South Korea became democratic, many Koreans began to take Japan's cozy relations with the dictators as one more piece of evidence of the country's exploitative nature. Protesting against Japan now became a way to celebrate the hard-won democracy.

Democratization without a Democratic Bond

Until South Korea's democratization, Japan added to rather than shed its heavy political capital deficit. At that point, all the problems that the military regimes had suppressed resurfaced. Instead of becoming a bonding factor, South Korea's democratic identity has become a new channel for releasing anger at Japan. On the Japanese side, despite the sensation that the cultural Korean wave has stirred up, the public remained tepid overall toward South Korea.

Poll numbers reflect this absence of charm. Japanese hostility toward South Korea lessened, but the majority of the Japanese respondents were willing to be neutral toward South Korea when surveys offered that option. In three polls jointly sponsored by two national newspapers in Japan and South Korea in 2000, 2001, and 2005 (thus covering the high-profile 2002 Soccer World Cup, co-hosted by Japan and Korea, as well as the Korean wave),[37] 60 percent of the Japanese said they neither liked nor disliked South Korea, a number that fluctuated by only 1 percentage point over the three polls. However, the percentage of those who disliked South Korea kept rising, topping the percentage of those who liked South Korea in 2005 (figure 9).

South Korean respondents consistently ranked Japan as the country they disliked the most. Even in 1999 and 2000, when hostility toward Japan dropped to its nadir, the percentages of those who disliked Japan remained markedly higher than those who liked Japan. In the 2001 and 2005 polls, six in ten respondents disliked Japan. An affection gap has apparently existed as the South Korean public invariably dislikes Japan much more than the Japanese public dislikes South Korea.

A long-term perspective is even more revealing. As figure 9 illustrates, between 1984 (the first year such data were available) and 2005, the percentage of South Koreans saying they liked Japan never topped 23 percent and declined from its 1984 high. And even when that number was at its peak, the number who disliked Japan was 16 points higher. By 2005, only 8 percent of the Koreans polled liked Japan, while 63 percent disliked Japan. Nearly 90 percent opposed Japan's bid for a permanent seat on the United Nations Security Council, and 93 percent expected relations with Japan to worsen. The two countries could at least agree in their pessimism: 61 percent of Japanese respondents said they expected relations with Korea to worsen.

With such numbers, it would be hard to claim that either country has done an impressive job of winning the other's hearts and minds, though Japan's failure was more pronounced. Such failures to woo can hardly be explained as a result of leaders or governments unaware of their counterparts' sensitivities: Japan and South Korea have dealt with each other long and known each other well. These numbers, therefore, offer powerful hints that leaders were constrained by domestic sentiments and that the need to appeal to such emotions compelled them to poke each other in the eye. This argument directly speaks to the causal chain laid out in the introduc-

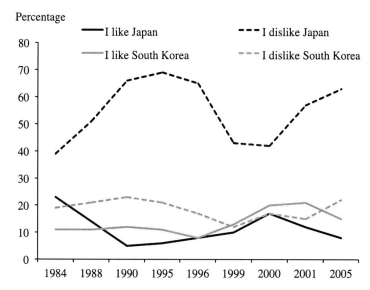

Fig. 9. South Korea and Japan's gap in mutual affection (1984–2005). (Data from *Asahi Shimbun*, "Miraishikoh to kakokaifuku yureru nikkan kokkoh 40nen" [Fortieth anniversary of Japan–South Korea relations: Shaken by collision between future and past], June 20, 2005.)

tion chapter—that is, a decision about whether to woo or to respond to wooing is often conditioned by domestic agendas. But of course, leaders are not mere prisoners: When they loudly echo popular appeals, they often intensify such views and make diplomatic compromises even harder to achieve.

Softening to Hardening: A Presidential Wooing Pattern

A closer examination of South Korean presidencies during the democratic era can shed some insight into the country's shifting between soft and hard diplomatic gestures toward Japan. Behind the ups and downs revealed by figure 9, there is a recurring pattern: Prior to Lee Myung-bak, all the presidents initially took a soft approach toward Japan. This pattern fits even Kim Young-sam (1993–98) and Roh Moo-hyun (2003–8), who are remembered for their assertiveness toward Japan. But each president eventually hardened, sometimes abruptly.

Kim Young-sam, South Korea's first democratically elected civilian president, was no stranger to Japan. Born in 1927, he is fluent in Japanese and, like many Koreans of his generation, was forced to acquire a Japanese name during the colonial period. But when Kim assumed the presidency, he made some wooing gestures toward Japan. One month prior to his in-auguration, Kim gave his first postvictory foreign interview to a group of Japanese journalists, pointing out that such preferential treatment symbol-ized the importance his administration would attach to Japan–South Korea relations.[38]

Some cordiality seemed to develop at the personal level between Kim and Japanese prime minister Hosokawa Morihiro. During his trip to South Korea in November 1993, Hosokawa apologized up-front for such colo-nial-era policies as depriving Koreans of their right to learn their own lan-guage, forcing them to bear Japanese names, and drafting Korean women to serve as sex slaves for the Japanese military. Hosokawa also expressed his goal of elevating bilateral relations to a level where "leaders could phone each other in a relaxed manner."[39] Kim in return highly praised Hoso-kawa's remarks on history.[40] On his trip to Japan in the following year, Kim further impressed the Japanese audience with his forward-looking stance, expressing on multiple occasions the idea that the two countries should no longer be haunted by the past.[41]

But Kim reserved another face for domestic consumption. Six months into his presidency, he announced a decision to tear down the national cen-tral museum, which was housed in a building that had originally served as the Japanese governor's mansion and hence symbolized humiliation for many Koreans. He explained that the destruction would "eliminate a sym-bol of Japanese imperialism and restore national self-pride."[42] As long as Kim hid this face from the Japanese, relations between the two countries remained tranquil. But in late 1994, Kim showed his more assertive vis-age to Japanese audiences. The trigger was a "problematic remark [*mondai hatsugen*]" by Eto Takami, a minister in the Murayama Tomiichi administra-tion: Takami suggested that "not everything Japan did in Korea during the colonial era was bad. Japan also did some good things."[43] Such comments by Japanese government officials could be counted on to provoke condemna-tion from China and South Korea, and like his predecessors who made such statements, Eto was forced to resign shortly thereafter. To quiet the storm, Murayama also wrote to Kim to admit the "imperialist nature" of the 1910 annexation treaty.[44] But Korean and Chinese feathers were ruffled again in the summer of 1995 when the Japanese Diet passed a vaguely worded reso-lution on history. The document did more harm than good, as both China and South Korea viewed it as glossing over Japan's historical sins.

Kim struck back with at least four hardening measures: In March 1995, he indeed tore down the old governor's mansion, proclaiming that he did so to take care of the "national feeling." He also ordered the removal of huge iron sticks that the Japanese had planted in mountains. Although Japanese military documents show that the sticks had mining and measuring purposes, many Koreans subscribed to a conspiracy theory that the sticks blocked *pungsu* (*feng shui* in Chinese) and thus sapped Korean spirit. Furthermore, Kim launched campaigns to eliminate Japanese-style place-names and Japanese words in everyday language. All these measures sought to achieve *hanpuri*, or the venting of national hatred of Japan.[45] Kim saw his diplomatic offensive as justified, arguing that "a democratically elected civilian government must righteously highlight its moral superiority to that of previous military dictatorships."[46]

Even more worryingly to Japan, a grievance alliance was in the making between China and South Korea. During Kim's November 1995 summit with Jiang Zemin, both leaders voiced their displeasure with Tokyo's lack of repentance. Kim used the term *borujammori*, a colloquialism often used by adults to scold children for being idiotic, to describe Japan's attitude toward the past.[47]

History was not the only war zone. In February 1996, Japan and South Korea also quarreled loudly over the border of their two-hundred-nautical-mile exclusive economic zone and thus possession of Dokto/Takeshima. Kim promised his people that he would not negotiate with the Japanese on this issue, a stance that earned him a reputation for being "ultra-harsh" in dealing with Japan.[48] His fervency in echoing populism also made some Koreans feel that their president was behaving more like an opposition party leader and that he was diverting public attention from his scandal-ridden cabinet.[49] The same *Asahi Shimbun* journalists who had just hailed the arrival of a promising era in Japan–South Korea relations thanks to the open-minded Kim, now described the status of the relations as "the worst ever" and complained that Japan had become Kim's campaign tactic.[50]

The softening-to-hardening trajectory also was replicated under President Roh Moo-hyun. Like Kim, Roh met with the Japanese press prior to his inauguration, just one week after Koizumi Jun'ichirō paid his third annual visit to the Yasukuni Shrine. Yet Roh sounded relaxed, telling Japanese journalists, "I like Mr. Koizumi's straightforwardness—He's just like me."[51]

Less than five months into his presidency, Roh paid a state visit to Japan. Roh reassured members of the Diet, "I am here to talk not about the past but about the future."[52] Even cordiality at the personal level seemed to be repeating itself, as Koizumi and Roh staged two no-tie summits in Korean and Japanese resort towns. At the summit in Ibusukishi, Koizumi was in such a good mood that he invited Roh for a sand bath; however, the Korean president worried that the image of him in a Japanese bathrobe bathing with a Japanese prime minister would be too much for the Korean public. Ban Ki-moon, who was then serving as Korean foreign minister, explained to his Japanese counterpart that the president had nothing against the bath itself and happily took it alone.[53] Despite such sore spots, the overall picture of Japan–South Korea relations looked encouraging. In September 2003, Roh lifted the ban on Japanese movies, completely opening the Korean market to Japanese cultural products. At a July 2004 summit, he pledged "not to raise history in the official realm with Japan during my presidential tenure."[54]

But softening came to a sudden halt in March 2005. In an open letter posted on his home page, Roh announced that he would bid farewell to his "quiet diplomacy" toward Japan and replace it with a "diplomatic war." Japan's Shimane prefectural government appeared to set off Roh's furor, as it announced to set February 22 as Takeshima Day to commemorate its jurisdiction over the disputed island (which remained under South Korea's control). But Roh's declaration of a diplomatic war with Japan was not based solely on this incident. Rather, Roh, who was riding on a populist agenda, eventually caved in to domestic pressure, and the "Three-Point Package" (Yasukuni Shrine, territorial dispute, and history textbooks) boomeranged back to disturb bilateral relations.

Indeed, as a pioneering politician known for mastering online mobilization, Roh was even more prone to sentiments of younger voters, who were unapologetically nationalistic.[55] In the initial phase of his presidency, Roh seemed to demonstrate courage to contain this virulent sentiment. Despite Korean press concerns that Roh was busy "bowing to Japan after bowing to America," he went ahead with his summer 2003 state visit to Japan, an act Koizumi praised.[56] But Roh eventually had to take the pressure into consideration. According to Chi Myong-gwan, former presidential counselor on Korea-Japan cultural exchanges, Roh had wanted to lift the ban on Japanese movies even earlier than September 2003, yet public opinion had held him back for another few months.[57]

Nationalist sentiment was not Roh's only trouble, Externally, his tolerance toward Japan hit a wall, as Koizumi was busy burnishing his own populist image by attacking not only the Chinese and South Korean governments but also Japan's diplomats for "joining the wrong side" when they tried to persuade him to stop visiting the Yasukuni Shrine.[58] By standing up to foreign governments and Japan's bureaucracy, Koizumi added to his defiant, antiestablishment image. But as Roh was squeezed by domestic stresses and foreign provocations, a hardening became inevitable. Once the route was chosen, antagonism and confrontation further fed on each other. The Roh who had promised not to put history on the table now said he had "no interest" in meeting again with Koizumi.[59] To counter Takeshima Day, Gyeongsangnam-do, the South Korean province that administered the disputed Dokto/Takeshima, announced Dokto Month. For Roh as for Kim Young-sam, bilateral relations chilled.

However, if there has ever been a honeymoon in bilateral Japan–South Korea relations, it occurred during Kim Dae-jung's presidency, which followed that of Kim Young-sam. The most crucial achievement was the 1998 Kim-Obuchi joint statement. The document was unprecedented, not only because the two countries vowed to establish a partnership but also because of the remarkable progress reached on recognizing history: The Japanese government offered a formal apology for colonial control, while the Korean side praised Japan's democracy and pacifist postwar path. Photographs of Kim visiting his frail Japanese teacher, published widely in Japanese newspapers, also conveyed a heartwarming image. In addition, China inadvertently helped: Kim Dae-jung showed little interest in joining with Chinese leaders to shame Japan. Jiang's November 1998 visit to Tokyo was a disaster. His incessant bashings of Japan on history and his refusal to sign the partnership statement contrasted sharply with Kim's behavior as a gracious guest.

Despite this positive episode, the general soft-hard trajectory held firm. Even Kim Dae-jung followed this patter to at least some extent. With Koizumi going to Yasukuni each year, Kim's frustration mounted, and his responses escalated from a mild "it's difficult for me to understand" the visits to "I feel indignant and strongly protest."[60] After Koizumi's third visit, with only a few weeks remaining in Kim's presidency, the moderate Korean president sent an "enough-is-enough" signal by refusing to meet with Japanese foreign minister Kawaguchi Junko to hear her explanation.[61]

Kim Dae-jung tried to lessen Korean popular disdain for Japan, but his efforts accomplished little. Even at the height of bilateral relations, leading up to the 2002 World Cup, the percentage of Koreans who disliked Japan still far outstripped those who felt otherwise (figure 9). Despite the outside world's high regard for Kim, as evidenced by his receipt of the Nobel Peace Prize, the Korean public's views of him remained divided along regional and ideological lines.[62] The only area on which the Korean people reached consensus was precisely the one that Kim worked hard yet failed to transcend: widespread hatred of Japan.

Lee Myung-bak's presidency has thus far not followed the softening-to-hardening path insofar as relations with Japan are concerned. Indeed, the Japanese-born Lee has offered the best hope to Japan in recent years, repeatedly stating that he would prefer to put history aside. Lee also benefited from good timing, as his tenure has coincided with the ascension of a less revisionist administration under the Democratic Party of Japan, which has avoided blatant insults to Korean sensibilities. Most important, North Korea's rising belligerence and attacks on the south have commanded Lee's attention. History-based quarrels with Japan became trivial, whereas a security-based alliance became imperative. The recent harmony between Japan and South Korea thus has resulted not from Japan's wooing success but from diminished Korean concerns: Koreans have something more urgent to worry about. Furthermore, Lee's departure from the previous presidential paths may not be as complete as popularly perceived. He is not the first president to say that he would prefer to let history rest. Korean popular perceptions of Japan remain hostile, and whatever Lee's claims about looking to the future, he must remain mindful of public sentiment. His attempts to do so sometimes bear a striking resemblance to the efforts of hawkish Chinese foreign minister Li Zhaoxing: Both love to bring up Germany as a "good example" to shame Japan.[63] In August 2008, Lee also repeated one of his predecessors' drastic diplomatic measures, recalling his ambassador to Japan to protest the publication of history textbooks stating that Dokto/Takeshima is Japanese territory.

It is not yet certain that Lee's presidency will ultimately not follow the same hardening pattern evidenced by the tenures of previous South Korean leaders, and any improvements are not certain to persist into subsequent administrations. Cordiality between Japan and South Korea cannot rely permanently on a menacing third party but will require effective wooing so that any decline in Korean suspicion of Japan should not come as a by-product of rising Korean suspicion of another country. In the absence of wooing, emotionally charged issues will inevitably return to upset bilateral relations.

Cultural Exchanges: Increasingly Vibrant, Increasingly Irrelevant

The past two decades have witnessed a significant loosening of cultural exchanges and an explosive growth in human connections between South Korea and Japan (figure 10). But even in this realm, Korean leaders have carefully balanced between opening their market to Japan and addressing national sensitivities.

In 1988, the two governments founded the Committee on Japan-Korea

Unit: 1,000 Persons

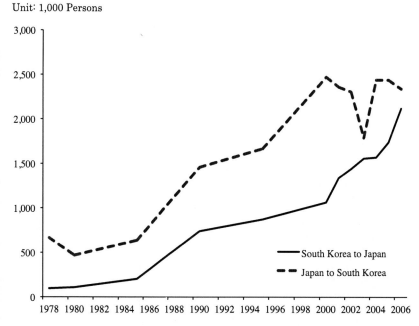

Fig. 10. Human exchanges between Japan and South Korea (1978–2006).
(Data for 1978 to 2003 from Japanese Embassy in Korea, http://www.kr.emb
-jpan.go.jp/rel/r_2002/r_20030607_01.htm; data from 2004 to 2006 from
Council of Local Authorities for International Relations, http://www.clair.or.kr/
info/info.asp?np=407.)

Relations for the Twenty-First Century, an organization charged with the
responsibility of promoting mutual understanding. Cultural exhibitions
were also regularly sponsored in major cities throughout the 1990s. Yet
South Korea's opening to Japan during this period remained timid and
inconsistent. Domestic resistance remained high. Two cultural ministers
in the Roh Tae-woo administration entertained the possibility of lifting
the ban on importing Japanese popular cultural products (music and movies), but others within the government voiced objections, with the opposition sticking to the arguments that Japan's "low-quality" culture could
spoil Korean youth and that the South Korean cultural industry might be
overwhelmed by its Japanese rival. Even the two committees set up by Kim
Yong-sam to study the feasibility of cultural opening offered contradic-
tory conclusions: One headed by Seoul University in 1998 claimed that the
country was ready for a comprehensive opening, while one under the In-

stitute of Policy Studies contended that the opening should be postponed indefinitely to protect the Korean cultural industry.[64] In addition, a string of acrimonious historical disputes and the 1997 Asian financial crisis put Kim's plan of phased opening on the shelf.

South Korea was meaningfully opened to Japanese popular culture during Kim Dae-jung's presidency, with the process completed by his successor, Roh Moo-hyun. From 1998 to 2004, the South Korean government completed a four-phase opening of its market to most Japanese cultural products: music CDs, movies (including animations), computer games, and television programs. Korean popular culture made significant inroads into Japan. As part of the Korean wave, sitcoms and celebrities swept across the Asian market, including Japan. Fans poured into South Korea, often seeking to visit sites where highly popular sitcoms were made. Joint production of movies and songs commenced. The Japan–South Korea partnership received global attention during this time as the two countries cohosted the 2002 Soccer World Cup, the world's most watched sports event.

Such cultural exchanges have attracted huge publicity and have prompted politicians and media pundits to proclaim that reconciliation between the two nations is blossoming.[65] Yet as the recurring presidential pattern of softening to hardening suggests, the wide availability of Japanese movies and songs may not really have softened the Korean perception of Japan.

In his insightful study of the power of Japanese popular culture in Asia, Nassim Kadosh Otmazgin reveals that as late as 2004–5, 81 of the 119 Korean respondents in one survey associated Japan's image with its war responsibilities, whereas only 7 of the 120 respondents in Hong Kong and Bangkok did so. Several of the South Koreans claimed to love Japan's culture but to dislike its "right-wing government" or "the way they [Japan] treat history."[66]

Accessibility to the Japanese culture is unlikely to have transformed Korean condescension toward it. When asked to compare Japanese and Korean animation, the South Korean public offered a mixture of positive and negative remarks, with "Japanese animation is more violent" generating the most responses. And 48.6 percent of respondents described Japanese animation as "in poor taste," while only 20 percent thought otherwise.[67]

Popular culture increasingly operates in a self-contained commercialized universe. The Japanese ways of spotting potential artists and transforming them into celebrities have been emulated throughout Asia.[68] With Korea's opening, such learning has become more efficient and increasingly mutual. Yet the identification has remained commercial rather than political. Consumers in South Korea, just like their Chinese counterparts, see no problems enjoying Japanese food and fashion while remaining suspicious of the country's politics. A lot of misreading of Japan's soft power probably has occurred as unrealistic expectations have been placed on the shoulders of Japanese cartoons. Cuteness (*kawaii*), a much-worshipped term in Japanese culture, may have a global market, yet as long as the past continues to haunt the Japanese government, the linkage between *kawaii* and power remains absent.

Moreover, soft exchanges may be distorted for harder usage. A few daring Korean nationalists took advantage of a new visa-waiver policy and staged a protest before the Shiname city government of its claim of jurisdiction over Dokto/Takeshima.[69] Furthermore, beyond the bilateral context, there is scant evidence that South Korea has supported Japan's diplomatic priorities elsewhere. No Korean presidents, including Lee, have offered support to Japan's bid for a permanent seat on the United Nations Security Council, a prime diplomatic goal that enjoys widespread support in Japan. Before North Korea's strikes in November 2010 South Korea had shown little interest in solidarity with Japan. Furthermore, although South Korean citizens were kidnapped by North Korean agents, it did little to respond to similar Japanese grievances, offering only infrequent rhetorical support. As late as 2005, far more South Koreans saw Japan as a bigger threat than North Korea.[70]

Softer exchanges have been unable to exert much influence on high-politics disputes. Furthermore, such exchanges are often among the first victims when the political atmosphere worsens. In the wake of the territorial dispute, for example, large numbers of Korean nongovernmental organizations cancelled exchange programs with their Japanese counterparts in the name of solidarity with their government.[71] Such disruptions have primarily occurred in the realm of people-to-people exchange programs rather than cultural penetration, and the former are often transient and ceremonial, with limited utility in fostering better understanding.[72] The best achievement for cultural exchanges in Japan-Korea relations may be commercialized independence. Such relations have yet to move diplomacy.

One more worrying trend for Japan is China's swift rise. China has already become South Korea's biggest trading partner and has passed the United States as the top destination for Korean students. Japan's democratic identity has never been a major theme in Korean popular perceptions of it, and Japan's role as an economic model, seldom openly acknowledged, has lost much aura. As Chang Dae-joong puts it, the lessening of Korean hostility toward Japan has resulted partly from the fact that the

Korean public no longer takes Japan as seriously. Japan-bashing is less frequent only because Japan-passing is on the rise.[73]

What does the trajectory of Japan's wooing efforts toward South Korea imply? Recipient contexts not only condition the effectiveness of wooing but can become decisive. In the case of South Korea, Japanese colonial control, coupled with the Korean superiority complex stemming from ancient times, left a deeper emotional wound than Southeast Asia suffered. Not surprisingly, Korean sensitivity to the Japanese handling of historical issues is much higher. From the perspective of diplomatic engineering, it makes little sense to debate the rationale behind such high sensitivity. Rather, effective wooing means accepting this fact and working with it. However, a series of Japanese governments has demonstrated little interest in accommodating such Korean sentiments. Efforts at fostering mutual understanding have increased yet are often interrupted by domestic agendas. Paradoxically, this phenomenon justifies the importance of leadership and political wisdom, without which mass-based exchanges may be numerous yet irrelevant or may reinforce stereotypes.

China: Ample Power, Scant Charm

China's rise has probably contributed to the Japan-passing thesis. But South Korea is not necessarily coming closer to China, at least not in emotional terms. Rather, the Korean appreciation of China's importance is almost entirely based on security and material considerations, thus reflecting China's hard power rather than its soft cousin.

South Koreans are indeed taking China seriously, and for good reason. In dealing with unpredictable North Korea, China has unparallel weight. China is the world's third-largest donor of food aid, and 90 percent of that aid goes to North Korea. In 2005, China and South Korea jointly provided one million tons of food aid to the north.[74] In addition, China reportedly provides an estimated 80 to 90 percent of North Korea's oil imports at "friendly prices" that are substantially lower than the world market price.[75] Beijing's willingness to use this leverage is debatable, but few observers would dispute China's pivotal role on the Korean Peninsula. The Chinese government has served as the host for the Six-Party Talks, at one time the main coordinating mechanism for addressing security concerns triggered by North Korea's nuclear weapons program.

China's significance to South Korea also lies in the economic area. What the two countries have achieved since 1992 is truly remarkable. Trade tells the most illuminating story (figure 11). From 1991 to 2008, the total value of South Korea's exports to Japan more than doubled, from $12.3 billion to $28.3 billion. Yet such gains look almost negligible compared to the growth in South Korean exports to China, which mushroomed from a little more than $1 billion in 1991 to $91.4 billion in 2008.[76] Since the beginning of the new century, the gap between China and Japan as export markets for South Korea has further widened. For Korean businesses, the Chinese market carried only one-quarter the weight of the Japanese market in 1992. But with an annual growth rate of more than 20 percent, by 2008, the Chinese market had expanded to more than three times the size of the Japanese market. In 2003, China alone accounted for nearly a quarter of the value of South Korea's total exports.[77] China has also become the top recipient of Korean businesses' international investment, receiving $25 billion, nearly half of the global total.[78]

Human exchanges are also vibrant. In 2010, 2.84 million South Koreans visited China, making China the most popular foreign destination for South Korean tourists; that year, 2.14 million Koreans visited Japan.[79] More South Koreans now choose to study overseas in China than in any other country. According to the China Association for International Education, 64,232 South Koreans studied in China in 2009. As figure 12 indicates, the number of South Korean students in China markedly outpaced those from other countries. The Confucius Institute, China's state-sponsored organization to promote Chinese language and culture, set up its first overseas branch in Seoul in November 2004, with twelve others following in South Korea by 2011.

With more and more Koreans living in China on a long-term basis, *Han Guo Cun* (Koreatowns) have sprung up in Beijing, Shanghai, Guangzhou, Chong Qing, and other major Chinese cities. China's popular entertainment has also been swept by the *Han liu* (Korean wave). TV dramas and films from South Korea have become immensely popular among the Chinese audience. The term *Ha han* (Koreaphiles) was coined to capture the obsessiveness with which some Chinese have devoted themselves to Korean clothing, music, and sitcoms. Some Chinese have even undergone cosmetic surgery to make them look more like Korean celebrities. Koreans have also taken key positions in China's booming sports industry, particularly in soccer, tae kwon do, handball, and field hockey. A Korean-born coach led the Chinese national team to the 2002 Asian Games field hockey championship, winning the gold medal by beating the Korean team in South Korea, a feat that made the coach appear selfless and heroic.[80] Cultural exchanges are not just one-way traffic, as such Chinese idols as Zhang Yimou, Jackie Chan, Zhang Ziyi, and Tang Wei are widely known

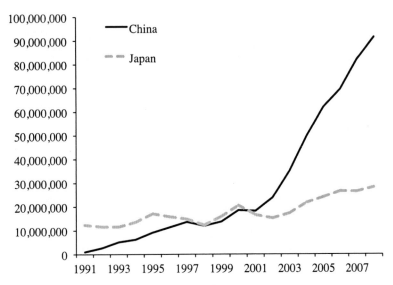

Fig. 11. "Japan passing"—South Korea's trade with China and Japan compared (1991–2008). (Data on South Korea–Japan trade from Korea International Trade Association [KITA] online statistics bulletin, http://www.kita.org/ [accessed April 1, 2009]; data on South Korea–China trade from Embassy of the Republic of Korea in China, "Statistics of Korea-China Exchanges" [Hanzhong jiaoliu tongji], http://china.koreanembassy.cn/politics/politics_01b.aspx?bm=2&sm=1&fm=1 [accessed April 5, 2009].)

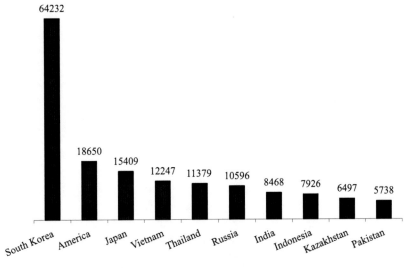

Fig. 12. Top ten sources of international students in China (2009). (Data from Chinese Association for International Education, "2009 nian laihua liuxue-sheng tongjijiankuang [Brief statistics of international students in China]," http://www.cafsa.org.cn/index.php?mid=6.

in South Korea. In early 2009, the epic Chinese movie *Red Cliff* was the most popular film in Korea, earning more revenue than the Hollywood blockbuster *Valkyrie*, starring Tom Cruise.

Despite vast material and human linkages, Beijing's efforts to woo South Korea have been haunted by the same factor obstructing Tokyo's wooing: South Korea offers a hostile atmosphere for China as well as Japan. In the Korean collective memory, China is far from innocent. Historical grievances and a mixture of condescension and humiliation impede South Korea–China relations, too. South Korea and China's shared suffering as a result of Japanese invasions has not led to any enduring victim alliance. Rather, Koreans see themselves as the sole victim and China as an Other that contributes to the tale of Korea's heroic quest for independence. As a result, China, like Japan, is permanently suspected and resented by their neighbor in the middle.

Prior to Normalization: All That Softens Is Not Wooing

Little English-language scholarship exists on Sino–South Korea relations prior to their normalization in 1992.[81] A series of conciliatory gestures reduced the level of mutual hostility prior to formal normalization, but the stunning subsequent development of Sino–South Korean relations has rendered this softening aspect underappreciated. The first sign of thawing of relations came in 1973. In the wake of Nixon's visit to China, Park Chung-hee announced that South Korea would open its door to "nonhostile" communist countries.[82] Deng Xiaoping's Reform and Open policy eliminated yet another contact barrier on the Chinese side. But what jump-started official contact between the two governments was an emergency situation rather than a premeditated plan. On May 5, 1983, a group of Chinese hijackers took control of a Chinese commercial flight and landed the plane in Seoul. A Chinese delegation headed by Shen Tu, director of the Civic Aviation Administration of China (CAAC), was granted entry to South Korea, accompanied by officials from China's National Security Bureau, foreign ministry, and Xinhua News Agency (all of whom bore nominal CAAC titles).[83] As a result of Taiwanese pressure, South Korea did not return the hijackers to China. Instead, they were tried and received relatively light sentences before being pardoned and sent to Taiwan. But South Korea returned the aircraft, its crew, and all the Chinese passengers to China in five days. As one member of the Chinese delegation recalled, the negotiating atmosphere could be described as cordial. Given the nature of the incident, South Korea's first deputy foreign minister welcomed the Chinese team by quoting Confucius: "Isn't it a delight to have friends coming from afar?"[84]

A crisis thus became an opportunity. Three months after the negotiation, China began to allow its citizens to attend conferences and sporting events in South Korea as long as these events were sponsored by international organizations. Another sign of lowered hostility occurred when two disgruntled Chinese soldiers hijacked a motor torpedo boat to South Korea in March 1985: The two governments agreed to frame the incident as an "accidental entry." China offered an apology. In exchange, despite protests from Taiwan, South Korea quickly returned the boat and its entire crew to China, where the two defectors were tried on charges of treason and swiftly executed.[85]

Beijing indicated its goodwill by sending large delegations to the 1986 Asian Games and the 1988 Olympic Games, both held in Seoul. China's official radio station began to refer to South Korea by its official title, Han Guo (Republic of Korea). rather than Nan Chao Xian (South Korea) even in domestic broadcasts. Such an adjustment should not be read as depoliticizing sports, which have always been highly political in China. During the Cultural Revolution, the Chinese ping-pong team refused to play against a Cambodian team sent by the "antirevolutionary" Lon Nol government. Hence the decision to use Han Guo to refer to a country China had not yet recognized was not random. Also in 1988, direct trade between the two countries commenced.[86]

All of these quieter developments indicated the thawing of relations between two officially hostile countries but did not constitute wooing to enhance soft power, for they had little to do with projecting positive state characters or improving an image among the target audience. To be sure, as Jae Ho Chong points out, popular Korean perceptions of China had an "affection" element as a consequence of Korean familiarity with Chinese civilization.[87] Chong may well be right in sensing this sentiment in the 1980s: At a time when South Korea was rapidly ascending to become "Asia's next giant,"[88] its people had little reason for anxiety about poor, weak China. Instead, they could safely feel romantic about ancient Chinese civilization and ponder the commercial opportunities a vast China could offer, matching Japanese feelings at the time. Hence, this affection had more to do with South Korean ambition than with Chinese reality. In retrospect, the current Korean sensitivity toward China did not spring out of nowhere but was a persistent undercurrent that surfaced as a result of China's rapid ascendance and Korea's economic blues. Affection and suspicion are, after all, simply two sides of the same emotional coin.

Both Beijing's and Seoul's softer stances were simply signaling devices, much in the same way as Mao stood beside Edgar Snow, a left-wing American writer, on the Tiananmen Gate to inform Washington of China's willingness to talk.[89] Both China's and South Korea's moves were utilitarian, either security- or trade-driven, with little value-based resonance. Chinese leaders might have held internal discussions about learning from the South Korean modernizing experience, but South Korea as a legitimate state was still largely blocked in media coverage. There was little popular-based adulation of South Korea as an example. Japan was much more attractive as well as politically safe to admire.

In the mutual approaching process, both China and South Korea had to be careful to avoid triggering suspicion from their junior yet official allies, North Korea and Taiwan, respectively. Normalization meetings were conducted in secret, while official envoys were dispatched to the allies to quell nerves.[90] Beijing's and Seoul's mutual approach hence was hesitant, two steps forward and one step back, leading to an inconsistent and time-consuming normalizing process.

Finally, as China stepped out of its self-imposed isolation, it came to realize that interaction with South Korea was unavoidable. As China began to bid to host a series of international events, including the 1990 Asian Games, the Chinese government found that regulations required that South Korea be treated as a legitimate state. A rigid alliance with North Korea became increasingly detrimental to China's Open Door policy. Moreover, normalizing relations with South Korea would deliver a decisive blow to Taipei, which would lose its last ally in the region.

In short, a series of conciliatory measures was quietly yet unmistakably lessening the hostility between China and South Korea, laying ground for the eventual normalization of relations. Yet all that softens is not wooing. Moves by both sides were employed largely to send signals of readiness rather than to create value-based bonding. Without that goal, the concept of soft power lost its relevance in this context.

China as Another Other

As the goal of normalization was achieved, deepening relations became a natural goal. This effort, however, made China's failure to woo South Korea glaring: Despite the two countries' expanding material and human connections, China has made little progress in winning the hearts and minds of the South Korean public—that is, in increasing South Koreans' voluntary acceptance of China's prestige and consequent willingness to jump on the Beijing bandwagon. Instead, the two countries' interactions have demonstrated some worrisome features that resemble those in Japan–South Korea relations. One Chinese scholar has lamented that China–South Korea relations are "walking the same path as South Korea–Japan relations, only one decade later."[91]

Value-based bonding is still absent, as the natures of China's and South Korea's political regimes diverged more than two decades ago. In addition, Korea's rising appreciation of China's importance has been accompanied by Korean suspicions. In the same polls that surveyed attitudes toward Japan, rising numbers of South Korean respondents also indicated they "disliked" China, passing the percentage of those who "liked" China in 2005 (though China registered much warmer than Japan on the Korean emotional thermometer). The importance of the Chinese market notwithstanding, nearly 60 percent of the South Korean public viewed the Chinese economy as a threat.[92]

These numbers hardly indicate that Sino–South Korean relations have reached a new level. China certainly matters to South Koreans, but they do not see it as a model for emulation. The recognition of China's importance drove Seoul to approach Beijing in the 1980s, and the country's rise has only vindicated this view. So what is new to their relations?

Chinese leaders should not be blamed for a lack of trying. The real issue is why their attempted wooing has failed. As a nondemocracy, China would find it impossible to bond politically with South Korea. However, it has an alternative in history, which would seem to be an ideal bonding factor. Chinese leaders have indeed adopted the habit of praising the "two-millennium" history of exchanges between the two countries.[93] For example, when China's propaganda chief, Li Changchun, visited South Korea in April 2009, he highlighted the positive role of history through speeches and his choice of venues. Li visited Jeju's Xufu Park, which commemorates a Chinese envoy, sent by Emperor Qin, who stopped in Korea, en route to the eastern seas. (Never mind that Xu Fu was seeking the elixir of life for the Chinese emperor, so his mission had little to do with Korean locals, or that Xu is believed to have landed in Japan.) Li's speech hailed Xu's journey as "a magnificent event in the long history of friendly exchanges between the Chinese and Korean peoples." Moreover, "through mutual learning, mutual borrowing, and mutual assimilating, our two peoples have jointly made a mighty contribution to the Oriental civilization."[94]

Recent history may be even more helpful. From the mid-nineteenth century to the mid-twentieth, both countries were traumatized by their common enemy, Japan. By colonizing Korea and invading China, Japan wreaked more damage on its two immediate neighbors than did any Western country, at least in China's and South Korea's collective memories. From this perspective, bonding with South Korea by evoking the recent past would seem an enticing strategy for Beijing: If successful, such a grievance alliance would pull South Korea further from the Japanese sphere of influence, satisfying China's entrenched desire to drive a wedge into the U.S.-led security alliance along China's coast.[95] In keeping with this approach, Jiang Zemin reached out to Kim Young-sam and bashed Japan for its lack of repentance, a practice Hu Jintao carried on when he became China's leader. Speaking before the Korean Parliament in 2005, Hu pointed out that "in recent history, people of our two countries mutually supported and aided each other in our respective great struggles to resist foreign invasions and to fight for national independence. These are chapters of friendship jointly written by our people. They are worthy of praise and tears."[96]

But history is a risky card. Leaders in Beijing can evoke the past but cannot define how far back South Koreans can remember and the terms on which they interpret those memories. And Koreans would not need to travel far before their anger would turn toward China. Just a little more than half a century before South Korea's independence, China's history becomes just as messy as Japan's. China fought the 1894 Sino-Japanese War not to protect Korea's independence from Japan but because China wanted to continue its control of Korea. China was the suzerain by default, while Japan was the challenger. In fact, when the Japanese troops set foot in Korea, they did so in the name of offering the country meaningful independence. At least initially, their stated goal fooled some aspiring Korean nationalists.

China has a much longer history of dominating Korea than does Japan. On several occasions, the Chinese imperial courts assimilated almost the entire Korean Peninsula. Chinese history textbooks always portray their country as the selfless outsider rushing to the scene to save Korea, typically from Japanese invaders. The 1598 Battle of Noryang (Luliang Haizhan), for example, is touted as a joint Chinese-Korean campaign against Japanese troops led by Toyotomi Hideyoshi, This interpretation caters to domestic tastes: By evoking a historical linkage to the Chinese intervention in the Korean War nearly four hundred years later, the Chinese government has sought to convince its youth that China has historically acted as a heroic and selfless protector of a weaker neighbor. Yet given the nature of the event—the Ming suzerain sent troops to its Korean protectorate at Korea's request—Korea would be expected to offer little contemporary appreciation for China's "valiant" deed. In the much more recent Korean War, widely perceived as a proxy war orchestrated by the two Cold War superpowers, South Korea went into a direct conflict with China.

Consequently, after invoking history, China soon found it a double-edged sword, and Korean anger turned not just to Japan but also to China. Indeed, China–South Korea relations deteriorated markedly in the later years of the Roh presidency by a chain of bitter clashes, primarily over history but also including territorial issues and Chinese hooligans who attacked Korean protesters during the Olympic Torch Relay in Seoul. At one point, an angry Roh openly bashed China to the visiting George W. Bush, telling the U.S. president that China had "invaded us hundreds of times, and how could we forget these bone-aching pains?"[97]

In short, Korean collective memory has seen a consistent pattern: Bigger powers have always tussled over Korea, while its people have courageously if not tragically rejected this fate. China was not innocent and certainly was not a victim on the same scale as Korea. The past becomes a haunting rather than facilitating factor, as Beijing has found itself reflected in the Korean memory simply as another domineering Other heroically resisted by the Korean people.

To Woo or Not to Woo: Tension between Domestic and Diplomatic Agendas

China and Korea's long, shared history has produced one more layer of sensitivity: Nearly two million ethnic Koreans live in China as Chinese citizens.[98] Their presence is particularly strong in the northeast province of Jilin, with nearly nine hundred thousand ethnic Koreans residing in the border town of Yanbian alone. Unlike Tibetans and Uighurs, most ethnic Koreans have embraced their Chinese identity. Quite a few have climbed to political, military, and cultural prominence in the Han-dominated China, including General Zhao Nanqi of the Chinese People's Liberation Army; Zheng Lücheng, who composed military anthems for both China and North Korea; Li Dezhu, chair of the State Ethnic Affairs Commission; and Cui Jian, a pioneering figure in Chinese rock music. Nevertheless, ethnic Koreans are also proud of their Korean roots. Many can still speak the language and wear traditional Korean attire. Further complicating the situation, they live in a region close to Baekdu Mountain (Chinese name, Changbai Mountain), a site sacred to many Koreans as their ancestral origin.

Any sort of Korean independence movement is almost unheard of inside China. But for a Beijing wary of the ongoing unrest in Tibet and Xinjiang, the strong ethnic identity that many ethnic Koreans carry and the fact that they live in a strategically vital border region warrant extra caution. The Chinese government's priority of maintaining stability and territorial integrity renders any compromise with South Korea on history exceedingly difficult.

The case that best reveals how Beijing has been caught in the middle between diplomatic wooing and domestic concern is the Goguryeo dispute with South Korea. On the surface, it is a scholarly debate about whether Goguryeo, an ancient kingdom with a history that can be traced back to 37 B.C., should be seen as a regional power of China (as the Chinese side contends) or an independent state in its own right (as the South Korean side argues).[99] The Chinese argument was part of a bigger $2.4 million Northeast Project (Dongbei Gongcheng) undertaken by the Chinese Academy of Social Sciences from 2001 to 2006.

Once published, the Chinese argument triggered strong protests from both politicians and academics in South Korea. Korean bloggers set up "Defend Goguryeo" websites to refute what they perceived as Chinese fabrications, and Korean activists called for a boycott of Chinese goods. Korean prime minister Lee Hai-chan convened an urgent cabinet meeting and announced funding for a state committee to study Goguryeo history.[100]

Such angry responses should not have surprised Beijing. As Peter H. Gries points out, the Chinese claim of Goguryeo as a regional kingdom was an effort to apply "Chineseness to the border, hence striking at the very heart of what it meant to be Korean today."[101] The Chinese move was, therefore, an irritant—precisely the opposite of wooing.

Has the Chinese government, driven by identity politics, stepped on a land mine by underestimating the intensity of the South Korean response?[102] The answer is probably more nuanced. Identity politics has yet to acquire a life in Chinese diplomacy; rather, Chinese identity is important because it connects closely to security, China's most sensitive nerve. According to the Chinese Social Science Academy's mission statement, the Northeast Project was defensive in nature, so an attitudinal showdown with Korea on the Goguryeo issue was undesirable yet unavoidable:

> Our country's northeast border region is located at the center of East Asia, hence carrying extremely important strategic significance. In such a situation, some countries' research projects and scholars, driven by their secretive agendas, distort historical facts in their so-called research on history-related topics. A small number of politicians, for political purposes, publicly propagate various ridiculous viewpoints to create chaos. [The Northeast Project is launched] to further promote the

founding and development of scholarship on the history and the current situation of the northeast border region and to further protect stability in the northeast border region.[103]

The message is clear: Concerns about ethnic tensions and border stability compelled Beijing to launch the Northeast Project, whatever South
Korea's response might be. However, Beijing obviously did not want to
push its relations with Seoul into an emotional corner. Once South Korea's storm of protest started, Li Sheng, director of the Northeast Project,
stressed its "academic" and "nonpolitical" nature. Yet he may have said a
bit more than he was supposed to to quell the Korean anger. Li admitted that the provincial Chinese Communist Party propaganda ministers
served on the project's advisory board, though they were only doing "some
coordinating work." In another blow to the project's credibility, Li said that
Chinese researchers "will definitely not get into any debate with Korean
scholars. Instead, we will proceed according to our own original plan."[104]

These answers hardly convinced non-Chinese listeners, particularly the
Koreans. What sort of "coordinating work" would demand the presence of
highly political propaganda ministers? And if the nature of the project were
academic, as Li insisted, why would the Chinese team not allow debate,
the essence of scholarship? Li's answers were nonetheless illuminating because their inconsistency inadvertently revealed an anxious Beijing caught
between its "peaceful rise" charm offensive and its everlasting paranoia regarding ethnic unrest. Hence, the Goguryeo dispute did not necessarily
backfire, though Li's words could be seen as an awkward effort to control
damage.

Overall, Beijing's conflicted handling of the Goguryeo dispute exposed
a Chinese government caught between wooing the world and fearing domestic stability. Even knowing that the area concealed a land mine, a para-
noid Beijing would have stepped there anyway, calculating that any diplomatic pain would be manageable whereas inaction would be much more
risky. The Northeast Project may allow Chinese leaders to sleep better, but
it also added some new bad blood to Sino–South Korean relations, further
dimming China's hopes of selling charm to the Korean public.

Contemporary Stereotypes and Mutual Condescension

Quarrels over history and territory are further exacerbated by contemporary stereotypes. In recent years, Chinese media's often sensational cov-

erage of the acrimonious historical disputes with South Korea has given rise to a new form of online entertainment—ridiculing South Korea and Koreans as an ethnic group. This shaming game even has a name, Hanguo Qiyuanlun (the Born in Korea Thesis). In fact, signs indicate that Korea may surpass Japan as the most popular target for ridicule by Chinese Internet users.

The Born in Korea game started with finding and publicizing claims that the Korean nation was the creator or inventor of certain technologies or products later adopted elsewhere (for example, the magnetic compass, paper-making, the Go game, and soy sauce) or that famous historical figures (such as Confucius and Genghis Khan) were actually of Korean ethnicity.[105] Chinese participants soon began to fabricate similar Korean claims, apparently to deride the perceived Korean obsession with national pride. The list of figures Koreans purportedly were attempting to claim as their own quickly became absurd—modern Chinese founding father Sun Yat-sen, basketball player Yao Ming, Chairman Mao, and American swimmer Michael Phelps.[106]

South Korea is not the first victim of such popular exaggerations, if not fabrications. Zhong Lisi, a Chinese writer based in Paris, wrote an account of how she and a Taiwanese student refuted a certain "French professor" who believed that Taiwan and China were two different countries. According to Zhong, after hearing passionate speeches arguing that Taiwan and the mainland belong to "one China," the professor took off his hat and announced, "I salute the Chinese. The class is adjourned."[107] Zhong's account was so vivid that the China Central Television later adapted it into a short drama and broadcast it nationwide during prime time. Yet Zhong never named the professor or anyone else who could verify her version of events.

Zhong is not the only self-propagated hero, as other Chinese have depicted themselves as vigorously defending their country while on foreign soil. In 2003, a report, "Japan's New Blueprint for Conquering China," began circulating on various Chinese websites. The author, who claimed to be a Japanese military officer, vows to "wipe China off the map" by 2015.[108] Yet the very different grammatical patterns of the Chinese and Japanese languages would make any Chinese translation of a Japanese work easily detectable to trained eyes. This article bears no linguistic connection with the Japanese language, and no original Japanese version has ever surfaced. Indeed, the tone of the article is so amateurish and its expression so Chinese that the author is probably one of China's *fenqing* (angry nationalist youths).

Online Chinese fabrications have victimized many other countries in addition to France, Japan, and South Korea. Linked together, these incidents may reveal Chinese sensitivities regarding national pride. Confucius's famous saying, "*Ji suo bu yu, wu shi yu ren* [Do not unto others as you would not have others do unto you]," apparently does not apply to these Chinese patriots.

It is not clear whether Chinese readers have taken seriously the anti-Korean fabrications. Yet as genuine and fictitious reports converge, few readers would have the interest or take the time to differentiate true from false. Such stories have strengthened Chinese stereotypes of Koreans as supersensitive to issues related to national prestige, while a few highly publicized events have offered a facade of vindication to the Chinese ridicule. A group of female South Korean skaters held up a sign in Korean that read "Baekdu Mountain Is Our Territory" during the awards ceremony for the 2007 Asian Winter Games, held in China. The Chinese crowd, most of whom did not understand the Korean language, initially assumed that the sign was offering friendship or appreciation and cheered. They became angry when they learned the truth.[109]

Condescension is also embedded in the daily use of language. Online commentators frequently use the term *gao li bang zi* (literally "Korean sticks") to describe Koreans, particularly males, as ill-mannered and stubborn. Koreans also are occasionally referred to as *bang zi* (sticks). Despite the Korean community's dislike for such terms, they have shown no sign of retreating from the Chinese colloquial vocabulary.

Sensitivity and stereotyping run both ways, of course. In January 2005, the mayor of Seoul, Lee Myung-bak, announced that his city's Chinese name would be changed from Han Cheng (Han City) to Shou'er (a neutral term that mimics the sound of *Seoul*). In the summer of 2008, a Korean pet shop used the image of Tiananmen in an advertisement, changing the famous Chinese slogan, "Long Live the People's Republic of China," into the Korean "White Dog Village" and replacing Mao's portrait with an image of a dog.[110] In March 2009, Chinese bloggers again became indignant about what they perceived as condescending portrayals of China in a Korean TV drama. Although the drama was set in contemporary Shanghai, netizens complained, there were no scenes of the city's modern skyline, only dark and narrow alleys. Chinese police and officials were portrayed as greedy and corrupt, and the male protagonist whined, "There are too many thieves here in China."[111] Such incidents have invariably drawn the anger of China's growing army of nationalists, who perceive these episodes as new evidence of Korean condescension toward China and the Chinese nation.

A New Obstacle to Wooing: Are We Still in the Same League?

Lee Myung-bak assumed South Korea's presidency at a time of escalating hostility toward both China and Japan. Lee reduced tensions with Tokyo, but has he improved emotional relations with China? His tenure in office did not get off to a promising start, as Beijing saw him as a much less welcoming figure as a consequence of his more explicit pro-U.S. stance and his eagerness to reach out to Japan based on "common values." But Lee has since made some unprecedented wooing gestures to lower Chinese hostility: Lee became the first head of a foreign state to visit the Sichuan earthquake site, hugging and crying with local residents. He also surprised Chinese college students by disclosing his love affair with a Chinese woman in an otherwise serious diplomatic speech. The two countries have signed a declaration elevating their relations to "strategic comprehensive partnership," a status Japan and South Korea have yet to achieve.

There is, however, a rising fear that may justify and strengthen historically based suspicions: Is China looking beyond Japan and South Korea for diplomatic partners (table 6)? With little affection present, both the Korean and the Japanese publics may be concerned whether China continues its regional chauvinism.

In short, combining the Chinese experience with that of Japan reveals a clear pattern: In spite of expanding material exchanges, a value-based embrace between South Korea and either country is largely missing. In late 2007, a Chinese newspaper polled twelve thousand Chinese and found that 40.1 percent selected South Korea as the country they disliked the most, with Japan receiving 30.2 percent of the votes. The result compelled the editors to call for "stopping the cold current at the people-to-people level in Sino-Korean relations."[112] Japan remained at the top of the list of coun-

TABLE 6. Chinese, Japanese, and South Korean Respondents' Answers to the Question "Choose ONE Country that you want your own country to develop good relations with" (2005)

	China	Japan	South Korea
(1)	Russia: 32% (29%)[a]	USA: 37% (41%)	North Korea: 36% (38%)
(2)	USA: 28% (31%)	China: 24% (21%)	USA: 29% (26%)
(3)	Japan: 11% (8%)	South Korea: 10% (9%)	China: 22% (15%)

Source: Asahi Shimbun, "Rekishi ninshiki ohkina mizo kyohzonkyoh'ei nao mosaku" (Huge gap on facing history; testing waters on coexistence and coprosperity), April 27, 2005; and "Growing China and Depressing Japan: Contrast between Optimism and Pessimism (Seichō chūgoku to teimei nihon: Rakkan to hikan kukkiri), September 27, 2002.

[a]Numbers in parentheses are results from the same poll in 2002.

tries South Koreans dislike the most (57 percent), followed by China (far behind at 13 percent). Both were more disliked than even North Korea, with a nearly bankrupt international reputation.[113]

Recipient context not only matters but matters decisively. The meaning of being Korean was substantially built on differentiating the country from its immediate neighbors China and Japan. The fact that South Korea has been the weakest of the three, coupled with a long history of being bullied by the two bigger powers, has contributed to a tragic yet heroic construction of Korean nationalism. Against this background, to expect South Koreans to undertake a value-based emotional embrace of either China or Japan would be unrealistic. In other words, the case of South Korea reveals why wooing cannot go very far in certain scenarios.

On the superficial level, lack of charm does not seem terribly significant. The ever-tightening connections among China, Japan, and South Korea imply that people can still do business without affinity for one another. Under popular pressure, governments may occasionally ratchet up their critical tone toward each another. But overall, no one seems to want to disrupt the bigger picture of economic and security interdependence. As one Japanese diplomat explained, he traveled to South Korea when Koizumi's visit to the Yasukuni Shrine triggered vociferous protests in Seoul. At official meetings, the Japanese delegation had to listen to the Korean government's protests about Japan's "wrong views on history." Yet at the evening cocktail session, after a few rounds of drinks, the diplomat's Korean friend put aside his official identity, patted the diplomat on the back, and said, "Don't worry. Everything will be fine."[114] The pattern reminds me of a popular Chinese saying, "*Mensheng fa dacai* [Make money by being quiet]." More often than not, governments of South Korea, Japan, and China adroitly seem to be following this wisdom.

If material relations continue to deepen among Japan, China, and South Korea, why should wooing matter? First, emotional acceptance is important because leaders in these three countries, particularly in China and South Korea, are still haunted by the abstract, intangible, yet very potent factor of national feeling, the bettering of which is a prime goal for wooing. National feeling may have little to do with reality (for example, the belief that Japan is revitalizing militarism and again dreaming about invading China and/or Korea), but it has real diplomatic consequences: Material and human exchanges may prevent antagonism from exploding but with sensitivities poked externally by former victimizers and utilized internally by votes- or legitimacy-seeking politicians, a long road remains to be traveled before the three powers can coordinate on security threats (like North

Korea) and to support each other's diplomatic priorities. Political scientist Ming Wan characterizes Sino-Japanese relations, caught in the middle of vast connections and tense feelings, as "dispute-prone" but "confrontation-averse."[115] Another framing commonly used by politicians or media pundits is "close-yet-distant relations." Both framings also apply to the bigger triangular setting as well. And such a "cold accommodation" is largely a result of trilateral emotional barriers.

I am not suggesting that wooing has totally failed. Rather, it may succeed in a bilateral setting; when it does so, it however, it dims the prospect of trilateral reconciliation. Governments have a tendency to perceive hostility in one pair of bilateral relations as a good opportunity for cordiality in another pair, a darker side of bilateral wooing. A zero-sum mentality still shadows the three powers' interactions, and governments often find incentives to utilize tensions in their counterpart's relations with the third country, as manifested by Beijing's urge to draw South Korea closer through the bond of historical grievance. Coming closer to one country inevitably entails moving further from another. In this sense, wooing seeks to create discordances elsewhere and gaining perks from them, thus attesting to the Othering theme that repeatedly appears in this book.

These two factors have rendered the three countries underachievers in regional integration. There is no shortage of aspiring slogans: "East Asia: Our Home," "East Asian Community," a "lover-like quasi-alliance."[116] But it is highly doubtful that citizens and the three governments are ready to accept the others as "lovers." If anything, *quasi* only adds a positive spin to a much less inspiring reality of keeping discontent at bay in order to do business, even when they realize the potential of achieving more if emotional barriers could be transcended. There is also the concern that the triangle may become structurally imbalanced in both material and perceptive terms. The Chinese public has shown a clear tendency to look beyond Japan and South Korea in searching for diplomatic partners of equal weights. The Japanese and Koreans suspect that China's rise out of the Northeast Asian minor league will only become stronger.

FOUR

Taiwan: Negotiating Self-Identity and Security

This chapter examines China and Japan's efforts to woo Taiwan, which differs in important ways from previously examples. Unlike South Korea and countries in Southeast Asia, the issue of national identity still hangs in Taiwan's air. Having ruled the island in the nineteenth century and for much of the first half of the twentieth, China and Japan have been particularly important in shaping Taiwan's political views on statehood and national identity. Indeed, China and Japan define the boundaries of that imagination: Moving closer to one means inevitable distancing from the other. Hence, the Taiwan case can reveal not only wooing but also the country's search for its place vis-à-vis China and Japan.

While Beijing is more eager than Japan to win Taiwanese hearts and minds, China's charm has been severely abridged by a number of factors. First, a significant (and growing) portion of the Taiwanese public rejects the national identity of Chineseness, the ultimate goal of Beijing's charm offensive. The Chinese government cannot possibly achieve any resonance with this sector of the Taiwanese population. Second, even Taiwanese who acknowledge their Chinese roots have a deeply entrenched fear and distrust of China's authoritarian nature. The Taiwanese see political fiascos such as the Great Leap Forward, the Cultural Revolution, and the 1989 Tiananmen Massacre as not only horrifying but also harbingers of what could befall them should reunification materialize. Third, economic gap between the two has created a sense of Taiwanese superiority to Chinese mainlanders. Human and cultural exchanges have become regular, yet stereotypes remain rampant. Overall, the Taiwanese public perceives China as a state with little charm.

By contrast, particularly since the 1990s, Japan and Taiwan have participated in a commingling process that has elevated their relations to an unofficial-in-name-only status. Three factors stand out in such mutual wooing: a positive interpretation of colonial experience, a new bond of democratic identity, and mutual cultural attractions with immense popular support. Jointly, these factors have created an upward spiral of bilateral relations that has deepened Taiwan's "independence legitimacy" among Japan's elites and public alike. Japan in return has enhanced its diplomatic leverage vis-à-vis China. Notwithstanding Japan's expanding connections with the mainland, Tokyo has become increasingly flexible in its execution of the One China policy in spite of Beijing's entrenched sensitivity and repeated warnings.

China-Taiwan Relations: Why Both Diplomacy and Wooing Are Relevant

The selection of Taiwan as a case invites a question: Would the island qualify for inclusion in a book on diplomatic wooing among sovereign nation-states? After all, China under the People's Republic has never renounced its claim to the island. Sticking to its eventual goal of reunification, Beijing vehemently insists that solving the Taiwan issue is a purely "domestic matter."[1]

It is highly unlikely that Beijing will admit the "diplomatic" nature of the Taiwan issue. But in substantive terms, the Chinese government must deal with the subject not only as a diplomatic matter but a core one. The role of the United States is particularly important: The Taiwan Relations Act passed by the Congress in April 1979 authorizes the U.S. government to maintain quasi-diplomatic relations with the Republic of China (ROC) on Taiwan and to provide the ROC government with defensive arms. It also states that any nonpeaceful means of resolving the Taiwan issue would be a matter of "grave concern" to the United States, though the exact form of the U.S. response is intentionally ambiguous. China's consistent and increasingly credible threats to Taiwan and the U.S. legal obligation could set the two world powers on a collision course. This catastrophic possibility has attracted the bulk of the existing scholarship on the Taiwan issue, as numerous arguments have been made regarding the possibility, the form, and the consequences of such a clash.

The mainland Chinese government is clearly aware of the tremendous weight the United States carries. While insisting on the domestic nature of Taiwan's future, the government's white paper claims that the Taiwan issue is the "most essential and most sensitive [*zui hexin zui mingan*]" area in Sino-U.S. relations.[2] It has also become a ritual for Chinese leaders to stress to their U.S. counterparts the issue's key position. Four days following Barack Obama's election as president, Chinese president Hu Jintao called to offer his congratulations and to remind Obama that China and the United States should "properly handle sensitive questions in bilateral relations, particularly that of Taiwan."[3]

In recent years, the Chinese government has signaled that it might seek to internationalize the Taiwan issue if it deems conditions right. Once again, the United States stands out in this new trend. Figuring that the United States cannot afford a costly conflict with China while bogged down in Iraq and Afghanistan, Beijing has obtained U.S. cooperation in its effort to curb the island's quest for a greater international presence.

One key tactic was to paint the Taiwanese administration under the Democratic Progressive Party (DPP) as the region's troublemaker, and U.S. help usually came in the form of open criticism of Taiwan's leaders, a slap in the face. Meeting with Chinese premier Wen Jiabao, President George W. Bush expressed his opposition to Taiwanese president Chen Shui-bian's decision to hold politically sensitive referendums.[4] The most scathing criticism, however, came from U.S. deputy assistant secretary Thomas Christensen, a China specialist by training. Commenting on Chen's decision to hold a referendum on joining the United Nations under the name Taiwan, Christensen chided Chen and his supporters for failing to "take seriously Taiwan's commitments to the United States and the international community, [being] willing to ignore the security interests of Taiwan's most steadfast friend, and [being] ready to put at some risk the security interests of the Taiwan people for short-term political gain."[5] Expressing U.S. displeasure, the Bush administration refused to allow Chen's presidential plane to land on the U.S. mainland while en route to South America in May 2006. Chen's subsequent refusal to land in Alaska produced midair drama: No one in the press corps accompanying the Taiwanese leader seemed to know their destination, and they dubbed the trip a "voyage lost in direction [*mi hang zhi lü*]."[6]

Beijing is not only waving sticks but also dangling carrots. "To place hopes in the Taiwanese people" has been a traditional slogan frequently uttered by Chinese leaders, particularly when governmental relations go awry.[7] To execute Taiwan-related policies on a day-to-day basis, the central government set up Taiwan Affairs Offices not only at national level but also in all provinces, including remote Tibet and Xinjiang. Such offices were also established in cities that have strong Taiwanese presences, such as Dalian, Ningbo, and Qingdao. The main goals of such offices, according to minister Wang Yi, are to "work for the well-being of our compatriots on both sides of the straits and for peace in the Taiwan Straits region, safeguard the fundamental interests of the Chinese nation, realize peaceful reunification of our motherland and the Chinese nation's rejuvenation."[8] To achieve such grand goals, offices at all levels work to reach out to and build rapport with Taiwanese communities. Between 2003 and March 2009, the central Taiwan Affairs Office posted nearly eighteen hundred entries on its official bulletin on Taiwan-related exchange activities.[9] Activities sponsored by local offices would raise that number considerably.

Before taking charge of Taiwan-related affairs, Wang, a Japan specialist, had been the party secretary of the Ministry of Foreign Affairs. Promoted to the rank of deputy minister at the age of fifty-three, he was perceived inside China as a charismatic and able diplomat, a rising star within Beijing's highly hierarchical diplomatic firmament.[10] Hence, his selection reveals the coexistence of diplomacy and wooing.

Beijing's wooing urge was also illustrated by the top-level treatment accorded to Kuomintang (KMT) president Lien Chan during his 2005 trip to the mainland. Lien's visit featured a meeting with Hu during which both sides reaffirmed the "92 Consensus," a compromise between the two sides that allowed them to retain the One China principle yet allowing different interpretations. The DPP and former president Lee Teng-hui previously had vehemently denied the consensus's existence. Following Lien's visit, Beijing offered three "goodwill" gifts: normalizing tourism, increasing sales of Taiwanese produce on the mainland, and presenting two pandas to the Taipei Zoo.

Wooing in the Shadow of Sword

Despite Beijing's superficial insistence on the "domestic" nature of the Taiwan issue, in practice both the diplomatic and the wooing dimensions are clearly at work. Yet Beijing's wooing has had unimpressive results. In fact, China was late to realize the importance of wooing and has little understanding of Taiwan as a recipient context.

The most obvious obstacle for China's wooing is the sword hanging above Taiwan's head—that is, the mainland Chinese government has never renounced its right to use military means to solve the Taiwan issue. Indeed,

China's military threat has become increasingly credible, and it formalized the right to use force by ratifying the Anti-Secession Law in March 2005, only a month before Lien's historic visit.[11]

Hence, China maintains the legal option of wiping Taiwan off the map. With its deepening pockets, China has also waged a diplomatic war to reduce the number of countries that recognize Taiwan: While Taiwan lost only four countries to Beijing in the 1980s, it has lost twenty since 1990, and as of March 2009 only twenty-three countries still recognized the island as a sovereign country, and most of them were small, weak states concentrated in Central America, Africa, and the South Pacific. Under the double threats of military takeover and international asphyxiation, China and Taiwan engaged in little policy coordination at the elite level. Even under the Ma Ying-jeou administration, which is much friendlier to China, confrontation and suspicion remain core components of government-to-government interactions.

At the popular level, the double threats have also hindered Beijing's efforts to woo. A 2008 poll sponsored by the Taiwanese government's Mainland Affairs Council revealed that despite the change in the presidency, the much-acclaimed Hu-Lien meeting, and Beijing's three major gifts, more than 53 percent of the Taiwanese respondents still felt that "the mainland government was treating our government in an unfriendly way," just a 5.6 percent drop from the previous year. Only 28 percent felt otherwise.[12]

Yet to expect Beijing to woo convincingly at the cost of renouncing swords or allowing simultaneous diplomatic recognition would be unrealistic. Beijing may even have reason to believe that the "noncharming" part of its image has kept the island from becoming fully independent. After all, surveys have shown that a commanding majority of the Taiwanese public has consistently preferred maintaining the status quo (that is, Taiwan's de facto independence) over full independence or reunification. Yet when the status quo was eliminated as an option, those who preferred independence outweighed those who preferred reunification by nearly five to one.[13] Such a gap may well imply that for the Taiwanese public, the predominant reason for keeping the status quo was to avoid the doomsday scenario: a Chinese invasion in the name of preventing the island's full independence. If Beijing really means what it says and places its hopes in the people of Taiwan, such a result would be frustrating. Yet it may end up solidifying Chinese leaders' faith in standing by the nonpeaceful options. Smiles may not bring Taiwan closer to China any time soon, but a fist is definitely necessary to keep it from floating away.

Taiwan Responds to Beijing's Wooing: Lick the Sugar Coating but Spit the Pill

China's major challenge is on national identification. Popular impression holds that the Taiwanese democratization movement has been coupled with the rise of the Taiwanese national identity to the exclusion of the Chinese identity. Polls over the past two decades have indeed shown an increasing tendency for people to identify themselves as Taiwanese rather than Chinese.[14]

But the Taiwanese public is ambivalent, even conflicted, about its collective identity. On one hand, poll data have shown that the Taiwanese people resoundingly reject Beijing's description of Taiwan as a part of the People's Republic; on the other hand, the Taiwanese are vague about whether people from mainland China should be seen as foreigners and even whether the Chinese government should be seen as a foreign government.

Answers sometimes depend on how the questions are framed. For example, in a May 2007 poll conducted by the Taiwanese government, 67.1 percent of island residents chose to identify themselves as Taiwanese rather than as Chinese or as both Chinese and Taiwanese (categories that totaled 28.8 percent of respondents); however, a poll taken two months earlier showed that nearly 60 percent of those surveyed identified themselves as ethnically Chinese (*zhong hua min zu*). Still another 2007 poll by the independence-leaning DPP revealed that only 27 percent viewed mainlanders as foreigners, whereas 37 percent viewed them as "compatriots" and another 29 percent viewed them as "neighbors," an ambivalent term.[15]

After negotiations regarding Taipei's hosting of a leg of the Olympic torch relay collapsed between the DPP-led Taiwanese government and its Chinese counterpart in 2007, Taiwan's Mainland Affairs Committee asked the public,

> In April this year, when Beijing announced the relay route for the 2008 Olympic Torch, it described Taipei as the first domestic leg inside the People's Republic of China. This measure, if implemented, would severely disgrace [*aihua*] us. On this ground, our government rejected the arrival of the Olympic torch to Taiwan. Do you support or not support our government's action taken at the time?

The framing of the question was loaded. However, the government's not-so-subtle hint did not produce a lopsided result in its favor. Whereas 38.7 percent of Taiwanese supported their government's handling of the issue,

33.8 percent did not support the government, and 27.5 percent did not know or care about the matter.[16]

Since Beijing has long stressed the idea of "placing hopes in the Taiwanese people," two questions arise: Have the people of Taiwan noticed Beijing's different wooing strategies, and has such wooing helped Beijing come closer to its goals—the growth of support for reunification among the Taiwanese and their acceptance of the "one country, two systems" formula?

Figure 13 provides an answer to the first question. In the eyes of the Taiwanese public, Beijing's hostilities toward "our government" and "our people" have largely moved in tandem. The people of Taiwan have difficulty seeing a government favorably if it is perceived as hostile to their government. In addition, a gap has persisted between Beijing's relatively low "people-targeted" hostility and its "government-targeted" hostility. This finding implies that the Taiwanese people are aware of China's effort to be somewhat more conciliatory and that although they dislike Beijing's heavy-handed approach to Taipei, they tend to see it first and foremost as a governmental issue.

Taking notice of Beijing's wooing is one thing. Whether such noticing has helped Beijing is quite another. Figures 14 and 15 address the effect of Beijing's wooing, which remains unimpressive. Figure 14 tracks the Taiwanese public's preferred future scenario for cross-strait relations: to achieve reunification with the People's Republic as soon as possible, to achieve full independence as soon as possible, or to maintain the status quo in a general sense.[17] The answers have remained strikingly coherent from 2001 to 2009 despite the changes in the presidency and other official ups and downs: A commanding majority has favored maintaining the status quo. Supporters of swift independence, despite their loud noise, have generally hovered between 6 and 7 percent and have never topped 15 percent. Perhaps most disheartening to Beijing, though, is the low percentage of those who choose "reunification," which has never surpassed 3.3 and usually has been almost zero.

Figure 15 further demonstrates the Taiwanese public's immunity to Beijing's wooing—that is, their consistent and resounding rejection of the "one country, two systems" formula, the only solution Beijing can imagine. Moreover, the past twenty years have also witnessed the resumption and explosion of material and human connections between the two sides, meaning that China can hardly blame the rejection of its wisdom on inaccessibility. Quite the contrary—as more contacts have brought China's realities to the Taiwanese doorstep, China has found itself further removed from Taiwanese identification. Not knowing the mainland has been replaced by not liking it—hardly a victory for China's wooing efforts.

Percentage

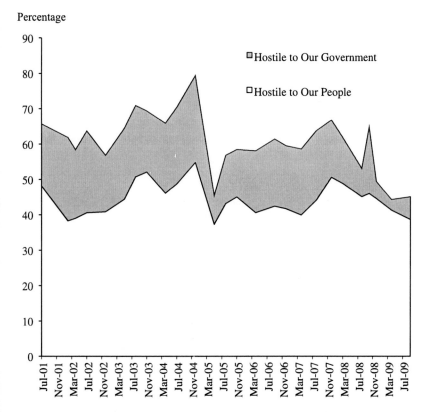

Fig. 13. Measuring China's hostility toward Taiwanese government and Taiwanese people (2001–9). (Data from surveys sponsored by Taiwan's Mainland Affairs Committee, http://www.mac.gov.tw/public/Attach ment/9103017175923.gif.)

The Taiwanese response to Beijing's wooing basically has been, "Nice try, but no, and still no." As a popular Chinese saying goes, the Taiwanese public gladly licks the sugar coating (the various policy incentives that the Chinese government has extended to lure Taiwan) but spits the pill of reunification back at Beijing.

"Grandpa Lien, You're Back!"

Leaders in Beijing love to denounce "a tiny group of Taiwan-independence elements [*yixiaocuo taidu shili*]" for obstructing the reunification process. But as the data demonstrate, China's lack of charm does not resonate only with Taiwan's independence-leaning sector. Even those who are willing to

Percentage

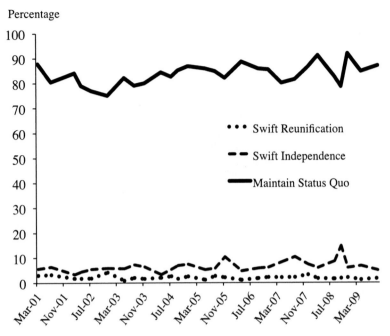

Fig. 14. Gauging Taiwan's future—swift reunification, swift independence, or maintaining status quo? (2001–9). (Data from surveys sponsored by Taiwan's Mainland Affairs Council, http://www.mac.gov.tw/public/Attach ment/9103017171958.gif.)

embrace the Chinese element of their identity see virtually no charm in China as a state. The possibility of reuniting with China under the People's Republic, when cast against the background of a chain of political disasters on the mainland since 1949, dims any attraction of a swift reunification. The idea of reuniting with the People's Republic simply has no market inside Taiwan, regardless of people's ideological leanings. That is the only explanation for the fact that in survey after survey, only single-digit percentages of the population favor accelerating the reunification process.

The Taiwanese public, of course, is not the only ethnic Chinese group suspicious of China as a result of its government's turbulent record of breaking promises. The 1989 Tiananmen incident was largely responsible for setting off mass emigration among the people of Hong Kong.[18] Having already secured a safe harbor, the people of Taiwan see little sense in being sucked into Beijing's unpredictable political world.

Indeed, the gap between a democratic Taiwan and an authoritarian

Percentage

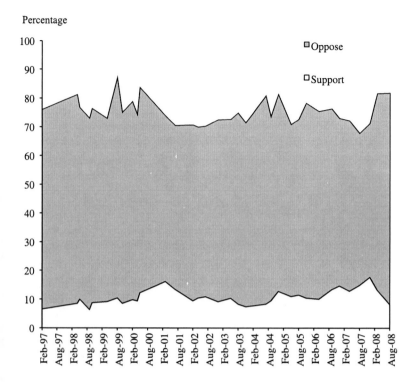

Fig. 15. Do you oppose or support using China's "one country two systems" formula to solve Taiwan's future? (1997–2008). (Data from surveys sponsored by Taiwan's Mainland Affairs Council, http://www.mac.gov.tw/public/Attachment/9111022215134/gif.)

China has added a new layer of resistance to reunification. On a daily level, this gap may be a source of humor for many Taiwanese. To demonstrate the eagerness with KMT chair Lien was received on a visit to his primary school in the mainland city of Xi'an, two pupils read a poem, "*Lian yeye, nin hui lai la* [Grandpa Lien, You're Back!]." Yet the traditional propaganda-style presentation, with its high-pitched sound and overflowing passion, dumbfounded the Taiwanese guests, and Lien became visibly embarrassed. The incident became a huge joke in Taiwan. A loud and childish voice screaming "Grandpa Lien, You're Back!" became a popular cell phone ring tone. Internet bloggers spoofed the poem in songs, slide shows, and skits. Those who opposed Lien's visit to China protested his return to the island with signs that read, "Grandpa Lien, Don't Come Back!" When asked to comment on the poem, Lien could only laugh.[19] Knowing little about how the media operate in a democratic environment, Beijing saw its eagerness to please backfire, justifying precisely the stereotype it had attempted to put to rest.

Choosing and reading a poem are only minor and technical manifestations of a much deeper institutional gap between the two sides. Beijing has long been trying to sell the "one country, two systems" formula, which it has already imposed on Hong Kong and Macau, to the Taiwanese public. Yet as figure 15 shows, the Taiwanese people have overwhelmingly and consistently rejected this formula, for a variety of reasons: for supporters of independence, any form of reunion with China would be unacceptable; those who embrace their Chineseness would hardly be enticed by the idea of rejoining an authoritarian China screaming "Grandpa Lien, You're Back!"

From Beijing's end, though, such intra-Taiwan differences would matter little. To woo Taiwan convincingly in this realm would require democratization, the strongest taboo in Chinese politics. The Chinese Communist Party has shown few signs that it would be willing to go this far to win Taiwanese hearts and minds. In fact, as recently as in March 2009, the chair of China's parliament, Wu Bangguo, told the National Congress that China "will never adopt Western-style democracy with a multi-party system"[20] Unwilling to renounce its political monopoly, the party cannot go beyond "one country, two systems," and its insistence on this formula exposes the exhaustion of its political imagination. Realizing that the term is deeply unpopular in Taiwan, the Chinese government avoided using those words in the Anti-Secession Law. Yet the solution remains the same: "Following peaceful reunification, Taiwan will enjoy a high level of autonomy and operate under a system different from mainland China." Yet whether the words are explicitly uttered makes no difference: Taiwanese at both the elite and mass levels have shown little interest in accepting this offer since its genesis thirty years ago. There is no reason to believe that they will alter their position any time soon.

Why Cultural Exchanges Have Not Helped

Cultural exchanges can either be applauded for their vibrancy or lamented for their irrelevance. Songs, movies, television dramas, and fashion trends from Taiwan all have tremendous markets in China. Taiwanese celebrities are often worshipped even more fervently by their mainland fans than by fellow Taiwanese. The Little Tigers [Xiaohudui], a Taiwanese boy band popular in the late 1980s and early 1990s, staged a comeback at the 2010

"Spring Festival Gala Show" hosted by China Central Television (CCTV). More than seven hundred million viewers watch the show each year, making it among the world's most-watched television programs. At approximately 10:00 P.M., hundreds of millions of people watched three middle-aged men perform, with their five minutes representing the climax of the five-hour show.[21]

The Little Tigers' experience is indicative: given the size of China's population, the mainland market carries markedly heavier weight than Taiwan's market. Not surprisingly, Taiwanese celebrities have joined their colleagues in Hong Kong, Singapore, and Malaysia in the northbound gold rush. Taiwanese pop singers now commonly give concerts in the People's Republic, and the island's actors take roles in movies or television dramas produced on the mainland. One female celebrity, Yi Neng Jing, even played a People's Liberation Army officer. Taiwanese writers made inroads into the mainland market even earlier, as romance novelists Chiung-Yao and Sanmao had cultlike followings inside China in the 1980s. More recently, the current has begun to flow both ways, as mainland celebrities have begun to penetrate the Taiwanese market. Both movies and actors from the mainland have also received awards from Taiwanese artistic organizations. Indeed, the one arena in which the "Greater China Sphere" appears to be taking shape is cultural exchange.

Yet before applauding the arrival of cultural reunification, two important qualifications are in order. First, cultural exchanges remain vulnerable to the political climate. Most Taiwanese celebrities interested in the mainland market are quiet about their political views, fearing that such exposures would hurt their commercial opportunities. Chang Hui-mei, an aboriginal Taiwanese pop singer, found herself at the center of a political storm after she sang the Republic of China's national anthem at President Chen Shui-bian's inauguration ceremony in March 2000. Beijing completely banned her music from television and radio as well as commercials in which she appeared. Chang was forced into seclusion in New York for the remainder of the year. In a 2004 CCTV interview, a remorseful Chang said, "I had to suffer the consequences of a decision that was not made by me. . . . I should have been more discreet in my behavior, which impacts so many people."[22] These words brought down another firestorm of outrage, this time from inside Taiwan, as Vice President Annette Lu and other independence-leaning politicians questioned the pop diva's loyalty.[23] Ironically, a month earlier, a group of Chinese protesters had disrupted Chang's plan to hold a concert in Hangzhou on the grounds that she was a traitor who supported Taiwanese independence.

Drawing lessons from Chang's ordeal, celebrities have tried their best to sound detached from political issues. In 2006, when a list of allegedly pro-independence Taiwanese celebrities (*shenlü Taiwan yiren*) began appearing on major Chinese web portals, many of those named quickly moved to announce their lack of interest in politics. Artists' prime concern remains shielding their business activities from political influence rather than effecting political change.

Second, the economic gap between the two sides has given some Taiwanese, including celebrities, a sense of superiority vis-à-vis mainlanders. Precisely because of the undisturbed flow of cultural programs, statements on one side are instantly heard and felt by the other. In September 2006, Taiwanese actress Meng Guangmei received enormous condemnation from within China after she sensationally talked about using public restrooms in China. Her description of "seeing hundreds of white buttocks" since "people seldom shut doors when defecating" brought roaring laughter from her Taiwanese audience, but over a million entries were posted on various Chinese web portals, with netizens demanding Meng's apology or her life.[24] To save her commercial career, Meng apologized for "not knowing what I was talking about."[25] She added, "Like everyone, I love China."[26]

Angry mainlanders might have seen Meng's remarks as evidence of Taiwanese disdain, but some Chinese echo this view of their compatriots as medieval barbarians, though with a more humorous edge. According to a verse popular among male Chinese college students,

Top-notch girls marry GIs [Americans]
Second-tier ones marry the [Japanese] Imperial Army
Third-tier ones marry the KMT [Taiwanese]
Whereas those at the bottom marry the commies [mainlanders].

In addition, mainlanders can be condescending toward those from the island, as the popular usage of *tai ba zi* (hicks from Taiwan) in Shanghai dialect demonstrates. Wang Shuo, a widely known writer from Beijing, has openly derided Taiwanese president Chen Shui-bian as "a ground beetle from southern Taiwan [*Tainan tubie*]." Beijingers have long used *tubie* (ground beetle) to describe those who appear unsophisticated and boorish, and such mainland perceptions of the Taiwanese are quite common.

However, people in mainland China may not be disparaging the Taiwanese uniformly. China's Taiwan experts often joke that "people in Beijing want war, people in Shanghai want peace, and people in Fujian want surrender." But it is unlikely that regional variances will change Beijing's official insistence on extreme popular solidarity on the Taiwan issue. According to various online and traditional polls whose scientific reliability cannot be confirmed, as much as 95 percent of the Chinese respondents see Taiwan as part of China and support resolving the issue at any cost. Furthermore, as the economic gap between coastal China and Taiwan narrows, the Taiwanese sense of superiority may cede even more ground to rising Chinese pride.

These institutional and emotional obstacles may lead to a new interpretation of Beijing's decision to "internationalize" the Taiwan issue. The strategy reveals the Chinese government's strength: It formed a tacit alliance with the United States to define the limits of Taiwan's political ambition. Yet it also reveals Beijing's lack of confidence in its influence over people it officially proclaims as compatriots. If Beijing really means that it wants "to place hopes in the people of Taiwan," it would need to change its policies completely, rendering the official slogan hollow if not ironic. From this perspective, China's requests for help from external powers reveal not strength but weakness. Neither banquets nor pandas have helped Beijing gain much political capital inside Taiwan. China's wooing effort has largely failed.

Japan-Taiwan Relations: Beyond the Shadow of the Big Two

As a result of normalization of Sino-Japanese relations in 1972, Japan cut off its diplomatic ties with Taiwan. What followed was nearly two decades of diplomatic tepidity between Tokyo and Taipei. Since the 1990s, however, Japan and Taiwan have been rapidly approaching each other again. In contrast to Taiwan-China relations, courting between Taiwan and Japan has been mutual and comprehensive, involving at least three dimensions: the reimagination of colonial ties, the sharing of a democratic identity, and a complete diffusion of popular culture. Such a commingling process has elevated their relations to a status that is unofficial in name only.

These three dimensions are particularly relevant to our understanding of softer elements of power. China and the United States have naturally dominated realists' discussions of the Taiwan issue. Other players in the region, most notably Taiwan and Japan, are accorded at best secondary importance even though they also have very high stakes. Only by discussing Taiwan's or Japan's relations with either China or the United States (the military sponsor for both island countries) could scholars meaningfully discuss the Taiwan issue.[27]

Nor can liberalism, which emphasizes how economic interdependence reduces the likelihood of violent conflicts, effectively supplement the incompleteness of realism.[28] In the past three decades, trade volume between Japan and China has increased astronomically, surpassing the trade volume between Japan and Taiwan by the mid-1990s.[29] However, the strengthening of Japan's economic ties with China has done little to disturb Japan's more comprehensive strengthening of economic, social, and political relations with Taiwan. Despite Beijing's warnings and protests, Tokyo has become increasingly assertive on the Taiwan issue, clearly indicating that Japan, just like the United States, is a stakeholder in this potentially explosive issue. Tokyo's assertiveness is manifested in its open support for Taiwan's participation as an observer at the World Health Organization, its elevated level of diplomatic contacts with Taiwan, its defiance of Beijing's warning about issuing visas to such prominent political figures as former president Lee Teng-hui, its deployment of personnel with military backgrounds as part of diplomatic missions to Taiwan, and its refusal to explicitly exclude Taiwan from the scope of revised United States–Japan security treaties. Indeed, while the Japanese government has remained much more quiet about China's human rights record than have other Western industrialized countries, the Taiwan issue has symbolized Japan's growing forcefulness vis-à-vis the rise of the Chinese power. Japan's much-increased economic ties with China have not intimidated Japan into silence regarding Taiwan.

Given the power-based constraints, security-dependent players such as Taiwan and Japan have come closer to each other through mutual wooing—that is, expanding the discourses that political elites in both countries share and mutual penetration of mass popular culture. The Japan-Taiwan case shows that for lesser powers, knowing their place does not mean being totally powerless. A shrewd use of soft power factors such as identity and culture values may enhance weaker countries' presences in international politics.

Taiwan's Cross-Generational Efforts to Reach Out to Japan

Although Taiwan today is known as the friendliest of Japan's immediate neighbors, it would be erroneous to see Taipei as Tokyo's natural ally. In fact, early Taiwanese nationalists were resistance fighters against the Japanese colonial rule. As Masahiro Wakabayashi points out, the concept of Taiwanese nationalism emerged as a result of Japanese colonization.[30] Japan's colonization of Taiwan happened roughly at the same time that modern concepts of the nation-state and nationalism began to reach East Asia. The early Japanese colonial rule was strongly militarist. All the governors had military backgrounds, treated the Taiwanese people as inferior, and subjected them to harsher laws than those in Japan.[31] Such discrimination caused Taiwanese intellectuals to call on all those being oppressed to unite and resist as Taiwanese. In Wakabayashi's terms, Japan became the "unforgettable Other" against which Taiwanese intellectuals constantly drew comparisons to imagine the island's future.[32] Early Taiwanese nationalism had an unambiguous Chinese leaning. The vision was not to achieve independence but to reunite with the Chinese fatherland and jointly pursue modernity.

But in Taiwan's current mainstream political mood, this anti-Japan strand of nationalism is much weaker than its rival sentiment, amity toward Japan and nostalgia about Japanese colonial rule. What caused this shift in attitude? First, political agenda matters. Approaching Japan serves the current Taiwanese government's overall agenda of highlighting the island's sovereign existence at a time when its economy is ever more tied to that of the People's Republic of China.

Japan may have triggered the emergence of Taiwanese nationalism, but it was not the only force. China stood at the other end of the nationalist spectrum. In other words, Japan and China defined the extremes of political imagination for early Taiwanese nationalists. In the contemporary context, the underlying rationale behind Taiwanese elites' efforts to stress Japan-Taiwan connections differs little from early Taiwanese nationalists' conception of a peculiar Taiwanese-made Chineseness to distance themselves from being Japanese subjects. To escape Chinese cultural and historical legacies, Taiwanese elites use the island's extensive linkages with Japan as a foundation on which Taiwan's "non-Chineseness" can be built. The only difference is that Japan has ceased to be the only pole that the Taiwanese government uses to pull the island away from the overarching Chinese shadow.

By the same token, as Beijing reaches out to Taiwan, "national resistance to Japan" has become a sacred bond. To Chinese leaders, however, such efforts have an ironic flavor. Chinese history textbooks long stuck to the tale that the Chinese Communist Party almost single-handedly beat the Japanese invaders with the KMT watching, if not fleeing. The party now needs to reinterpret history. It has begun to issue military honor badges to all veterans, including those serving in the KMT troops. In his speech at a 2005 national ceremony, President Hu not only mentioned the KMT but also acknowledged that it was "in charge of fighting the Japanese invaders as the main force" and "won many heroic major battles."[33] To echo the Chinese overture, the KMT president Ma Ying-jeou proclaimed that even during the colonial years, the people of Taiwan "never forgot that they were descendants of the Chinese nation."[34]

While the Taiwanese government's position may shift depending on the agenda of the governing party, the private realm has constituted a more consistently pro-Japan force. Scholars note that there is a high pro-Japan sentiment among Taiwanese born in the 1930s.[35] Most people of this generation lack clear memories of the early resistance movement. Instead, they have more vivid memories of receiving intensified naturalization education from Japanese teachers and fighting side by side with Japan, seeing Japan as a "motherland" sharing Taiwan's fate. Resistance to Japan was dwarfed by joining Japan in resisting other powers. Indeed, a recent poll indicates that people of this generation still have fond memories of their Japanese teachers and Japanese police, two positive influences. According to Tsai Chin-tang, 94.47 percent of the 203 respondents in one poll said that their impressions of their childhood Japanese teachers were "good" or "quite good."[36]

This pro-Japan nostalgia, however, is as much a Chinese-induced product as a direct Japanese legacy. The return of Taiwan to the Chinese fatherland brought an extremely corrupt and oppressive regime into the lives of many Taiwanese. Many found themselves experiencing as much discrimination from their so-called compatriots as from the previous Japanese colonial administration. But the KMT government was much more corrupt and much less effective in maintaining law and order. Chiang Kai-shek's decision to use force to put down a February 28, 1947, popular protest may have consolidated his control of the island, but the massacre and the subsequent mass arrests also firmed up Taiwan's hidden resistance to mainland rule. The KMT government's decision to ban virtually everything related to the Japanese culture (movies, radio and television programs, songs, even Japanese-language education at public universities) perversely connected nostalgia for Japanese colonial rule with the hidden antipathy to the KMT as a part of cultural resistance movement. When Taiwanese democratization was in full swing under the leadership of President Lee Teng-hui, himself a member of this pro-Japan generation, this long suppressed emotion was finally set free, acquiring significance both as a weapon to address historical grievances under the KMT's authoritarian rule and as a celebration of Taiwan's democratic achievement.

The members of the colonial generation, driven by their fond childhood memories, are not the only force pushing Taiwan closer to Japan. Taiwan's ruling elites have no personal experience with Japanese colonization but are actively creating new connections. They strike Japanese chords by frequently stressing the discourses of democratization and security. Uchida Yoshihisa, Japan's de facto ambassador to Taiwan from 2003 to

2005,[37] recalls that in his first meeting with Chen Shui-bian, the Taiwanese president emphasized the importance of triangular security cooperation among the United States, Japan, and Taiwan and praised Japan for refusing to place Taiwan outside the protective scope of United States–Japan security despite Beijing's repeated demands.[38] When the Japanese government expressed concern about Chen's decision to hold a 2004 referendum on cross-strait relations, the general secretary of the Presidential Office, Chiou I-jen, also called on the Japanese side to realize that Taiwan provides a buffer between Beijing and Tokyo without which Chinese missiles would be targeted against Japan.[39]

In addition to underlining Taiwan's security significance to Japan, accentuating Taiwan's democratic achievements has also brought the two countries closer. Japanese diplomats have noticed that when receiving Japanese delegations, government officials at all levels tend to highlight Taiwan's democratizing achievements, frequently contrasting them with practices in China, where the government has ruled out any possibility of fundamental political reform.[40] One natural extension of this contrast is a feeling in Japan that a democratic Taiwan should not be wiped out by an authoritarian China and that the Taiwanese demand for independence represents the will of the people and deserves other democracies' respect. While the security discourses strike Japanese nerves about the consequences of a Chinese invasion, the democratic discourses bring Japan and Taiwan closer by highlighting a value-based common identity—that is, Japan is no longer the lone democracy in the region but has been joined by a democratic, gracious, and friendly Taiwan.

Finally, Japanese popular culture has created a cultlike following among Taiwan's younger people, many of whom proudly label themselves *ha ri zu* (Japan-loving geeks). In Mandarin, *ha* imitates the sound a dog makes when pleasing its owners. But the *ha ri zu* use the word not to imply self-degradation but instead to capture their fervor. These Japanophiles, mostly in their twenties and thirties, regard Japan as their cultural Mecca, the source of all inspiration for new fashions, songs, movies, TV dramas, video games, cuisines, sports, and even words. The boom started with the publication of a series of manga-style travelogues by a female essayist who became so infatuated with Japanese culture that she decided to use a pseudo-Japanese pen name, Ha Ri (Japanophile) and Kyōko (an ordinary Japanese female name). Though it is difficult to estimate the number of young Japanophiles, they are visible in the scenery of Taiwanese popular culture. With an army of *ha ri zu* and the absence of vocal anti-Japan segments in the younger generation (unlike China), the Taiwanese government's attempt to build new ties with Japan meets with little public resistance. In contrast to China, Southeast Asia, and South Korea, where cultural attraction remains in its commercialized space, in Taiwan the popular fascination with Japanese culture provides the government with the best momentum for furthering its agenda.

In short, Japan holds wide-ranging charms for Taiwan. Japan is vital for political and security reasons as well as attractive on cultural grounds. The cultural Japan has never faded from the memories of members of the older generation. Democratization only set free and amplified their long-suppressed nostalgia for their onetime motherland. Although the current ruling elites lack personal experiences with Japanese rule, they certainly realize Japan's vital security importance, and they seek to build new ties by calling Japanese attention to the two countries' shared democratic identity vis-à-vis an authoritarian China. For the younger generation, Japan is attractive as the Paris next door. The anti-Japan voices, conversely, have largely become ostracized in all three generations.

Willing Recipients on the Other Side: Rise of Pro-Taiwan Voices in Japan

Taiwan's cross-generational efforts to reach out to Japan would not succeed without a corresponding pro-Taiwan movement in Japan. The Japanese side also features a growing group of actors who are willing to lend their sympathy and support to the Taiwanese quest for international recognition. The widening of this pro-Taiwan coalition is remarkable, for it marks a gradual yet far-reaching transformation of Japanese perceptions of China and Taiwan and of Japan's place in this vital diplomatic question. In 1972, public mood was among the major factors that compelled Tanaka Kakuei to normalize relations with the People's Republic shortly after he took office.[41] But pro-Taiwan voices were never completely silenced. One staunch anti–People's Republic politician, Ishihara Shintarō, joined like-minded young lawmakers in organizing the Blue Storm Society [Seirankai] to oppose Tanaka's decision to abandon Taiwan. Though the group's effort failed to reverse the normalization, it did restrain the Tanaka government from going too far in accepting the One China principle. Instead, the Tanaka government merely expressed that Japan "fully understands" and "respects" the Chinese position on Taiwan without endorsing it.

The Blue Storm Society's organizational structure survived its failed mission. As the Tanaka government began a series of negotiation with China over such functional issues like fishing and aviation, its members continued to act as gatekeepers, checking the government to minimize Taiwan's losses. The Blue Storm Society gradually evolved into a more encompassing conservative political club, addressing a variety of domestic and foreign policy issues. Though strengthening Japan-Taiwan relations is no longer the group's sole mission, the group's continued existence has guaranteed the persistence of pro-Taiwan voices among Japanese elites during difficult times. By joining other conservative visions (for example, historical revisionism, nationalism, and anticommunism), they contribute to the articulation of an assertive and independent Japanese state.

Taiwanese president Lee Teng-hui was particularly important in broadening his country's appeal on Japanese soil. Lee reached out to Japan's cultural and scholarly elite and utilized his charisma to recruit them as enthusiastic interpreters of Taiwan's charm. His interactions with Shiba Ryōtarō, a famed Japanese essayist, were particularly important in presenting Japanese readers with a positive image of Taiwan. Shiba wrote a bestselling travel essay in which he praised Lee, framing him as the perfect embodiment of Japanese-style integrity. Shiba also conveyed Lee's pride and appreciation for his Japanese roots. He stressed Lee's lament on the "sadness of being a Taiwanese," which both admirers and attackers have used as evidence of Lee's rejection of the Chinese identity.[42] Lee's reputation was also enhanced by Shiba's popularity, which has persisted after his death, and the fact that Shiba was not a right-winger but was known as a knowledgeable historical writer and philosopher. Recruiting such a highly respected interpreter of Taiwan's charm constituted a major wooing victory for Lee.

Japan also has a visible group of Taiwan-born pro-independence activists who have spent most of their lives exiled to Japan by the KMT government. Jin Meiling, Huang Wenxiong, Huang Zhaotang, and others have worked as professors and authors and published profusely on the Taiwan issue, offering clear pro-independence, pro-Japan, and anti-China rhetoric. They speak publicly and are frequently quoted in the press, often in the form of dialogues with friendly Japanese conservative politicians and authors in which they jointly lambast China and Japan's timid policy toward China and Taiwan. Their views may not be in the mainstream—a partial list of Huang Wenxiong's publications includes *The Ugly Chinaman* [Minikui Chūgokujin], *Japan—Falling into the Trap of Sinocentrism* [Chūkashisō no wana ni hamatta nihon], *Taiwan Was Built by the Japanese* [Taiwan ha nihonjin'ni tsukutta], *South Korea Was Built by the Japanese* [Kankoku ha nihonjin'ni tsukutta], and *Seven Reasons Why China Cannot Prevail over Japan Even When China Fights to the Death* [Chūgoku ga shindemo nihon ni katenai nanatsu no riyū]. Such books have helped these activists gain a following at Japan's major conservative publication houses, among them Fusōsha and Kōdansha, and thus are featured prominently in bookstores throughout Japan. Sales figures for these books are unclear, but these Taiwanese activists have a solid base of Japanese conservative and nationalist readers and have certainly reached other people via television.

Taiwan's democratization further empowered these activists. The DPP government no longer treated them as traitors but welcomed them as heroes. President Chen appointed Jin and Huang Zhaotang as personal counselors. Together with Japanese conservatives, these pro-independence activists helped to ensure the survival and ultimately revitalization of Japanese sympathy for Taiwan. This revitalization was propelled not only by Taiwan's democratization but also by China's 1989 political debacle. Following the signing of the Japan-China Friendship Treaty in 1978, Japan and post–Cultural Revolution China experienced a brief era of cordiality, as many Japanese genuinely believed that China was eagerly learning from Japan and becoming an open and democratizing society. As figure 2 illustrates (chapter 1), the number of Japanese who felt friendly toward China reached an all-time high of 78.6 percent in 1982 and remained above 70 percent for much of the 1980s.[43] Even China's 1986 anti-Japan protest did not have a major impact on Japanese perceptions. These years also represented the nadir of Japanese awareness of Taiwan: In Japan's media-saturated society, only one national newspaper, the *Sankei Shimbun*, the smallest of the national Big Five, noted for its right-leaning position, posted correspondents in Taiwan.[44] But the Tiananmen Massacre shocked the Japanese and resulted in a drastic decline in the number of people who felt friendly toward China. Japanese perceptions of China have subsequently continued their drop.[45] Taiwan's democratic progress, contrasted with China's rising nationalist fervor and intensified anti-Japan patriotic education, has further tipped Japanese popular sympathy toward the Taiwanese side. Support for Taiwan, once the almost exclusive domain of conservative nationalists, now enjoys tremendous support across the ideological spectrum.

During the 1990s, the major Japanese media outlets returned journalists to Taiwan, and tourism to the island has also boomed. Each week, approximately 150 regular flights and 50 charter flights link the two island nations. Japanese women have joined what was once a predominantly male tourist stream and have begun to show interest in popular trends initiated in Taiwan. The number of Japanese visitors to Taiwan surpassed one million in 2005, now accounting for about one-third of all of the country's foreign tourists. People-to-people exchanges have brought a democratic and culturally vibrant Taiwanese society into the personal worlds of numerous Japanese. As a result, the transmission of popular culture is no longer unidirectional. Taiwanese movies and pop stars have begun to penetrate into the Japanese market, leading to the emergence of *ha tai zu*, the Japanese counterpart of the Taiwanese *ha ri zu*. For example, the Taiwanese all-male group F4 (Flower-4), which was named after a Japanese manga series, *Hana yori danshi* [Boys over Flowers] by Kamio Yōko, has fan clubs all over Japan. Their 2001 TV presentation of the manga series, "Meteor Garden [*Liu xing hua yuan*]," was a major hit in Japan and a Japanese adaptation of the story. In politics, the translation of Lee Teng-hui's major works and Kobayashi Yoshinori's comic book, *On Taiwan*, also make Taiwan's pro-independence and pro-Japan stance more accessible to average Japanese readers.

Finally, the Japanese government has become more tolerant, if not implicitly supportive, of closer ties with Taiwan. As of May 2006, 240 Japanese lawmakers were members of Nikka Gi'in Renmei [the Japan-Taiwan Legislators Panel], many of whom have overlapping memberships in Nicchūyūkō Gi'in Renmei [the Japan-China Friendship Legislators Panel] and see little conflict between membership in the two groups. The Japanese government began to support Taiwan's effort to gain observer status at the World Health Organization in 2002, even before the outbreak of the SARS pandemic in 2003. Japan also elevated the level of official contact with Taiwan from *fukukachō* [assistant division chief] to *kachō* [division chief]. To improve security cooperation, retired Self-Defense Force officers were stationed in Tokyo's de facto diplomatic missions inside Taiwan. The influential think tank Taigaikankei Tasukufōsu [Foreign Relations Task Force], which consists of current and recently retired officials, prominent intellectuals, and entrepreneurs and acts as foreign policy consulting agency to Prime Minister Koizumi Jun'ichirō, proposed strengthening ties with Taiwan as a result of its democratization progress.[46] On the mass level, visa exemptions for Taiwanese tourists, first implemented during the World Expo in Aichi Prefecture in 2005, have remained in effect. This policy clears away the legal obstacle for inviting prominent private citizens such as Lee Teng-hui to visit Japan.

Local governments have become even more assertive in promoting exchanges with Taiwan. Ishihara Shintarō, now the governor of Tokyo, has visited Taiwan multiple times since assuming office, openly defying China's protests, while Tokyo's sister relationship with Beijing has been largely put aside. When Ogihara Seiji, the mayor of Okayama, decided to establish sister city relations with Taiwan's Hsinchu City in 2003, the mayor of

Luoyang, Okayama's Chinese sister city for twenty years, sent multiple letters to warn his Japanese counterpart not to violate the One China policy. Ogihara directly appealed to his people by posting all his correspondence with the mayor of Luoyang on the city's web site. Ogihara pointed out that if U.S. cities such as Los Angeles can maintain sister city relations with both Chinese and Taiwanese cities, Japanese cities could also do so.[47] He urged the Chinese side to stop using one standard to monitor U.S. abidance by the One China policy and another, more stringent standard for other countries, especially Japan. The Okayama city government launched its sister city relations with Hsinchu; in response, Luoyang froze its relationship with Okayama.[48]

In the end, Beijing's One-China paranoia and the economic prospect of bringing in Taiwanese tourists compelled the mayor of Okayama to reach out to Taiwan at the cost of cutting off ceremonial linkages with China. In essence, Ogihara called for greater Japanese foreign policy autonomy vis-à-vis Chinese intimidation, much like the Taiwanese quest to build closer ties with Japan. In short, the mutual wooing between the two countries is an indigenous process driven by political needs, security concerns, and cultural attractions. Unlike in Southeast Asia and South Korea, where neither China nor Japan enjoys a clear upper hand, efforts to woo Taiwan have elevated Japan's image but have done little help to China's.

Obstacles and Challenges in Mutual Wooing

Yet obstacles remain for further courting between Japan and Taiwan. First, pro-independence elites' efforts to reach out to Japan may become overly utilitarian. Uchida Yoshihisa, Japan's de facto ambassador to Taiwan from 2002 to 2005, admitted in his memoir that on occasions the DPP government under President Chen Shui-bian sought to provoke China and to escalate cross-strait relations as electoral strategies. Such moves led the Japanese government to issue an official warning to Chen's government in January 2004, with Tokyo expressing "grave concern" regarding Chen's referendum initiative.[49] Citing the lack of progress on a free trade agreement between Taiwan and Japan, Uchida also pointed out that pro-independence forces are sometimes too eager to politicize purely economic issues as a way of asserting Taiwan's sovereignty. Such overeagerness to politicize functional issue areas may alarm Japanese officials who prioritize the smooth functioning of Japan-China relations ahead of any substantial improvement in Japan-Taiwan relations.

This recognition brings the second obstacle to spotlight—namely the so-called *Chaina-sukūru* [China School] segment in the Japanese government, especially in the Ministry of Foreign Affairs (MOFA). The term China School originated from the language-training program at MOFA that sought to produce China-focused diplomats. The Japanese press later picked up the term to describe Japanese officials who prioritize the importance of the Japanese-Chinese friendship and emphasize the need to reach compromises with the Chinese government.

This faction was largely marginalized during the Koizumi years.[50] Yet signs indicate that the China School is returning from its Siberia. If the trend continues, the urge to court Taiwan may be weakened. Despite the press's earlier speculation that the Japanese government would appoint Iimura Yutaka, former Japanese ambassador to Indonesia who had little experience in China affairs, as its new ambassador to Beijing, the post went to Miyamoto Yūji, a veteran specializing in Japan-China relations and commonly perceived as a member of the China School. Miyamoto's successor, Niwa Uichirō, also has extensive connections with China's top policymakers as a consequence of his background as the president of Japan's enormous Itochu Corporation. More important, MOFA still insists on placing its Taiwan-related staff under the direct administrative control of the China Division, leading Uchida to complain that MOFA created obstacles to his efforts to escalate Japan-Taiwan relations.[51]

Politicians are not usually placed into the China School category, but some are known for anchoring moderate voices to Beijing. Representative figures include political veterans like Tanaka Makiko, the daughter of former prime minister Tanaka Kakuei as well as Koizumi's first foreign minister. Soon after taking office, Tanaka Makiko angered Taiwan by suggesting that following Hong Kong's footsteps in returning to China was not a bad idea.[52] Fukuda Yasuo, Koizumi's longtime cabinet office secretary who became prime minister in 2007, and Katō Kōichi, who also served as cabinet office secretary and as secretary of the ruling Liberal Democratic Party, are also commonly perceived as pro-China politicians.[53]

Third, Japanese business and media sectors also hesitate to improve ties with Taiwan if doing so might antagonize China. Japan's national broadcaster, the NHK, repeatedly declined Taiwanese invitations to host a widely watched annual Japanese folk song contest held in Taiwan. The NHK is believed to have feared that if it accepted the Taiwanese invitation, the Chinese government would retaliate by prohibiting the NHK from broadcasting the 2008 Beijing Olympics.[54] With the world economy plunging into recession and China's important role in shifting the tide, Beijing may have a new leverage in limiting the scope of mutual courting between Japan and Taiwan (or between any major economies and Taiwan).

Fourth, Taiwan's political situation remains highly fluid, and its quest for identity has become increasingly diversified. While strongly pro-independence forces are eager to please Japan, with some supporters even visiting the Yasukuni Shrine,[55] other sectors, most notably the Taiwanese military, remain deeply suspicious of Japan. Uchida recalled a somewhat unpleasant meeting with Taiwan's vice defense minister, who used a supposedly ceremonial greeting to criticize Japan's colonial occupation and for its diplomatic betrayal of Taiwan in 1972.[56] Such hostility took the Japanese ambassador by surprise, especially after a series of highly amiable meetings with other government officials.

Anti-Japan sentiment also continues among Taiwanese aboriginals and is reflected in their highly publicized on-site protests against Koizumi's visit to the Yasukuni Shrine and their request to withdraw their ancestors' names from the shrine's worship list of heroes who died for the Japanese empire. A tiny yet highly vocal minority makes annual pilgrimages to the Japanese-occupied Diaoyu/Senkaku Islands. In recent years, these activists have joined forces with similar organizations in mainland China and Hong Kong to create a pan-China nationalist coalition that demands that Japan return the islands back to Chinese sovereign control. In short, nearly two decades into Taiwanese democratization, one word no longer captures the panoramic picture of Taiwanese sentiments toward Japan.

In addition, generational leadership change does not always work in Japan's favor. Former president Lee Teng-hui remains an iconic figure for the Japanese conservatives. The Friends of Lee Teng-hui Association in Japan, set up by a few well-known Japanese conservative writers and politicians, boasts nineteen regional chapters as well as a chapter in Los Angeles. But Lee's political utility is dwindling inside Taiwan: Incidents such as his latest remarks that the disputed Diaoyu/Senkaku Islands belong to Japan and a visit by the president of the Taiwan Solidarity Union (TSU), a party that worships Lee as its "spiritual leader," to the Yasukuni Shrine made Lee sound extremist if not treasonous to many Taiwanese. Despite Lee's hard campaigning, the TSU was eliminated in the national legislature in 2005, and its marginalization attests to his evaporating political capital.

Overall, the Taiwanese are indeed friendlier toward the Japanese than Japan's other neighbors, but such amiable feeling may become uncertain as Taiwan's partisan warfare becomes increasingly malicious. Burdened with a tremendously unpopular president mired in scandals, the DPP lost the 2008 presidential race to the main opposition party, the KMT, by a wide margin. Given the groundbreaking rapprochement between the KMT and the Chinese Communist Party symbolized by Lien's visit to China in 2005, a KMT government may no longer be eager to reach out to Japan to distance itself from the People's Republic. In an interview with the Japanese press, President Ma Ying-jeou has clearly stated that he opposes Taiwanese independence and sees both Taiwan and the mainland as "belonging to our territory [*wei wo ling tu*]."[57] In addition, Ma's experience as a vocal protester of Japanese control of the Diaoyu/Senkaku Islands has made him even suspicious in Tokyo's eyes. Ma attempted to assuage Japanese concerns by visiting the country before taking office and delivering a speech in Japanese, but purely ceremonial gestures would not allay those fears.

And Japan may feel its fear vindicated after all. Since Ma took the presidency, Japan-Taiwan relations have indeed chilled, while Taiwan's connection with China has tightened. Despite Ma's trip to Japan and his "special partnership" proposal, tension has been on the rise. Bilateral discordance even led to the forced resignation of Saitō Masaki, the de facto Japanese ambassador to Taipei, on December 1, 2009. Speaking before an audience at a Taiwanese university, Saitō stated that Taiwan's legal status was "undecided." Japan has always remained vague about Taiwan's legal status, but the DPP government never felt any pressure to intervene. Realizing China's threat, President Chen even expressed appreciation that Japan had done its best under serious constraints.[58] But Saitō's speech generated angry responses from both the Taiwanese and the Chinese governments. Ma declared that Taiwan has always belonged to the Republic of China, while the Chinese foreign ministry stated that Saitō's speech challenged China's "core interest." To punish Saitō, Ma and other high-ranking officials refused to meet with him, leaving Tokyo with no choice but to recall him. That a high-ranking diplomat would be punished for remaining vague on Taiwan's statehood would have been unthinkable under the pro-independence DPP government.

Finally, Japan and Taiwan lack a mechanism for dealing with unexpected incidents. The territorial dispute over the Diaoyu/Senkaku Islands is compounded by the fact that Taiwan is not accepted as a member of the international regime of the high seas, so its legal claim over the exclusive economic zone is not recognized by other countries, including Japan. Occasional clashes between Taiwanese fishermen and the Japanese coast guard have forced some Taiwanese fishermen to hang the Chinese national flag on their boats to reduce the likelihood of being attacked.[59]

On June 10, 2008, a Japanese coast guard ship collided with and sunk a Taiwanese fishing boat. Tokyo initially insisted that the ship did nothing wrong and that the fishing crew bore full responsibility for the incident.

Only when Ma withdrew Taiwan's de facto ambassador, Ko Se-kai, from Japan and the Taiwanese military announced its decision to send warships to the disputed area did Tokyo back down. It expressed "regrets" three days later, formally apologized for the incident, and agreed to offer compensation to the fishing crew.[60] In addition, Tokyo tacitly allowed the Taiwanese navy to cruise near the disputed islands as a face-saving gesture.

But damage was significant. The drama cost Japan a friendly messenger in Ko, who had called for calmer responses from his government right after the incident and was thus denounced by some as a traitor to the Chinese nation (*Han jian*). After returning to Taiwan, Ko refused to attend legislative questioning sessions, was physically attacked by a protester, and angrily resigned his post. Taiwanese foreign minister Francisco Ou permitted Ko's resignation but criticized his refusal to testify as "greatly irresponsible."[61] The Ma administration also eliminated the Japan Affairs Council [Riben Shiwuhui], a presidential advisory body set up by Chen and operating independently of the foreign ministry.

Such acrimonious incidents apparently poisoned the cordial atmosphere between Japan and Taiwan. Unless the current case-by-case mode of conflict management is replaced by a more formalized mechanism, accidental clashes may lead to real crises. Furthermore, the two governments' clumsy handling of the fishing boat incident, combined with the forced resignation of Japan's chief diplomat in Taiwan, clearly demonstrates the cooling between the two countries.

In the arena of popular culture, South Korea has become a formidable challenger to Japan in luring the attention of young Taiwanese. Korean television dramas and movies, though they do not necessarily paint an accurate picture of real life in that country, have resonated with countless East and Southeast Asian viewers. Korean pop singers and movie stars are fresh faces in the greater Asian market, and their popularity has triggered an increase in general interest in Korean culture and language. The Japanese entertainment industry, which has for decades remained the driving force behind regional trends, is feeling the pressure. The "Korean wave" has already produced an army of *ha han zu* (Korea lovers) in Taiwan as well as elsewhere in the region. With the lack of an equally impressive advancement of Japanese popular culture, will the *ha han zu* lead to the decline of the *ha ri zu?* In an increasingly crowded international cultural stage, can Japanese popular culture continue to surprise the Taiwanese? If not, even if Japanese cultural elements are likely to maintain a sizable presence in Taiwan, a unique cultural linkage will become markedly weaker. In this sense, Taiwan may eventually join China, South Korea, and Southeast

Asia as places where transnational cultural exchanges are increasingly commercialized and depoliticized—not necessarily good news for diplomatic wooing.

China and Japan's wooing trajectories toward Taiwan could not be more different, as China has yet to find plausible ground on which to connect with the Taiwanese audience. As long as China remains as a one-party state, the contrast between a democratic Taiwan and an authoritarian China will enhance Taiwan's soft power by tipping international sympathy (including that of Japan) toward the Taiwanese side.

However, Taipei may have to constantly reconcile its aspiration for international recognition with the cold, hard facts of a rising Chinese power insistent on its sovereign claim to the island. In practice, therefore, the Taiwanese ruling elite may have to resist the temptation to overuse positive international social capital, accumulated through years of democratic bonding and courting, beyond the limits imposed by power politics. To varying degrees, such tendencies recently has been present in United States–Taiwan relations. Taiwan's limited international place is indeed a dictate of power politics. But making the best use of this limited place requires the political wisdom of leaders, especially in the case of Taiwan. For the foreseeable future, the country's leaders may have to constantly balance between aspirations for international recognition and the danger of biting off more than Taiwan can chew.

Conclusion:
The Dynamic Wooing Game

Most recently, China's wooing campaign has become more selective about whom to attract. Burned by a series of public relations debacles, the Chinese government has realized that it has only a slim chance of making itself appealing to "the West," a concept vaguely defined in Chinese popular discourse as the industrialized democracies of Europe, North America, and the South Pacific as well as Japan. Consequently, Beijing has shown signs that it is abandoning its courting of this market. Instead, by taking an unapologetic and assertive tone, it seeks to enhance its political capital elsewhere, as in its "fight with the West for the right to speak" campaign, which was launched by the Chinese government with strong popular backing.

In Japan, the LDP government in the post–Koizumi era attempted to build an ideological alliance, using value-oriented diplomacy [*kachikan gaikō*] as a new slogan. Such effort was particularly salient under the Abe and Asō administrations. Though the campaign never explicitly mentioned China as an outsider, the emphasis on democracy spoke for itself. Yet this concept generated little enthusiasm beyond Kasumigaseki, Japan's bureaucratic quarter. Furthermore, the new Democratic Party of Japan (DPJ) government has offered more confusion than hope. Overwhelmed by its domestic reform agenda, a series of scandals, and natural disasters, the DPJ government appeared hesitant and chaotic, and voices questioning its viability are becoming louder.

Binding together these two Asian powers has both theoretical and empirical implications. First, such a pairing permits an examination of the common tasks and different challenges that a democracy and a nondemocracy face as they seek to woo diplomatically. Both the Chinese government and its public have demonstrated a strong interest in promoting the country's charm in order to enhance its *ruan shi li* (soft power). The internal passion for and external attention to China's soft power should serve as a caution: domestic and international values should not be casually equated. Depending on the audience, the legitimacy of a country's diplomacy may have little to do with how it organizes its internal politics. On the other side of the coin, for Japan, although its democratic reputation has been well established and the country earns consistently high remarks in global polls conducted by the BBC World Survey, the country still runs an emotional debt with the neighbors that matter most.

These observations should certainly not be read as implying that nondemocracies are stronger candidates for making charm offensives. For certain recipients, a nondemocratic, repressive nature could be an insurmountable obstacle in the path of achieving emotional embrace. In addition, such countries tend to bounce unpredictably and drastically between wooing and menacing. When authoritarian leaders become erratic, no electoral constraints are in place to tame them. Despite these qualifications, nondemocracies are in the game of enhancing soft power through wooing, and they should be taken seriously.

In addition to this theoretical angle, there is also an empirical need to bind together Japan's and China's wooing campaigns. Though these two Asian powers are materially interdependent, their emotional antagonism has been on the rise. To make matters worse, the confrontation encompasses both the official and private realms. When people of two countries are suspicious and distrustful of each other, governments have much less room to be flexible and moderate. For legitimacy- or votes-seeking politicians focused on short-term gains, heeding such public sentiment would look easier and safer, though domestic courting would bear a huge diplomatic price tag.

In the context of the Sino-Japanese rivalry, an Othering or belittling component is part of diplomacy. Wooing no longer is just about constructing a positive self but also involves hurting the other country's reputation. This tendency is clearly visible in the two countries' courting efforts toward Southeast Asia, South Korea, and Taiwan. For the soft power literature, this phenomenon implies that the darker, zero-sum dimension of this concept must be explored. The adjective *soft* stresses a very different outer appearance, yet, at its core, soft power shares its harder counterpart's nature: Both are calculating and interest-driven devices to enhance one country's interest in a world of competing actors fighting for limited resources.

2008: A Cursed Year for China?

One Chinese journalist lamented to me that 2008 was "cursed"—
"Everything went wrong" that year. Such frustration was widely shared
among various Chinese to whom I talked.[1] In fact, with the world economy
plunging into recession, such complaints may even resonate with global
audiences.

The Chinese in particular had had high expectations for the year. With
the Olympics coming to Beijing, the Chinese government had touted 2008
as the pinnacle of China's rise.[2] Yet the year started on a bad note: A series
of blizzards hit central and southern China, causing extensive damage to
hundreds of thousands of homes and at least 169 deaths, most of them
caused by roofs collapsing under the weight of snow and ice. The blizzards
also caused a major disruption of the country's transportation network
right before the Spring Festival, with two million passengers stranded at
the Guangzhou Railway Station alone and the Jing-Zhu Highway linking
northern and southern China blocked by massive chunks of ice.[3]

The blizzards were just the beginning of a string of calamities. Between
March and the end of May, an outbreak of hand, foot, and mouth disease
in central China caused 170,000 infections and 40 deaths.[4] Also in May,
four rounds of torrential rains flooded five central and southern provinces, killing 55.[5] One month earlier, two trains collided on a busy route in
Shandong Province, resulting in 72 deaths and 416 injuries.[6] The human
and economic losses of these incidents were dwarfed by the devastation
caused by the May 12 Wenchuan Earthquake. Reaching 8.5 on the Richter
scale, the tremor killed nearly 70,000 people and caused economic losses
estimated at 845 billion yuan (approximately $123 billion).[7] Less than one
hundred days before the Olympics, the entire nation plunged into shock
and grief.

China also found itself engulfed in an international image crisis, precisely the opposite of its Olympic goal. In March, unrest broke out in
Tibet. The following month, activists seized on the Olympic Torch Relay
as a prime opportunity to vent their anger at China's Tibet policy, taking
to the streets of London, Paris, and San Francisco to disrupt the relay.
The Free Tibet activists attracted the most media coverage, but the relay was also dogged by protesters who wanted to draw attention to the
Darfur Crisis, the persecution of political dissidents, the one-child policy, sweatshops, environmental deterioration, and animal rights. Chinese
counterdemonstrators also turned out to "protect" the relay, adding to the
chaos. In cities around the world, Chinese residents waved Chinese flags,

shouted patriotic slogans, and occasionally engaged in physical skirmishes with the anti-China protesters. Chinese diplomats stationed in the countries through which the torch relay passed frantically wired Beijing for instructions, negotiated with host governments about enhancing security measures, and arranged to transport busloads of their compatriots to relay sites to overwhelm the protesters. What had been advertised as a "trip of harmony," echoing the new leadership's domestic agenda of establishing a "harmonious society," turned into total disarray. One Chinese journalist bemoaned, "What a joke," but neither he nor most other people found it funny.[8]

Other Olympic-related setbacks also frustrated Chinese leaders. In February, noted Hollywood director Steven Spielberg withdrew from the Beijing Olympics Art Advisory Committee to protest China's policy on Darfur, claiming that his "conscience" would not allow him to "continue business as usual."[9] To lessen the government's acute embarrassment, Liu Guijin, China's special envoy on the Darfur Crisis, quickly announced that Spielberg had never signed his contract and was therefore never really a committee member.[10]

The Olympics themselves also generated some negative moments. Chen Qigang, musical director of the opening ceremony, ultimately revealed that Lin Miaoke, the nine-year-old girl who had become a celebrity after singing "Ode to the Motherland" at the ceremony, was actually lip-synching, while the voice belonged to Yang Peiyi, a seven-year-old whom authorities had declared "less cute" than Lin. Chen's explanation that the change had been made "for the national interest. The child on camera should be flawless in image, internal feeling, and expression," did not go over well outside China, leaving a bad taste in the world's mouth.[11] The gold-medal-winning performance by China's female gymnasts was tainted by allegations, fueled by conflicting reports in the Chinese media, that some of the athletes were underage. Such incidents strengthened the international audience's stereotypes regarding Chinese government manipulations.

Six months after the games, a BBC World Service Poll of thirteen thousand respondents in twenty-one countries presented a rather discouraging picture for Beijing: The Olympics had worsened rather than improved the global attitude toward China. China's positive ratings dropped from 45 to 39 percent, while 40 percent viewed China negatively. The findings prompted Doug Miller, director of the polling program, to say that "a successful Olympic Games has not been enough to offset other concerns that people have" and that "China has much to learn about winning hearts and minds in the world."[12]

"Well-Fed Foreigners"—China's Partial Abandoning of Wooing

Has China's diplomatic wooing failed? Chinese officials and scholars have offered their reflections on the lessons of the entire Olympic drama. One piece of suggestion, largely tactical, is to shun Hollywood. Commenting on Spielberg's much-publicized resignation, one scholar close to the Chinese government stated, "We have nobody but ourselves to blame. The real lesson is this: Our feudalist and hierarchical mentality really hurts [*Fengjian dengji yishi haisi ren*]. We still tend to think our popularity will get a boost from adding some Western celebrities on board, even nominally. But does it really? How many preparatory meetings did Spielberg attend to discuss the opening ceremony? How many people knew he was an artistic adviser in the first place? But now he resigned, it became a huge loss of face for us. We picked up the stone and dropped it on our own feet."[13] Asked the same question, a journalist working for the state media simply shrugged off Spielberg and his ilk as "erratic" "time bombs": "You know these Hollywood celebrities are unreliable, but you don't know when they will betray you. So just stay away from them."[14]

Other lessons can also be learned. As this book consistently shows, recipient context matters—sometimes decisively. If the value cherished most by the recipient is an institutional taboo for the courting initiator, the bonding effect will be severely abridged. London, Paris, and San Francisco were the three stops on the Olympic torch's global trip that most humiliated Beijing. The relay proceeded relatively smoothly in Australia and India, at least in part as a consequence of unprecedented security levels. In New Delhi, fifteen thousand police created a cordon around the seventy or so relay runners as they ran along an empty and much shortened route.[15] In Canberra, moreover, ten thousand Chinese supporters rallied along the route, outnumbering protesters by more than thirteen to one.[16]

But the number of protesters in Russia, Turkey, Argentina, Tanzania, Oman, and, most notably, China's Southeast Asian and East Asian neighbors was much smaller than in Western Europe and America. A city official in Nagano, Japan, ridiculed the protests as "a stupid thing to do [*baka na koto wo yatteiru*]." The city government later contended that the official had been referring to "violent protest measures" as stupid, not questioning the right to protest.[17] However, my conversations with Japanese diplomats and officials suggest that opposition to protest in general has a market among the governing elites even at the national level. When asked to comment on how democracy can be used as soft power, one official in the Cabinet Office said, "In my opinion, China is already more democratic than America thinks of it. American democracy is *one*, not *the*, version of democracy. But they tend to think theirs is the only one." He further explained, "In Japan we emphasize the importance of hierarchy. Not everyone is equal in a group. But we are democratic nonetheless."[18]

The level of sensitivity toward whether a country is democratic varies across contexts. In Southeast and East Asia, indifference or even a sense of resistance to Western democratization is not uncommon. Mainstream scholarship has dismissed "Asian values" for their shaky intellectual coherence, seeing the concept as nothing more than a deception coined by authoritarian leaders unwilling to relinquish their control of power.[19] Though such criticisms have at least a grain of truth, political elites in East and Southeast Asia also see "Western democracy" as a concept bearing a sense of self-righteousness and interventionism and claim that they can better appreciate the "democratic" nuances of countries commonly perceived as authoritarian.[20] While Lee Kuan Yew of Singapore and Mahathir bin Mohamad of Malaysia frequently are targets of scholarly critiques of "Asian values," this viewpoint is neither new nor peculiar.[21] Instead, such a mentality has a historical pattern in the region. Yoshida Shigeru frequently vented his frustration that "crass" Americans lacked Japan's ability to appreciate China's cultural and political delicateness.[22]

Beijing appears to be drawing cues from this tendency and has not abandoned its wooing effort. Yet the campaign has increasingly acquired a selective hardening edge toward democracies in Europe and North America. In other words, the Chinese government has realized that effective echoing with Western democracies[23] in the political realm is virtually impossible, because doing so would require China to compromise on key issues such as Tibet, Taiwan, and press freedom. Instead, Beijing has launched a new campaign to "fight with the West for the right to speak [*yu xifang zhengduo huayuquan*]." Prudence has ceded some ground to cockiness. In a clear departure from the usually dull yet conciliatory rhetoric, Chinese vice president Xi Jinping delivered a stinging criticism during a February 2009 trip to Mexico:

> There are some well-fed foreigners who have nothing better to do [*chibaole meishigan*] than pointing fingers at us. First, China doesn't export revolution; second, China doesn't export hunger and poverty; third, China doesn't come and cause you headaches, what more to be said?[24]

Xi's unexpectedly hard-line rant triggered heated online discussions inside China. Both supporters and opponents were surprised at the apparently colloquial manner in which Xi delivered his punch. "Well fed with nothing better to do" is well-known Beijing slang commonly associated with the image of a hooligan. Supporters cheered China's new boss for his straightforwardness, whereas opponents doubted whether China's No. 1–in–waiting has the basic diplomatic etiquette needed for such a high post.[25] Beijing's messages were confusing: Xi's speech was broadcast on the nation's most-watched news program, but online discussions were banned a few hours later. Media outlets were ordered to use only coverage from the *People's Daily* and Xinhua News Agency, which did not mention Xi's controversial speech.

It is thus unclear whether Xi's remarks on "well-fed foreigners" were premeditated or whether he was being creative, though the current leadership seldom demonstrates the latter trait on diplomatic occasions.[26] But the Chinese government's ambition to speak out is much less ambivalent. Xinhua News Agency, China's state media outlet, planned to nearly double the number of overseas correspondent stations it maintains from around 100 to 180. The organization further set up the goal of becoming an Al-Jazeera–like media outlet with "credibility and influence." The *Huan Qiu Shi Bao* [Global Times], a nationalist tabloid affiliated with the *People's Daily*, also announced its plan to publish in English. Meanwhile, China's national broadcaster, China Central Television, planned to add Arabic and Russian channels to its current lineup of English, Japanese, Spanish, and French channels.[27] The "right to speak" campaign has enjoyed considerable domestic backing. China's nationalist netizens have set up Anti-CNN .com and other websites to "gather righteous forces" and "refute lies and distortions" by the Western media.[28] Anti-CNN.com's home page is entirely in Mandarin except for one English phrase: "Just Another Voice."

Furthermore, overseas Chinese have participated in this "right to speak" campaign. Those who turned out to support China during the Olympic Torch Relay included an army of Chinese students, businesspeople, professionals, and tourists, all joining what they perceived as the heroic cause of protecting the holy flame from China haters. In the wake of the unrest in Tibet, a slide show, "Tibet Was, Is, and Will Always Be a Part of China," began circulating widely on the Internet, attracting nearly 3.5 million views on YouTube.[29] The slide show is in passable English (with minor typos and abundant expletives) and not only defends China but bashes the United States, Canada, Australia, and Japan, among others, as hypocritical. The video's creator argues that these countries should offer independence to their own indigenous groups before meddling in China. In another publicity-seeking gesture, hundreds of pro-China supporters took to the Seattle streets to protest Dalai Lama's April 2008 visit, hiring a small plane to fly overhead with a banner reading, "Dalai, Your Smiles Charm but Your Actions Harm."[30]

It is hard to believe that the Chinese government and its supporters are fighting only for the right to speak to themselves. After all, China's media market remains largely closed, and the Communist Party still has a near monopoly on the right to speak to China's citizens. This state of affairs implies a greater ambition behind China's quest for its right to speak. Such attitudinal hardening in the political realm may usher in a new round of diplomatic Othering by Beijing—a new, confrontational framing of a China-led world versus the West is emerging. By proclaiming the right to speak on behalf of non-Western developing countries, China is abandoning attempts to court the Western market as a means of enlarging its value resonance elsewhere. China's self-promoted charm may thus acquire a harder edge. China's national broadcaster hailed its government's action at the Copenhagen Climate Change Conference as "leading a broad scope of developing countries to break [Western] encirclement."[31] Delegations from Japan and the European Union blamed Beijing for wrecking the deal, whereas the United States saw Beijing's dispatching of a vice minister to meet with President Barack Obama as intentionally insulting.[32]

Beijing's rising assertiveness toward the West in the areas of democratization and human rights is also demonstrated by its handling of human rights activist Liu Xiaobo's receipt of the 2010 Nobel Peace Award and the arrest of artist and political activist Ai Weiwei in April 2011. On both occasions, the Chinese government loudly invoked its noninterference mantra. China persuaded eighteen other countries to decline to attend the Nobel ceremony in Oslo, where a vacant chair symbolized Liu's forced absence. In late April 2011, Sino-Norwegian relations remained strained by the incident, and Chinese ambassador to Oslo Tang Guoqiang sternly reiterated that Norway would have to apologize before the situation could return to normal. And the *People's Daily* warned U.S. secretary of state Hillary Clinton to speak carefully after she cited the abduction of Ai as an example of Chinese government's effort to "stop history," which Clinton described as a "fool's errand."[33]

Both cases reveal the limitations of China's soft power. Because enduring soft power demands bonding based on common values, the fundamental clash of political values indicates China's slim chance of winning over Western audiences. Furthermore, Beijing's hostile responses propelled

Liu, Ai, and other enemies to greater international fame, much as Beijing inadvertently helped to boost the Dalai Lama's popularity. Unless China democratizes, its soft power cannot go very far in certain markets.

But Beijing no longer seems particularly to care. Its loud and unapologetic responses are more than purely a defensive measure. The two latest cases, combined with the hard-line remarks by Chinese leaders, hint at the Chinese government's attitudinal hardening toward the West. China is abandoning wooing the West on political and developmental issues to enlarge its value resonance elsewhere.

The "right to speak" campaign does not mean an all-out propaganda war with Western industrialized democracies. Sensing that the democracies cannot maintain policy solidarity toward a huge country such as China, Beijing is extending olive branches to some Western countries (often in the form of government-sponsored shopping sprees) while punishing others. For much of 2008, France seemed to be attracting most of Beijing's ire for a chain of incidents: Paris was the only international leg where the Olympic torch was doused; French president Nicolas Sarkozy defied China and met with the Dalai Lama when France was serving as the chair of the European Union; and in February 2009, Christie's in Paris went ahead with an auction of two bronze artifacts looted from a Chinese palace 150 years ago. Pierre Berge, the two bronzes' current owner, did not help the situation by claiming that he would return them to China if Beijing would allow the Dalai Lama to return to Tibet.[34]

Apparently to punish France, Chinese premier Wen Jiabao chose to visit Spain, Switzerland, Germany, Belgium, and Britain in early 2009 on what was officially touted as the "Trip of Trust [Xinxin zhilü]" but jokingly dubbed the "Trip around France [Huanfa zhilü]" by the Chinese media. Wen did not attempt to hide his intent to shame France, telling a group of Hong Kong journalists, "While in the plane, I did look at the map carefully. My trip this time is to circle around France. However, everyone knows why France was not arranged for my visit. The responsibility does not lie on the Chinese side."[35]

In the summer of 2009, China again made its anger known, this time toward Australia. Less than two years earlier, China's official Xinhua News Agency hailed the election of Kevin Rudd, a fluent Mandarin-speaker, as Australia's prime minister as reflecting China's rising global influence.[36] Some were quick to link Rudd's victory with China's rising soft power, calling him Lao Lu (Old Rudd), an affectionate way of referring to a senior colleague or an old friend.[37]

However, there is a fundamental difference between knowing China (*zhihua*) and being a supporter of the Chinese government (*qinhua*),[38] a point that these enthusiastic voices soon found out, to their frustration. In July 2009, when the Melbourne International Film Festival planned to screen a documentary about Rebiya Kadeer, a Uighur activist in exile, Chinese attaché Chen Chunmei phoned festival director Richard Moore and urged him to drop the film. Moore resisted the Chinese demand and called Chen's effort "strident," "arrogant," and "ill advised."[39] When Rudd's government issued Kadeer a visa, the Xinhua News Agency began bashing "Lao Lu" as "inconsistent" and "domineering" and described Beijing as "disappointed" at his China policy.[40] Coverage of Australia's anti-China wave [*fanhua chao*] appeared in major Chinese media outlets. China's populist *Global Times* quoted Shen Shishun, a researcher associated with the foreign ministry, as describing Rudd as "a little kid who is having a tantrum [*naopiqi de xiaohaizi*]."[41]

This condescending tone did not mean that Beijing would be more tolerant of Australia. All Chinese directors withdrew their movies from the festival in solidarity with their government, though Beijing denied exerting any pressure on them. A few weeks later, the Shanghai government arrested four employees of Australian mining giant Rio Tinto on espionage charges, tried them without permitting Australian diplomat to be present, and sentenced them to prison terms ranging from seven to fourteen years.

The experiences of France and Australia paled in comparison to what Japan confronted in the autumn of 2010, when China's ire escalated to unprecedented levels. On September 8, Japan arrested a Chinese captain whose trawler had rammed into two Japanese coast guard vessels near the disputed Diaoyu/Senkaku Islands the preceding day. In response, the Chinese government suspended all exchanges with Japan above the ministerial and provincial levels, summoned Japanese ambassador Niwa Uichirō five times to demand the captain's release, revoked the invitations of one thousand young Japanese to visit the Shanghai Expo, warned Chinese citizens not to visit Japan, and unofficially banned Japan-bound export of rare-earth metals. On September 21, China's formerly reticent premier, Wen, warned Japan that "further actions" would follow if Japan did not release the captain "immediately and unconditionally."[42] Three days later, four Japanese working for the private Fujita Corporation were arrested in Hebei Province on suspicion of videotaping military installations.[43]

The severity of these measures and the speed with which Beijing carried them out were extraordinary. Indeed, when prosecutors in Okinawa released the captain on September 24, they admitted that they had made this decision in light of "the well-being of our citizens and the future of

Japan-China relations."[44] Yet the release did not bring the drama to a quick end. After staging a hero's welcome for the captain, Beijing again turned on Tokyo, this time demanding an "apology" and "compensation."[45]

A plethora of voices in China, Japan, and beyond weighed in to announce the winner and loser of this feud. While some observers believed that Japan had blinked, others contended that China had overplayed its hand.[46] But as leaders in Beijing imposed the string of unilateral sanctions, they could not have failed to foresee the damage these actions would create to the recent, hard-earned improvements in China-Japan relations. They also must have anticipated that their "retaliation" would send Japanese popular emotions on China, which had just warmed up a bit, back to icy levels. But the harshness and swiftness of these measures reveals a vehement Beijing that did not care about the consequences for public opinion.

As chapter 2 demonstrated, with two of the three sources of soft power—legitimacy of foreign policy and domestic values—despised, China as a state holds little charm for Japan, and vice versa. The absence of these two sources has stripped Japan-China relations of moderating mechanisms that could have slowed down the escalation of a minor incident into an adrenaline-propelled and costly diplomatic crisis. Popular interest in cultural items such as cuisine, fashion, movies, and so forth is likely to persist, but its diplomatic utility is diminishing.

This crisis reached a dramatic ending on October 4: At the Asia-Europe Meeting, the Japanese prime minister, Kan Naoto, and Chinese premier, Wen, "happened to" meet in a hallway and "happened to" find two vacant chairs, and a translator "happened to" be present.[47] According to Kan, it was thus "natural" for the two leaders to sit down and talk for twenty-five minutes, during which time they agreed that the "current state of [Japan-China] relations is undesirable" and that they should return to advancing "mutually beneficial strategic relations."[48]

No one would really perceive such an encounter as "natural." The fact that both Wen and Kan had to follow their diplomats' script to bump into each other has almost made Japan-China diplomacy a jointly produced dark comedy, but few of their compatriots would be amused. Hardened emotions and mutual disdain drove the leaders of the world's second- and third-biggest economies to the hallway for a most unnatural conversation. One week later, Chinese defense minister Liang Guanglie and his Japanese counterpart, Kitazawa Toshimi, claimed that they "happened to" run into each other in an elevator in Hanoi and "naturally" talked for twenty minutes about repairing relations.[49] Chinese and Japanese diplomats used great creativity in finding unlikely places to force their leaders to face each other.

Japan's Continuing Search for a Courting Strategy

Recent LDP and DPJ administrations have continued to promote Japan's charm. Such efforts, however, confront challenges from two realms: Externally, value-based courting resonated only tepidly with the desired; internally, the danger of economic decay may cause the public to wonder how much attraction remains in the Japanese way.

One recent move was an emphasis on a democracy-based charm offensive, with Prime Ministers Abe Shinzō and Asō Tarō particularly active proponents for this wooing agenda. The government's publicizing effort was hard to miss: on its web page under the headline "Expanding Diplomatic Horizon," the Ministry of Foreign Affairs listed "value-oriented diplomacy [*kachikan gaikō*]" as the pillar of Japan's future diplomacy.[50] To convince both Japanese and external audiences that the term was not just a slogan, Asō, serving as foreign minister at the time, explained the idea's broadly defined geographical scope, an "Arc of Freedom and Prosperity" that would stretch "from Northeast Asia to Central Asia and the Caucasus, Turkey, Central and Eastern Europe and the Baltic states."[51] Based on this strategy, Japan was to increase its efforts to reach out to democracies and international organizations whose members were democracies. Specific targets to be courted would include the United States, Australia, India, the European Union, and the members of the North Atlantic Treaty Organization (NATO). The list was not random, for in Asō's signature speech on value-oriented diplomacy, he identified exactly the same group of countries and organizations as friends with whom Japan would seek to work.

Did Japan's democracy-based wooing construct a self-confident, peace-loving, and democratic Japan, a country with which anyone would have difficulty finding fault? This democratic arc was not frictionless. For example, the European Union sporadically criticized Japan's continued use of the death penalty.[52] Clashes between Japanese whaling vessels and their opponents also created high-profile incidents.[53] Yet such annoyances were by no means on the same scale as the troubles confronting Beijing. Indeed, polls have shown that people in Western Europe and North America approve of Japan, seeing it as a good player in international politics.[54] The Japanese Ministry of Foreign Affairs also granted India, another major member of the democratic arc, the "pro-Japan [*shin'nichiteki*]" title in its 2008 annual report.[55]

Japan's charm within this arc was thus well accepted. However, those left out of this arc were as important as those included. In fact, the countries and regions not on the list better reveal the obstacles facing Japan's democracy-based charm offensive. Japan's positive image among democratic friends notwithstanding, neither Abe nor Asō tackled the challenge of transforming such views into political capital elsewhere.

Africa was one noteworthy absence. Data show that Japan invested markedly fewer resources in Africa than did China. On the surface level, Japan has formal relations with more African countries (fifty-one as of March 2009) than does China (forty-one), largely as a result of the Taiwan factor. Yet while China has embassies in every African country with which it has diplomatic relations, Japan has no embassies in twenty-five smaller African countries, and relations are handled by embassies in larger countries (table 7).[56] There are more Chinese diplomats than Japanese representatives working on the ground. Between December 1963 and February 1964, Zhou Enlai toured ten African countries, six of them south of the Sahara Desert; in contrast, no Japanese leader set foot beyond the Sahara until 2001, when Mori Yoshirō visited South Africa, Kenya, Nigeria, and Tunisia.

The absence of Latin America and the inclusion of Central Asia in Asō's "Arc map" were equally perplexing. Arbitrary groupings thus created more questions than answers to Japan's diplomatic ambition.

Equally noteworthy was the absence of some major players from this arc. As a nondemocracy, China was excluded by definition, but for its leaders, the real concern was whether this arc marked the beginning of a new round of Othering by Japan. Scholars close to the Chinese government denounced the arc as a "Cold War remnant" that sought to "form a shield over China from west to east."[57] Nationalist bloggers also took Asō's speech as testifying to the long-held truth that Japan had never abandoned its ambition to wipe China off the map.[58]

China's fear should not be dismissed as pure paranoia. Japanese schol-

TABLE 7.   Japan's Embassy Centers in Africa (2009)

Embassy Location	Countries under Jurisdiction
Kenya	Kenya, Burundi, Eritrea, Seychelles, Somalia, Rwanda
Senegal	Senegal, Cape Verde, Gambia, Guinea-Bissau, Mauritania
Côte d'Ivoire	Côte d'Ivoire, Benin, Niger, Togo
South Africa	South Africa, Lesotho, Namibia, Swaziland
Gabon	Gabon, Equatorial Guinea, Republic of the Congo, São Tomé and Principe
Cameroon	Cameroon, Chad, Central Africa
Madagascar	Madagascar, Comoros, Mauritius
Ghana	Ghana, Liberia, Sierra Leone
Ethiopia	Ethiopia, Djibouti

ars and diplomats have suggested that containing China's rise was "intuitively [*hon'noteki*]" a consideration in Japan's democratic courting and that the arc concept was developed to counter China's "peaceful development" catchphrase.[59] This recognition, though largely tacit, attests to the contending nature of these two Asian powers' latest charm offensives. Japan's showcasing of its democracy thus acquired a duality, as it avoided naming China explicitly as a nondemocratic outsider yet sought to boost policy coordination with democratic friends to contain China. Making the first visit to NATO's headquarters by a Japanese prime minister, Abe discussed the security threat China poses as a result of its ever-expanding military. He also stressed the need for a value-based partnership between Japan and NATO to counter Chinese uncertainties.[60] Japan also became a key proponent of the continuation of the arms embargo imposed on China in the wake of the 1989 Tiananmen incident. Depending on one's position, the nature of Japan's democracy-based courting would be offensive (for Beijing) or defensive (for Tokyo). But the two sides seemed to concur on the non-Chineseness of this value-based concept, thus confirming the wooing strategy of enhancing in-group bonding while ostracizing those outside.

Understanding target countries' domestic agendas and the variances in what values to cherish or to prioritize enables countries not only to make their wooing more effective but also to realize the boundaries of such efforts. Japan's "democratic arc" was not, as the conventional wisdom holds, merely a response to China's peaceful development plan. Japan's concept was more ambitious: Whereas peaceful development involved convincing others of China's nonthreatening nature, the democratic arc was about asking others to join. Japan's concept thus was more sensitive to other countries' acceptance. In other words, a crucial standard for judging the effectiveness of Japan's value-oriented diplomatic courting would be to see whether its democratic friends identified themselves as proud members of this arc. Throughout the idea's life cycle, however, Abe and Asō's pet concept remained a largely Japanese product, with little foreign buy-in.

Japan's wooing effort also has one more danger, though it is by no means new. Japan is more than just an economic superpower. However, polls have shown that much of its allure as a state still rests on its use as a model of modernization. The bursting of the economic bubble certainly took away some of that appeal. The global recession that began in 2008 may cause further damage. Although the recession started in the United States, Japan was hit particularly hard. Its economy shrank 3.3 percent in the final quarter of 2008 (an annual rate of 12.7 percent), three times the drop experienced by the U.S. economy during the same period and the biggest Japanese economic dive since 1974.[61]

Japan remains an economic giant, and it is too early to toll the death knell for the Japanese model.[62] Yet both domestic and international audiences tend to view trajectories, and this perspective is not working to Japan's favor. As chapter 3 illustrates, the Southeast Asian public currently remains divided about whether Japan or China is the region's most important player. Predictions would seem to indicate that China will take a big lead. The same trajectory has also made Korean scholars suspect that the decline of hostility toward Japan has resulted partly from the fact that the Korean public no longer takes the island nation as seriously as was previously the case. Recent trends may also hint at the weakening of Japan's political clout in Taiwan, as the 2008 presidential election saw the defeat of the pro-Japan Democratic Progressive Party. Against this background, it no longer seemed purely incidental that China decided to shake its fist at Japan over the fishing boat, an incident that occurred right after China's economy officially surpassed Japan's as the world's second-largest. Japan's handling of the dispute offered a microcosm of what has been wrong with the country over the past two decades: Though the government desperately wants to turn the tide, it has no clear agenda, lacks self-confidence, and often feels doomed at its unmistakable decline.

Indeed, the sense of pessimism is apparent inside Japan, as reflected by the popular outlook for the future (figure 6, chapter 2). Such pessimism can even twist seemingly positive developments for Japan's prestige into self-derision. After taking office, U.S. secretary of state Hillary Clinton made Japan the first country she visited, and President Obama invited Asō to be his first guest to the White House. Japan's national broadcaster, NHK, however, dismissed these arrangements as merely "face-saving" measures resulting from intensive Japanese diplomatic efforts. The network's journalists also predicted that China–United States relations would undoubtedly surpass Japan–United States relations in importance.[63]

I do not challenge the argument that Japan matters. Rather, pessimism and lack of confidence are present in both popular discourses and at the elite level. Such sentiments have led to inconsistent and confusing policies. The problem has become even more apparent under the DPJ. Changes are certainly occurring, though disoriented and chaotic seem apt descriptions. During the Hatoyama administration, the first non-LDP government in fourteen years, Japan–United States relations chilled as a consequence of an increasingly acrimonious dispute over relocating Okinawa's Futenma

Military Base. In contrast, the new administration sought to warm up Japanese relations with China. DPJ party chief Ozawa Ichirō led a delegation to China that included 600 people, among them 143 lawmakers. The delegation was so large that it had to charter five commercial jets to fly from three Japanese airports into Beijing, where seventeen buses awaited.[64] The Chinese accorded Ozawa's army the highest level of diplomatic etiquette, and President Hu shook hands and posed for pictures with numerous lawmakers. The delegation later went to South Korea, though the second leg received much less Japanese press coverage.

One week later, the Hatoyama administration arranged a meeting between the Japanese emperor and visiting Chinese vice president Xi Jinping. In so doing, the Hatoyama administration ignored a tradition of consulting the emperor one month before such meetings, since the Chinese side requested the meeting on short notice. The incident triggered a storm of conservative anger, and with the Futenma Military Base dispute and Ozawa's China tour, invited heated discussions on whether the administration had crossed the line in wooing China. When asked about the appropriateness of "forcing" the emperor to meet Xi, Ozawa, the "shadow shogun," defiantly told the reporter to shut up and read the constitution and said that the disgruntled chief administrator of the imperial house should resign before whining.[65]

But the fishing boat incident brought this rapprochement to a sudden end. Superficial wooing, with no backing of shared values or mutual appreciation for foreign policy priorities, is bound to be fragile. Even before the incident, Beijing had responded only tepidly to Hatoyama's diplomatic message regarding the establishment of an "East Asia community." China remains suspicious of any "community" framing, which implies value convergence. Furthermore, implementing such a grand concept would require, at a minimum, a Japanese government that can last longer than has recently been the case for the country's administrations. Otherwise, the concept risks the same fate as Abe's "value-oriented diplomacy" and Asō's "Arc of Freedom and Prosperity," terms once in vogue but soon forgotten when their promoters left office.

Amid scandals and crises, the DPJ has seemed increasingly shaky as a viable governing party. The Kan administration's clumsy handling of the fishing boat incident provided the opposition and the public alike with new ways of attacking the government's incompetence. In the fall of 2009, the DPJ's "open budget debate [*jigyōshiwake*]" turned theatrical and created a rising sense of antagonism between bureaucrats (who likened the process to a "public execution") and the party. Government officials complained that such debates were exhausting their energy and that they were constantly worrying about how to use their ever-shallower pockets to fund Japan's wooing initiatives.[66]

All these incidents were eclipsed by the triple catastrophes that hit Japan in the spring of 2011, when northeastern Honshū was devastated by a major earthquake, a tsunami, and a nuclear crisis. In the wake of these calamities, the people of Japan impressed the world with their calm, discipline, and endurance. Yet equally glaring were the weak and occasionally chaotic responses from the Japanese government. Four months after the earthquake, the Kan administration's support barely topped 12 percent, with 71.2 percent of respondents in one poll urging the prime minister to quit.[67] In this unrelenting political climate, the Kan administration had to shelve diplomatic wooing in favor of more urgent issues, and he ultimately resigned amid mounting pressure in August 2011.

A Thematic Summary

This book starts by examining the conventional wisdom's preoccupation with cultural or commercial components of international exchanges and its view of these resources as equivalent to soft power. As the number of definitions for *soft power* grows, we need to ask whether our understanding is also expanding.

My answer is no. In fact, I am concerned that as our usage of the term widens, our understanding of it has become shallower and narrower. Journalists may have a better excuse for resorting to a few convenient cultural shortcuts as they contemplate soft power. To talk about songs, cuisines, fashion, sports, TV dramas, and celebrities simply produces more interesting news, which in turn boosts ratings or attracts readers. But scholars need to resist the temptation to compete with journalists to sensationalize world politics. As cultural and commercial products have become equivalent to soft power, two caveats emerge. At the factual level, people everywhere have shown no tension with loving another country's food or movies but not admiring that country's government. Otherwise, one would expect that the popularity of Coca-Cola in the Arab world or the mania for Japanese cartoons among Chinese and Korean youths would boost support for Washington's and Tokyo's diplomatic agendas. That support, however, has not arrived.

At the theoretical level, to assume that the love of a cultural or commercial product can naturally influence politics confuses the key difference between capability and power. International relations scholars, particularly those in the nonrealist tradition, have long noted that power lacks fungibility—that is, strength in one area does not automatically flow into other areas—and that contextualizing should be the essence of power analysis.[68] The magical transformation of culture into power—the Midas touch in international relations—has not occurred in many cases, and its absence has rightfully attracted scholarly suspicion of soft power's relevance. In other words, equating soft power with cultural affection and a resultant fixation on studying cultural/commercial products becomes a distraction. It hurts soft power's credibility as a useful concept. From this perspective, dwelling too much on culture and commerce is not only empirically inaccurate but also theoretically self-defeating for soft power studies.

This project was thus inspired by the concept of soft power but disagrees with its current direction. I seek to make the soft power literature less soft and to stress its intellectual connections with established international relations theories. One such connection is in the area of who possesses power. Despite the rise of nonstate actors, states remain most important parties in international relations. Fashion trends come and go, and loving Japanese animation has apparently not softened Chinese and Korean disdain for the Japanese state. The implication is that governments, not cultural agents, let alone commercial products, possess and execute power, hard and soft. Hence, talking about soft power still requires making governments and leaders the center of inquiries and enhancing interest the standard for assessing their effects.

This recognition should not be construed as a departure from soft power's conceptual framework. After all, Joseph Nye's concept, which this book employs, states that two of soft power's three sources are statist—domestic political values and legitimacy of foreign policy. Thus, the most effective way of enhancing a country's soft power is to convincingly propagate to a targeted foreign audience these values that the wooing country claims to embody, with the goal of soliciting trust and acceptance from this audience and consequently persuading it to voluntarily embrace the wooing country's policy agendas.

Nonfungibility also applies to intra–soft power analysis: That is, the three sources of soft power are not necessarily fluid and transformable, as revealed by the irrelevance of vibrant cultural exchanges in the East Asian setting. If a country has something desirable to offer in each arena, its soft power will certainly be more comprehensive and lasting. Conversely, enhancing soft power is still possible if desirable values in one area are highlighted and resonate with a foreign audience.

The nonfungibility of soft power's three sources suggests that a country's domestic values do not necessarily translate into charm or hinder it on the international stage. Both legitimacy and value are contested notions, and their global usage should not make one blind to localized interpretations. What is cherished domestically may not be treasured to the same extent overseas and may even become a source of tension. From a value-laden perspective, this idea sounds dispiriting to a democracy such as Japan but seems to offer an opportunity to a nondemocracy such as China. In practice, the Chinese government has indeed chosen to underscore its economic achievement and "sovereignty first" principle in foreign policy. Its continued breakneck growth, cast against the backdrop of the global economic recession, further helped Beijing's model gain currency and led policymakers and scholars to ponder the rise of a "Beijing consensus," with "to be truly independent [and] to protect [one's] way of life and political choices" as its essence.[69] In deconstructing this concept, China specialist Arif Dirlik calls it a "sales gimmick."[70] Indeed—the term may be full of holes, but its rapid adoption by the popular media attests to its marketing power, particularly among its intended "Third World constituencies."[71]

The statist focus and nonfungibility thus suggest that wooing targets prioritize values differently. The need to woo may be global, but markets are always local. The appreciation of recipient contexts entails understanding that successful wooing demands customized efforts—that is, prioritizing different values to appeal to different audiences. In the case of Southeast Asia, for example, the values of noninterference and equality outweigh concerns about domestic political values. One does not even have to use communist Vietnam or the junta government in Burma as an example to substantiate this point—ASEAN's silence on Thailand's recent political turmoil is equally revealing. Customizing values is not always possible. Where it is not, it exposes the limit of wooing. In both China's largely failed attempt to woo the Taiwanese public and its aborted effort to create a "harmonious world" with the West, Beijing knows what its audience wants to hear and see but has decided that complying with such wishes would be too costly.

The concept of recipient context also invites comparisons among the wooing targets. It is true that many scholars have studied Korea's and Taiwan's different colonial experiences under Japan, with the conventional wisdom viewing Japan's policies as generally more lenient on Taiwan. A study of wooing can introduce a new comparative angle: Ethnic and linguistic uniqueness, coupled with a much longer history of national independence and a self-awareness of such a history, created a much higher level of Korean sensitivity toward any hint of Chinese or Japanese domination.

Korean nationalist myths hence depend on defining Korean traditions as independently of, if not superior to, those of China and Japan. Taiwan, by contrast, must rely on China and Japan as two poles defining its nationalist imagination. It is not unusual for pro-independence elites to define Taiwan's uniqueness by stressing how the Taiwanese ways of thinking and doing things differ from China's and are more like Japan's. Even as the island searches for its own identity, it constantly finds itself in a self-imposed tug-of-war between the two identity poles, and navigating its place often occurs in the form of adjusting its distances from these two imaginary ends.

The need to customize wooing requires political wisdom. In designing and executing wooing strategies, leaders matter greatly. As powerful agents, they deserve more scholarly attention in the study of soft power. They can either lead or frustrate their country's wooing effort. As chapter 1 discusses, despite the new United States–Japan military alliance, Mao Zedong and Zhou Enlai sought to reach out to Japan, even using their authority to suppress popular anti-Japan sentiment. Taiwan's Lee Teng-hui skillfully packaged himself to Japanese cultural celebrities as the personal embodiment of Taiwan's heroic quest for its destiny, even comparing himself to Moses, who led his people out of Egypt. Lee also repeatedly expressed his appreciation for Japan, attributing his resoluteness to his Japanese education. And instead of resorting to the convenient "Japan as scapegoat" thesis embraced by his predecessors, Fukuda Takeo chose to appeal to emotion, envisioning a "heart-to-heart" relationship between Japan and the Southeast Asian countries. The Fukuda Doctrine not only turned the page in Japan–Southeast Asia relations but also became a cherished concept still pursued by the Japanese government.

Less positive examples also exist. Driven primarily by domestic needs, leaders such as Jiang Zemin, Koizumi Jun'ichirō, and Kim Young-sam chose to poke international rivals in the eye to gain domestic applause. But such acclaim is notoriously transient, and these efforts often backfire. In those cases, these leaders or their successors often must pay for the bullying or insulting.[72]

In either scenario, leaders matter greatly, though of course they are not omnipotent. They are structurally constrained and may only move things forward gradually whatever their personal desires. Asked why he took an active approach to reconciling with Japan, Kim Dae-jung answered that he was fully aware of the anti-Japan sentiment among Korean citizens but that a leader needs to be "half a step" ahead of his people or else he cannot lead.[73] Jiang, Koizumi, and Kim Young-sam, however, seemed to be a full step behind their people.

Like mainstream power, soft power has its darker side, a dimension that scholars have so far neglected. Indeed, even a casual observer of coverage of soft power can acquire the impression it is a "nice" power. In contrast to hard power, the adjective *soft* implies harmless, innocent, and even up-lifting possibilities for international relations. It is a competition to see which countries can become more attractive by becoming better versions of themselves. A flavor of sportsmanship tinges popular expectations of what we can achieve through soft power—a more harmonious future for international relations. It is a "good" power that countries should learn to possess.

This project serves as a wake-up call regarding this idealistic percep-tion. Soft power is embedded in international relations realities: States are still competing for limited resources, contemporary interactions are often entangled with historical grievances, wars are still happening, and threats of use of force are real. Against such a background, to promote soft power is not to enter a diplomatic pageant. Rather, it is a utilitarian approach with the potential to be confrontational. Even its execution may become ugly, because appearing attractive is not solely about becoming a better self but can also be achieved by making another player look bad—the Other-ing/belittling tactics. Wooing therefore can be just another new tool in a state's power kit. The competitive and calculating angle of soft power certainly speaks to its connection with the mainstream scholarship's take on its harder counterpart.

Finally, soft power has its limitations, which can be understood on mul-tiple levels. First, culture has much-exaggerated potency as a source of soft power and in reality can offer little diplomatic help to the wooing country, as the rapid worldwide expansion of the Confucius Institute network illus-trates. Between November 2004, when the first institute opened in Seoul, and July 2010, 316 Confucius institutes and another 337 Confucius class-rooms were set up in 94 countries.[74] There is no doubt that when leaders in Beijing decided to set up this global network, they did so to facilitate for-eign audiences' embrace of China.[75] While the network's rapid expansion indeed proves the global consensus on China's importance and the rising need to learn its language, it is a big leap to equate interest in learning a language with increased Chinese soft power.[76] Most of the branches are in North America (with eighty in the United States alone), Western Europe, Japan, and South Korea. But China's dismal state image in these parts of the world exposes the questionable soft power utility of such cultural institutes.

Second, soft power is not a substitute for hard power but can only be built on the foundation of credible hard power. Scholars have noted that

Tokyo did not intensify its efforts to propagate Japan's charm until the country's harder might had begun to decline.[77] From this perspective, the promotion of Japan's charm-based soft power has become a last resort for maintaining its dimming grandeur. A sense of desperation pervades Japanese politicians' hopes of promoting Japan's soft power with cute cartoon figures and sleek consumer gadgets. And indeed, these popular items have proved largely ineffective at helping Japan achieve political acceptance beyond friendly territories.

China's experience offers still more insight into the connection between soft and hard power. On the surface, China's trajectory is the opposite of Japan's, as China attempts to synchronize the simultaneous rises of its hard and soft powers. As China rapidly ascends to global stardom, its government has consciously stepped up efforts to promote soft power as a means of alleviating external concerns about the threats the country poses. But the Chinese task of using soft power to soothe others has proved no easier than the Japanese attempt to use soft power to excite them. China's recent row with Japan and its assertive territorial claims in the South China Sea expose the difficulty of curbing ambition for the sake of placating neighbors. Such wrestling is likely to continue, and with the continued rise of hard power, the balance may tip toward fists rather than smiles, as revealed by China's recent rising territorial assertiveness toward Japan as well as the Southeast Asian countries.

A comparison of the Japanese and Chinese experiences with soft power illustrates that hard power is a necessary but not sufficient precondition for its softer counterpart. A synergy of soft and hard powers is only possible when the wooing country's domestic and international missions do not conflict with each other. For a Japanese government that is busy reviving its economy, selling the country's charm convincingly would be a tall order. The problem is even more apparent for China. The prioritized need to serve its domestic agenda may drive China's diplomats to act in ways that can only hurt its charm in certain external markets. By phoning organizers of a second-tier film festival and sending a stern warning to the Nobel Committee, Chinese diplomats propelled Rebiya Kadeer and Liu Xiaobo to global fame and helped their causes in a way no others could. In other words, Chinese leaders became the best cheerleaders for their enemies. Such seemingly clumsy menacing acts cannot simply be blamed on ignorance. After more than three decades of deepening engagement with the rest of the world, Chinese diplomats have become reasonably familiar with how Western democracies function.[78] They must have foreseen that they were unlikely to intimidate nongovernmental actors in democracies into surrendering by threatening harm to their governments. These menacing gestures hence served the domestic purpose of conflating opposition to Chinese government with opposition to China. As figure 1 in the introduction indicates, decisions about whether to woo and how to do it are unmistakably conditioned by domestic agendas. Chinese diplomats knowingly pick up the rock and drop it on their own feet, understanding that considerations of soft power must be sacrificed to the agenda of maintaining domestic stability. Once again, these acts prove that unless China democratizes, its soft power cannot go very far in these markets.

Finally, as Nye points out, even when successful, soft power is more helpful for achieving general, long-term goals than short-term, issue-specific aims. In essence, soft power creates and sustains an amiable atmosphere in which the wooing country's agenda and policy preferences will be willingly shared and supported by the wooing target. But soft power in itself cannot be expected to make all the difference, and making a country's soft power encompassing and lasting is no easy task. For scholars, therefore, a trajectory-based, historical approach is particularly useful for studying soft power.

The Search for the Magic Adjective

As a result of Hillary Clinton's frequent references during her Senate confirmation hearings, the term *smart power* gained instant fame in popular discourse. The phrase was created by Nye, who defined it as "the ability to combine hard and soft power into a winning strategy."[79] Clinton elaborated by suggesting that it would include "the full range of tools at our disposal—diplomatic, economic, military, political, legal, and cultural—picking the right tool, or combination of tools, for each situation."[80]

The term is certainly catchy and easy to remember. It also reflects the popular frustration with the George W. Bush administration's "dumb" use of power, most obviously in the Iraq War. Politicians had strong incentive to adopt the term as an attacking tool to frame their opponents' policies, a time-honored strategy. But how much intellectual utility can the idea of *smart power* bring to the study of international relations? The word *smart* is loaded with subjective meaning. To use it invites a string of questions: Who makes the judgment? What are the standards for assessing smartness? Using what time span? Unless there is a wide consensus on the answers (there is not), the debate may start with the statement, "I am smart and you are not," and end with the same sentence. Although the Bush presidency became deeply unpopular toward the end, presidential historians suggest that it is simply too soon to evaluate its legacy and that history may have a different and certainly more nuanced take on the Bush years.[81]

What is new about Nye's concept? A "winning strategy?" This has eternally been the goal for nation-states: No country yearns to lose. "The ability to combine hard and soft power?" Again, nation-states have always been on that quest, and no country has survived for long by sheer intimidation or unconditioned appeasing. For centuries, governments and leaders have been searching for and testing the proper combinations of hard and soft elements of power. Scholars have been asking the same questions as the reservoir of diplomatic practices expands.

The lessons learned from this study of Japan and China apply to cases beyond Asia. With ever-tightening political, economic, cultural, and environmental changes binding people to a common fate, mutual accommodation will become an increasingly important diplomatic practice. This process leans toward the softer use of power. But as the preceding chapters demonstrate, hard-power-based considerations regarding security and relative position still exert their influence in the form of ostracization. And understanding the recipient's value structure is vital, leading not only to framing or prioritizing certain values over others but also to a realization of wooing's limited utility in cases no value resonance exists. In short, scholars need to examine what diplomatic wooing can and cannot do to promote national interests. At the same time, politicians and pundits will probably continue their search for the magical adjective to decorate the word *power.*

Notes

INTRODUCTION

1. Xun Mou and Jie Song, "Zhongguo de biaozhi keneng buzaishi long [Dragon May No Longer Fit to Serve as China's Symbol]," *Xinwen Chenbao* [News Morning Daily], December 4, 2006.

2. Han Han, *Guanyu Shanghai.*

3. Wen Jiabao speech.

4. Shihao Zhang, "Zhuchiren jianyi xiong mao qu dai long zuo wei minzu tuteng [Anchor Stirs Up Controversy by Suggesting Panda as National Symbol]," *Chengdu Shangbao*, December 27, 2008, http://news.163 .com/08/1227/03/4U519EG400011229.html.

5. Ibid.

6. As one journalist at *Dongfang Zaobao* [Oriental Morning Daily] told me (interview, November 22, 2008), such stories are "ridiculous," and "ridiculous stories sell papers," an opinion with which an editor at *Dongfang Guangbo Diantai* [Oriental Radio] concurred.

7. Chinese State Council Information Office, *White Paper on China's Peaceful Development* (Beijing, 2005), http://news.xinhuanet.com/politics/2005-12/22/con tent_3954937.htm.

8. "Besutoserā kaiko 2006: Kyōyō shinsho kōchō wo iji [Review of Bestsellers in 2006: Character-Building Books Remain Popular]," *Yomiuri Shimbun*, December 20, 2006.

9. Sasaki, "Commercial Cultivation of Tradition."

10. Asō, "New Look at Cultural Diplomacy."

11. McGray, "Japan's Gross National Cool."

12. Diamond, *Spirit of Democracy*, 318–20.

13. For an analysis of how in-group bonding depends on negatively defining external relations with other groups, see De Vries, "Self, In-Group, and Out-Group Evaluation."

14. Nye, *Soft Power*, 7.

15. Ibid., 8.

16. Hobbs, *Leviathan*, 94–98.

17. Machiavelli, *Prince*, 48–51, 57–59.

18. Russett, "Mysterious Case."

19. Baldwin, "Power Analysis and World Politics." See also Keohane, *After Hegemony*, 49, 51–64. For a critique on the limited fungibility of power, see Art, "American Foreign Policy."

20. Baldwin, "Power Analysis and World Politics."

21. Nye, *Soft Power*, 4.

22. O'Neil, Fields, and Share, "Germany," 192–93.

23. "The Polish Farewell," *Economist*, December 1–7, 2007, 67.

24. See, for example, Kirshner, "States, Markets, and Great Power Relations."

25. Nye, *Soft Power*, 6.

26. "Special Report: China: Culture, Economy, and Military Power—The New Giant Flexes Its Muscles," *Newsweek*, April 1, 1996.

27. Nye, *Soft Power*, 12–14.

28. Japanese Cabinet Office, *Gaikō ni kansuru yoron chōsa* [Annual Survey on Foreign Policy], http://www8.cao.go.jp/survey/h21/h21-gaiko/2-1.html.

29. "Seichō chūgoku to teimeinihon: Rakkan to hikan kukkiri [Growing China and Depressing Japan: Contrast between Optimism and Pessimism]," *Asahi Shimbun*, September 27, 2002.

30. Konno, "Sofuto pawā to nihon no senryaku," 5–7.

31. For a recent example of a book on American soft power almost exclusively reliant on these cultural and commercial images, see Fraser, *Weapons of Mass Distraction*.

32. For a discussion why commercial products should not be counted as power, see Ferguson, "Think Again."

33. Nye, *Soft Power*, 11.

34. Harding, speech.

35. "Chaoxian dapuo yiguan zuofa guli nüxing chuan kuzi dan bu tichang jinshenku [Korea Lifts Old Ban and Encourages Women to Wear Pants but Discourages Tight Ones]," *Dongfang Wang* [East Day News], August 20, 2008, http://news.eastday.com/w/20090820/u1a4595423.html.

36. Schneider, *Culture Communicates*, 7.

37. Kurlantzick, *Charm Offensive*, 18.

38. Kuniya Hiroko, "Kurozu appu gendai [Today's Close-Up]," *NHK*, April 3, 2004.

39. Anthony Faiola, "Japanese Women Catch the 'Korean Wave,'" *Washington Post*, August 30, 2006.

40. Zhang, "Dang qian taiguoren de zhongguoguan," 61–62.

41. U.S. Department of State, *Dictionary of International Relations Terms*, 85. For a thorough exploration of the evolution of public diplomacy as a concept, with its focus on communicating with publics of other countries, see University of Southern California Center on Public Diplomacy, "What Is Public Diplomacy?," http://uscpublicdiplomacy.org/index.php/about/what_is_pd.

42. U.S. Department of State, *Dictionary of International Relations Terms*, 85.

43. In fact, a glance at Chinese media coverage gives the impression that Japanese politicians developed a habit of saying that China was "not a threat" to Japan.

See, for example, "Xiaoquan 2005 zongjie: Zhongguo fazhan bushi weixie [Koizumi Sums up 2005: China's Development Is Not a Threat]," *Dongfang Zaobao*, December 29, 2005; "Futiankangfu: Zhongguo fazhan shi jihui bushi weixie [Fukuda Yasuo: China's Development Is Opportunity, Not Threat]," *Nanfang Zhoumo*, September 27, 2007; "Masheng fandui zhongguo weixielun [Asō opposes 'China Threat Thesis']," *China News Agency*, April 29, 2009.

44. Fraser, *Weapons of Mass Distraction*, and Kurlantzick, *Charm Offensive*, are examples of this short-term-oriented trend. See also Watanabe and McConnell, *Soft Power Superpowers*.

45. Nye, *Soft Power*, 8.

46. The term *Xifang minzhu guojia* (Western democracies) frequently appears in both popular and scholarly discourses in China. Although the term's exact scope is vague, different versions invariably include the United States, Canada, the EU member states, Australia, New Zealand, and Japan.

47. Tarō Asō, "Arc of Freedom and Prosperity: Japan's Expanding Diplomatic Horizons," speech at the Japan Institute of International Affairs Seminar, November 30, 2006, http://www.mofa.go.jp/announce/fm/aso/speech0611.html.

CHAPTER I

1. Mao, *Selected Works*, 439.

2. "Situleideng hun'gui Hangzhou [Leighton Stuart's Soul Returns to Hangzhou]," *China News Agency*, November 18, 2008, http://news.163.com/08/1118/08/4R14FDUF00011229.html.

3. Daizhao Lin, *Zhanhou zhongri guanxishi*, 46.

4. See, for example, "Lun zhongri guanxi [On China-Japan Relations]," *People's Daily*, October 30, 1953; "Lun Riben yu Zhongguo huifu guanxi zhengchanghua [On Normalization of Japan-China Relations]," *People's Daily*, December 30, 1954.

5. Weibin Wang, *Chūgoku to Nihon*, 73–85.

6. See, for example, Feng and Lin, *Zhongri guanxi baogao*, 311–68.

7. Chinese Communist Party Central Archive Bureau, *Mao Zedong waijiao wenxuan*, 219–20, 222, 226.

8. Ibid., 460–61.

9. Jiadong Qian and Xiaoxian Wang, "Zhou Enlai zongli he zhongri guanxi [Premier Zhou Enlai and Sino-Japanese Relations]," *Renwu Journal* 3 (2008), http://www.qikan.com.cn/Article/rewu/rewu200803/rewu20080301.html.

10. Yongxiang Wang and Gao, *Shū Onrai to Nihon*, 382.

11. Chinese Communist Party Central Archive Bureau, *Zhou Enlai waijiao wenxuan*, 87–89.

12. This reparation amount was roughly equal to twenty-one million dollars, one-third of the Qing government's annual revenue.

13. Takeiri, "Rekishi no haguruma ga mawatta," 201–2.

14. Nakasone and Satō, *Tenchiyūjō*, 280.

15. Ibid., 277.

16. Interview with a Chinese prison administrator, in *Ninzai: Chūgoku senpan-kanrisho rokunen* [Confession: Six Years in China's War-Criminals Internment Bureau], *NHK*, December 8, 2008.

17. Sai'onji, "Inshōbukai Shūonraisōri no hanashi," 253.

18. Weibin Wang, *Chūgoku to Nihon*, 159–60.

19. Jin, *Zhou Enlai zhuan*, 424.

20. Hu, *Zhou Enlai molüe daquan*, 16.

21. Kazankai Foundation, *Nicchūkankei kihon shiryōshū*, 28.

22. *Asahi Shimbun*, December 19, 1954.

23. Liberal Democratic Party, "Period of President Ikeda's Leadership."

24. See, for example, Mao, "Yao shengli jiu yao gaohao tongyizhanxian [To Achieve Victory Demands Good Management of the United Front]," in Mao, *Mao Zedong wenxuan disijuan*, 198.

25. Tian, *Zhanhou zhongriguanxi wenxianji*, 304.

26. Ibid., 237.

27. For Beijing's criticism of Yoshida for obstructing normal relations with China, see, for example, "Nan Hanchen, Chairman of the China Council for the Promotion of International Trade, Addresses the Xinhua News Agency on the Renewal of China-Japan Trade Treaty," in Weibin Wang, *Chūgoku to Nihon*, 40. For Beijing's criticism of Kishi, see, for example, "Shelun: Zaibo an xinjie [Editorial: To Refute Kishi Nobusuke Once Again]," *People's Daily*, May 11, 1958.

28. Japanese Ministry of Foreign Affairs, "Chūkyō no taigaikankei [Chinese Communist Party's Foreign Relations]," quoted in Weibin Wang, *Chūgoku to Nihon*, 89.

29. For an excellent analysis of the Japanese conservative and liberal thought on Asianism, see Koschmann, "Asianism's Ambivalent Legacy."

30. Yoshida, *Kaisō jū'nen*, 3:72. See also U.S. Department of State, "China and Japan," 1074.

31. Yoshida, *Kaisō jū'nen*, 1:267.

32. U.S. Department of State, "Asia and the Pacific," 828.

33. Yoshida, *Kaisō jū'nen*, 1:270.

34. Kō'ichi Katō, "Aji'a no seiki'no nicchūkankei," 57.

35. Yu, *Bing yan kan riben*.

36. Miyamoto, "Mōtakutō tono saigo no kaidan" [Last Meeting with Mao Zedong], *Shūkan Asahi*, June 24, 1966.

37. In fact, Zhou Enlai made it clear in his meeting with Nakasone in 1973 that he still thought of the JCP as "a faction of the Soviet revisionism." See Nakasone and Satō, *Tenchiyūjō*, 280.

38. "Keizai kyōryoku no kiso ni: chūgoku tono sekiyū yu'nyū kōshō [Foundation of Economic Cooperation: Negotiation with China over Importing Oil]," *Yomiuri Shimbun*, September 29, 1974.

39. "Nicchūkankei no zenshin o hakaro [Let Us Seek to Further Improve Japanese-Chinese Relations]," *Yomiuri Shimbun*, March 30, 1973.

40. Minoru Kusuda, chief secretary to Prime Minister Eisaku Satō, vividly recalled the impact of Nixon's sudden announcement of his forthcoming visit to China on the Japanese government: "It seemed as if [Satō] were fighting a thousand emotions in one frozen minute in time. His verbal reaction was only one word of acknowledgment, 'Sōka?' or literally translated, 'Is that so?' He fell silent afterwards" (Kusuda, U.S.-Japanese Relations").

41. See, for example, Krauss and Lambert, "Press and Japan's Attempts." See also Jing Sun, "Covering a Non-Democracy."

42. For a detailed analysis of the *Yomiuri Shimbun*'s misleadingly positive portrayal of China during the Cultural Revolution, see Jing Sun, "China as Funhouse Mirror: The *Yomiuri Shimbun*'s China Coverage."

43. "Korekara no sekai to nihon no kadai [The World from Now On and Japan's Challenges]," *Yomiuri Shimbun*, January 1, 1973.

44. Suzuki, *Nashonarisumu to masukomi*, 161–63.

45. "Chūgoku: Dokuritsu no rinjin [China: Independent Neighbor]," *Sankei Shimbun*, September 30, 1972.

46. "Keizai kyōryoku no kiso ni: chūgoku tono sekiyū yu'nyū kōshō [Foundation of Economic Cooperation: Negotiation with China over Importing Oil]," *Yomiuri Shimbun*, September 29, 1974.

47. "A Guide to Nixon's China Journey," *Time*, February 21, 1972, 30.

48. Ibid.

49. See, for example, "Bunkaku rosen wo kaku'ninshita shūonrai hōkoku [Zhou Enlai's Statement Confirms the Course of the Cultural Revolution]," *Asahi Shimbun*, September 2, 1973; "Kenkoku 25shūnen wo mukaeta chūgoku [China Welcomes 25th Anniversary of Independence]," *Yomiuri Shimbun*, October 1, 1974.

50. Jing Sun, "China as Funhouse Mirror: How Japanese National Dailies Watch China," 190–92.

51. Amako, "Dui 21shiji zhongriguanxi de jianyi."

52. Whiting, *China Eyes Japan*, 1–8.

53. Lifeng Jiang, "Zhongri lianhe jinxingde shehui yulun diaocha," 22–23.

54. Dreyer, *China's Political System*, 110–22.

55. "Naniga detanto no tameni hitsuyōka [What Is Necessary for Detente]," *Yomiuri Shimbun*, January 1, 1983.

56. Nakasone and Satō, *Tenchiyūjō*, 497.

57. Ibid., 490.

58. "Koshi hihan rokukōmoku no kōsai [Details of Six Indictments of Hu]," *Yomiuri Shimbun*, January 23, 1987.

59. Nakasone and Satō, *Tenchiyūjō*, 465.

60. Ibid., 494.

61. "Zhongri yulun guanzhu ODA, huarenxuezhe jie riyuandaikuan juece neimu [Chinese and Japanese Media Turn Eyes to ODA, Chinese Scholar Reveals Decision-Making Process of Japanese Loans]," *China News Agency*, December 16, 2004, http://news.163.com/41216/4/17NT1IU70001124T.html.

62. Shan Yu, "Renminshiping: Pingjing duidai riyuandaikuan 'biye' nayitian [Brief Comment by *People's Daily* on Contemporary Issues: Calmly Face Japanese ODA's 'Graduation Day']," *People's Daily*, March 16, 2004.

63. Kawashima, *Japanese Foreign Policy*, 98–99.

64. "Shakaishugi kaikaku to kojin no kaihō [Socialist Reform and Liberation for Individuals]," *Asahi Shimbun*, January 5, 1987.

65. "Kaname jiki wo mukaeru chugoku [China Enters Pivotal Era]," *Yomiuri Shimbun*, April 15, 1986.

66. "Chūgoku tōkyoku ni kasanete jisei wo nozomu [Expect the Chinese Authority to Exercise Restraint]," *Yomiuri Shimbun*, June 23, 1989.

67. See, for example, Ke Zhou, "Yaobang tongzhi bang wo pingfan"; Shuo Wang, "Teshiteban."

68. For a detailed account of the incident, see Whiting, *China Eyes Japan*, 48–49.

69. Chinese Communist Party Central Archive Bureau, *Deng Xiaoping nianpu*, 1:407.

70. Ibid., 368.

71. Ibid., 411.

72. Ibid., 1192–93.

73. Ibid., 1175.

74. Deng, *Deng Xiaoping wenxuan*, 292–93.

75. Yabuki, "Nicchū gokai."

76. Hitoshi Tanaka, former deputy minister of foreign affairs, in Tanaka and Tahara, *Kokka to gaikō*, 164.

77. "Kibishisa wo masu chūgoku no tainichi seisaku [China's Japan Policy Increasingly Tough]," *Yomiuri Shimbun*, September 5, 1982.

78. "Chūgoku no gunkokushugi keikairon to nihon [The Chinese Argument against Militarism and Japan]," *Asahi Shimbun*, September 5, 1984.

79. Nakasone and Satō, *Tenchiyūjō*, 497.

80. Yabuki, "Nicchū gokai."

81. Manabe, "Nihonjin no chūgoku imēji," 7–8.

82. For an excellent analysis of the Chinese government's effort to promote ultranationalism with Japan as its prime target, see Shirk, *China*, 140–80.

83. "One Hundred Patriotic Movies," http://zhidao.baidu.com/question/37098331.html.

84. Noboru Umaba, "Doyō manhyō [Saturday Cartoon Comment]," *Yomiuri Shimbun*, November 28, 1998.

85. Zemin Jiang, *Jiang Zemin wenxuan*, 2:241.

86. Ibid., 204.

87. Feng and Lin, *Zhongri guanxi Baogao*, 402.

88. Ibid., 405.

89. For a detailed yet sensational account of Jiang Zemin's "anti-Japan" sentiment that represents this strand of analysis, see, for example, Tori'i, *"Hannichi"de ikinobiru chūgoku*.

90. See, for example, Feng and Lin, *Zhongri guanxi baogao*, 400–403. Feng and Lin lay out Jiang's numerous speeches on history's importance in Japan-China relations without making any comment on whether those speeches helped or hindered relations; the authors merely cite the foreign press's words regarding China and Japan's dispute over history. Huang, *Riben daguohua qushi he zhongriguanxi*, does not even mention Jiang's trip.

91. Zhenjiang Lin, *Shounao waijiao*, 121.

92. Personal conversations with a Chinese diplomat on August 2, 2004, and with a scholar close to the Chinese government on January 15, 2009.

93. In the 2002 poll, only 2 percent of the Chinese respondents chose "Japan is a democracy" as their top impression of the country. "Japan is selfish" topped the chart at 33 percent, followed by "Japan is an economic power" with 27 percent. See "Seichō chūgoku to teimeinihon."

94. See, for example, Shirk, *China*, esp. chapter 6; Wan, *Sino-Japanese Relations*.

95. Personal interview with Ikuko Toyonaga, December 26, 2009.

96. At the height of the criticism campaign, a public forum was organized

by China's Japan Studies Association, the Sino-Japanese Friendship Association, and the Chinese Academy of Social Sciences, and some Japanese specialists used the occasion to issue harsh criticisms of Ma. The Central Propaganda Department praised *China Youth Daily*'s report on this forum. See http://www.wqtw.gov.cn/Article/wqr/200805/7.html. Jin Xide, a chief organizer of the criticism campaign, was arrested in 2008 on charges of spying for South Korea.

97. Feng and Lin, *Zhongri guanxi Baogao*, 394–410.

98. Ibid., 419.

99. Personal interview with a Japanese diplomat, March 12, 2009.

100. Tu, "Zhou Enlai yu Mei Lanfang Ersanshi."

101. Fu, "Zhongri baleiwaijiao chongxian."

102. Daizhao Lin, *Zhanghou zhongri guanxishi*, 53.

103. Koschmann, "Asianism's Ambivalent Legacy," 103–4.

104. Xu, "Shoupi duihua riyuandaikuan de zhongri jueceyuanyin," 220.

105. Te'an Chen, "Shijie xuyao heping: Jiangzhuxi canguan zhenzhugang yalisangna ji'nianguan [The World Needs Peace: President Jiang Visits USS Arizona Memorial at Pearl Harbor]," *People's Daily*, October 28, 1997.

106. "Chūgokugaishōhatsugen kōgi no yobidashi wo chū'nichidaishi ga kyōi [Chinese Ambassador Refuses to Apologize Despite Japan's Protest at Chinese Foreign Minister's Speech]," *Yomiuri Shimbun*, March 9, 2006.

CHAPTER 2

1. Unless otherwise noted, in this chapter *Southeast Asia* is defined as the region that includes and is limited to all the current members of the Association of Southeast Asian Nations.

2. Japanese Ministry of Foreign Affairs, *Surveys*.

3. The full member states of ASEAN as of 2006 were Brunei, Cambodia, Indonesia, Laos, Malaysia, Myanmar, the Philippines, Singapore, Thailand, and Vietnam.

4. Secretariat of the Association of Southeast Asian Nations (ASEAN), *ASEAN Statistical Yearbook 2006*, http://www.aseansec.org/13100.htm.

5. Data for 1995–2005 obtained from *ASEAN Statistical Yearbook 2006*, http://www.aseanorg/13100.htm; data for 2006–10 obtained from ASEAN Tourism Statistics, http://www.aseansec.org/stat/Table28.pdf.

6. U.S. Energy Information Administration. *World Oil Transit Chokepoints*.

7. Gungwu Wang, "Early Ming Relations." For a more comprehensive review, see Stuart-Fox, *Short History*.

8. Zha and Hu, *Building a Neighborly Community*, 55–83.

9. Arai, *ASEAN to Nihon*, 165–66.

10. Goto, *Kindai nihon to tonan'ajia*, 8.

11. Matsumoto, *Chūgokugaikō to tō'nan'ajia*, 10.

12. "Zhongguo qian zhu miandian dashi zishu: wo gei maozhuxi zuo fanyi [Former Chinese Ambassador to Myanmar: My Work as Translator for Chairman Mao]," *Guoji Xianqudaobao*, December 26, 2003.

13. Wanzhen Liu and Li, *Mao Zedong guoji jiaowang lu*.

14. Stuart-Fox, "Communism and the Cold War," 7.

15. Li, "Zhanhou zhongguo yu yinni de guanxi," 49.

16. Yuanxing Cheng, *Waijiao wangshi*.

17. Bingquan Xu, "Zhou Enlai wanlonghuiyi jingdiangonglüe [Zhou Enlai's Mastery Strategies at the Bandung Conference]" in *Zhou Enlai*, China Central Television, February 28, 2008.

18. Chinese Ministry of Foreign Affairs, *Yafeihuiyi Wenjianxuanji*, 36.

19. Zhang, "Zhongtai guanxi sishinian," 4.

20. *People's Daily*, July 21, 1957.

21. A partial list of post-1955 aid recipients includes Nepal ($13 million over three years), Cambodia ($22.9 million over two years), Ceylon ($27 million over two years), Burma ($4 million), Indonesia ($41 million), and Yemen ($16 million). See Matsumoto, *Chūgokugaikō to tō'nan'ajia*, 17.

22. For a photographic record of Zhou and Chen's participation in this festival, see Sina.com, "Zhou Enlai canjia poshuijie [Zhou Enlai Joins Sangkran]," http://news.sina.com.cn/c/p/2008-02-04/120314901146.shtml.

23. Weichi Shang and Weiwei Kou, "Bujinjin shi wenhua chayi: Xifang weihe wudu zhongguo [Not Just Cultural Difference: Why the West Is Misreading China], *Huanqiu Shibao* [Global Times], April 16, 2007.

24. This incident appeared in some Chinese history books and media coverage as the "Incident of Dulles Refusing to Shake Hands with Zhou," but even the Chinese media now admit that the story was fabricated. See Bingnan Wang, "Nine Years of Sino-U.S. Talks in Retrospect," *Guangzhou Ribao*, September 29, 1984–February 3, 1985, translated in U.S. Joint Publication Research Service, JPRS-CPS-85-079, August 7, 1985, 12–13.

25. "Memorandum of Conversation, Monday, February 21, 1972, 5:58 p.m.–6:55 p.m," in "Record of Historic Richard Nixon–Zhou Enlai Talks."

26. See, for example, Zhang, "Zhongtai guanxi sishinian," 5–7; Li, "Zhanhou zhongguo yu yinni de guanxi," 53.

27. *People's Daily*, April 20, 1965.

28. For an excellent review of China's intervention in Southeast Asia during the 1960s and 1970s, see Heaton, "China and Southeast Asian Communist Movements," 779–800.

29. Stuart-Fox, "Communism and the Cold War," 18, 26.

30. Suryadinata, "'Overseas Chinese,'" 45.

31. *People's Daily*, September 26, 1968.

32. Xu, "Zhongguo dongmeng guanxi sishinian," 55.

33. Hatano and Satō, *Gendai nihon no tō'nan'ajia seisaku*, 5.

34. Ibid., 49–50.

35. Ibid., 17. See also Miyagi, *Sengo ajia chitsujo no mosaku to nihon*, 29–36.

36. Japanese Ministry of Foreign Affairs, *Proceedings*.

37. Hatano and Satō, *Gendai nihon no tō'nan'ajia seisaku*, 9.

38. Ibid., 37.

39. Khalid and Lee, *Whither the Look East Policy*, 49.

40. Arai, *ASEAN to Nihon*, 184.

41. Kishi, *Kishi Nobusuke kaikoroku*, 312.

42. Fujisawa, *Fujisawa Nobuyuki tsuisō*, 76.

43. Hatano and Satō, *Gendai nihon no tō'nan'ajia seisaku*, 58–59.

44. Japanese Ministry of Foreign Affairs, *Key Notes.*

45. Japanese Ministry of Foreign Affairs, *Tanaka.*

46. Yamamoto and Takagi, "Tō'nan'ajia shokoku no nihon imēji saikō," 173–75.

47. Japanese Ministry of Foreign Affairs, *ASEAN to Nihon: Ajia no heiwa to han'ei no tameni* [ASEAN and Japan: For Peace and Prosperity of Asia], http://www.mofa.go.jp/mofaj/press/pr/wakaru/topics/vol64/index.html.

48. Kōnō, *Heiwa kōsaku*, 25.

49. Fukuda, *Kaiko kyūjunen*, 280.

50. Junpei Katō, *Japan's Cultural Exchange*, 54. As a result of the administrative reform, the Japan Foundation became an "independent administrative institution [*dokuritsu hōjin*]" in October 2003. Yet it has still maintained close ties with the Japanese government, particularly the Ministry of Foreign Affairs.

51. Japanese Ministry of Foreign Affairs, *Ni-ASEAN shuyōkyōryoku jigō.*

52. Koizumi, "Japan and ASEAN in East Asia," 5.

53. In 2002 and 2008, the poll expanded to include Vietnam.

54. Japanese Ministry of Foreign Affairs, *Tō'nan'ajia shokoku ni okeru yoronchōsa* [Surveys on Southeast Asian Countries], http://www.mofa.go.jp/mofaj/area/asean/pdfs/yoron08_03.pdf.

55. Qiao, *Riben duiwaizhengce yu dongmeng*, 249.

56. Yamamoto and Takagi, "Tō'nan'ajia shokoku no nihon imēji saikō," 171.

57. Mahathir, *Malay Dilemma*, 30, 98.

58. Khalid and Lee, *Whither the Look East Policy*, 93.

59. Ibid., 95.

60. Ibid., 121.

61. See, for example, Thand and Gan, "Deconstructing Japanisation."

62. Khalid and Lee, *Whither the Look East Policy*, 24.

63. Ibid., 26.

64. Arai, *ASEAN to Nihon*, 193–94.

65. Yamamoto and Takagi, "Tō'nan'ajia shokoku no nihon imēji saikō," 173–75.

66. Japanese Ministry of Foreign Affairs, *Tō'nan'ajia shokoku ni okeru yoronchōsa.*

67. For scholarly discussions of the reasons for Japan's economic malaise, see Katz, *Japan.*

68. Clarissa Oon, "The Dragon and the Little Red Dot: 20th Anniversary of China-Singapore Diplomatic Ties," *Strait Times*, October 2, 2010.

69. Ibid., November 16, 1978.

70. Ruisheng Cheng, *Mulin youhao sishi nian*, 137–53.

71. Interview with a Chinese diplomat, August 4, 2004.

72. Xu, "Zhongguo dongmeng guanxi sishinian," 56.

73. Karaki, "Chūgoku no taigaikaihō seisaku to tōnan'ajia bō'eki," 408.

74. For a firsthand record of China's efforts to break its international isolation, see the memoir by Chinese foreign minister Qichen Qian, *Waijiao shiji.*

75. Kurlantzick, *Charm Offensive*, 45.

76. See, for example, Meng, "Yali, renzhi yu guojixingxiang," 167. See also Qin, "Shijie gejü yu zhongguo waijiao."

77. Chinese Ministry of Foreign Affairs, *Pro-Active Policies*.

78. John M. Broder, "Clinton in China: The Overview: Clinton Vows to Help Asia on Crisis," *New York Times*, July 3, 1998.

79. Tingman Huang, "Haixiao ningjin zhongguo-dong'nanya liyigongtongti [Tsunami Binds China and Southeast Asia Tight on Common Interest]," *Jingjicankaobao*, January 10, 2005, http://www.china.com.cn/zhuanti2005/txt/2005-01/10/content_5752547.htm.

80. Ibid.

81. Yamamoto and Takagi, "Tō'nan'ajia shokoku no nihon imēji saikō," 182–83.

82. "'Wanlongjingsheng' jixu yinling zhongguo he yafeiguojia hezuo [The 'Bandung Spirit' Continues to Guide Long-Term Cooperation between China and Asian-African Countries]," China Central Television, http://www.cctv.com/news/china/20050418/102159.shtml.

83. In the wake of the riot, a graphic picture of a group of Asian men gang-raping an Asian woman was widely circulated on websites in China and was cited by Chinese nationalists as a disturbing illustration of the Indonesian riot. The image was later revealed to have been taken from a Japanese pornographic video.

84. Japanese Ministry of Foreign Affairs, *Tokyo Declaration*.

85. "Riben zaici guchui zhongguo weixielun [Japan Once Again Advertises 'China Threat' Thesis]," *Xinhua News Agency*, March 4, 2006.

86. Press conference by Prime Minister Fukuda Yasuo following his visits to the United States and Singapore, November 21, 2007, Japanese Politics and International Relations Database, University of Tokyo, http://www.ioc.u-tokyo.ac.jp/~worldjpn/documents/texts/asean/20071121.O2E.html.

87. Personal interview with a Japanese diplomat, October 12, 2008.

88. Tanaka and Tahara, *Kokka to gaikō*, 186.

89. Ibid., 185–87, 206–10.

90. Abe Shinzō, for example, stated in an August 2007 speech in Indonesia that Japanese diplomacy would "seek to strengthen relations with countries that share [our] values of freedom, democracy, human rights, and the rule of law." See "Abe shushō 'kachikan gaikō'de chūgoku kensei [Prime Minister Abe seeks to Contain China through 'Value-Based Diplomacy']," *Sankei Shimbun*, August 20, 2007. See also Koizumi, "Japan and ASEAN in East Asia," 6.

91. Zhang, "Dangqian taiguoren de zhongguoguan," 62–63.

92. Mingwei Zhou, *Guojia xingxiang yanjiu luncong*, 493–501.

93. Personal conversation with an adviser to the Chinese Foreign Ministry, January 15, 2009.

94. Hatano and Satō, *Gendai nihon no tō'nan'ajia seisaku*, 229.

95. See, for example, "No Escape from History," *Jakarta Post*, quoted by "Meiguo, Taiguo he Yinni meiti fenfen piping Xiaoquan canbai jingguo shenshe [American, Thai, and Indonesian Press Criticize Koizumi for Yasukuni Visit]," *Xinhua News Agency*, October 19, 2005. See also "Bai zhanfan yinhun bu chunshu neizheng [Worshipping War Criminals' Evil Souls Is Not Entirely a Matter of Domestic Politics]," *Lian He Zao Bao*, October 27, 2005; "Dui zhanfan de shenpan burong fouding [Trial of War Criminals Cannot Be Denied]," *Lian He Zao Bao*, October 29, 2005.

96. Ma, "Li Guangyao de ribenguan," 12–17.

97. "Koizumi, Singapore's Lee Agree Yasukuni Not to Hurt Sino-Japan Ties," *Kyodo News International*, May 30, 2006, http://findarticles.com/p/articles/mi_m0WDQ/is_/ai_n26880492.

98. Mondejar and Chu, "ASEAN-China Relations," 226.

99. Mingwei Zhou, *Guojia xingxiang yanjiu luncong*, 495.

100. Beiyan Wen, "Zhongguo-yinni zhanlue huobanguanxi de xianzhuang he zhanwang,," 37.

CHAPTER 3

1. Kane, "Potential Futures," 706.

2. Chang, "Gurōbaruka to minzokushugika no nagare no nikkan kankei," 11–23.

3. Weiguo Sun, *Daming qihao yü xiaozhonghua yishi*.

4. Young-jak Kim, "Nihon(jin) toha Kankoku(jin) nitotte nan'nanoka?," 5–6.

5. For documents employing these condescending terms, see, for example, *Tōbunsen* [Selection of Essays on the Country to the East of China] and *Kaitō shokokuki* [Record on Countries to the East of the Sea]; both were compiled by Korean sinologists in the fifteenth century.

6. Office of the Korean Prime Minister, "Early Joseon Period."

7. Yung-sik Kim, "Problems and Possibilities."

8. Young-jak Kim, "Nihon(jin) toha Kankoku(jin) nitotte nan'nanoka?," 5.

9. See, for example, Ogura, "Nikkan no shutaiteki jigoishiki to rekishi nin'shiki mondai," 76. For similar views, see also Hong, *Zhuxi yu ligu zhexue bijiao yanjiu*.

10. Ogura, "Nikkan no shutaiteki jigoishiki to rekishi nin'shiki mondai," 76.

11. Kyung-koo Han, "Nikkan no chiteki," 135.

12. Young-jak Kim, "Nihon(jin) toha Kankoku(jin) nitotte nan'nanoka?," 12.

13. Fukuzawa, "Jiji shōgen," 226–29.

14. *Jiji Shimpō*, August 13, 1885.

15. See, for example, Ishida, "Cultural Genocide."

16. For an insightful analysis of Korean historical positivism, see Jie-hyun Lim, "Antagonistic Complicity."

17. Nam, "Kankoku minzokushugi no tenkai to nikkan kankei," 99.

18. In, *Jitsuroku*.

19. "Kan'ichi kyōtei bunsho kōkai: Park Chung-hee Daitōryō 'Doktu mondai' yūtsūsei mattaku'nai [Documents on South Korea–Japan Treaty Open to the Public: President Park Chung-hee Allowed No Flexibility on the Doktu Problem]," *JoongAng Daily*, August 27, 2005, http://japanese.joins.com/article/article.php?aid=67065&servcode=200&sectcode=200.

20. Shimane Prefectural Government, "Rontenseiri."

21. Japanese Politics and International Relations Database, *Nikkan kaidan "Kuboda Hatsugen" ni kansuru sangi'in suisan i'inkai shitsugi*.

22. Yanagimachi, "Sengo nikkan kankei no keisei to sono keizaiteki sokumen," 63.

23. Cheol-on Park, *Nikkan kōryū kagede sasaeta okoto*.

24. Kimiya, "Nikkan kankei no rikigaku to tenbō."

25. Nam, "Kankoku minzokushugi no tenkai to nikkan kankei," 105.

26. Won-dok Yi, "Rekishi mondai wo meguru nikkan no kattō mekanizumu," 28–29.

27. "Nikkan jōyaku hijunsho kōkan nikansuru Park Chung-hee daitōryō danwa [President Park's Speech on the Signing of Japan-ROK Treaty]," in Japanese Ministry of Foreign Affairs, *Nihon gaikō*, 629–39.

28. Hayashi, "Taishu bunka kōryū kara miru gendai nikkan kankei," 231–32.

29. Ibid., 233.

30. Nam, "Kankoku minzokushugi no tenkai to nikkan kankei," 93.

31. Kyung-koo Han, "Nikkan no chiteki," 138.

32. Colbert, "Japan and the Republic of Korea," 274.

33. Shimokawa, *Showa Heisei kateishi nenbyō*.

34. *Korean Herald*, September 8, 1984.

35. Lee, "Japan's Expansionist Cultural Policy."

36. Chang, "Gurōbaruka to minzokushugika no nagare no nikkan kankei," 17.

37. The polls were sponsored by the *Asahi Shimbun* and the *Dong-a Ilbo*, and results were published by the *Asahi Shimbun* on June 20, 2005.

38. "Kimu Yon-samu: Kankoku jiki daitōryō no kaiken [Meeting with Republic of Korea's Next President Kim Young-sam]," *Asahi Shimbun*, January 10, 1993.

39. "Nikkan shunō kaidan yōshi [Summary of Japan-Korea Summit]," *Asahi Shimbun*, November 7, 1993.

40. Ibid.

41. "Mi'no aru 'miraishikō' no nikkan ni [Toward Meaningful 'Future-Oriented' Japan-Korea Relations]," *Asahi Shimbun*, March 26, 1994.

42. "Atarashi nikkan kankei wo tsukuru tokida [Time to Build New Japan-Korea Relations]," *Asahi Shimbun*, August 22, 1993.

43. "Murayama seiken de no rekishi'ninshiki wo meguru ugoki [Major Happenings on Historical Recognition under the Murayama Administration]," *Asahi Shimbun*, November 19, 1995.

44. Ibid.

45. "'Kaihō 50nen' mukaeru kankoku [Korea Welcomes 50th Anniversary of Liberation]," *Asahi Shimbun*, March 1, 1995.

46. "Chūkan shunō kaidan: tai'nichi hihan irei no kyōdōhochō [China-Korea Summit: Unusual Coordination in Criticizing Japan]," *Asahi Shimbun*, November 15, 1995.

47. Japanese Diet Archive, No. 140-5, February 3, 1997, http://kokkai.ndl .go.jp/SENTAKU/syugiin/140/0380/14002030380005a.html.

48. Yi, "Rekishi mondai wo meguru nikkan no kattō mekanizumu," 37–38.

49. Ji, *Kankoku daitōryo retten*, 212–13.

50. "Nikkan ni hashi wa kakaruka? [Can a Bridge Be Built between Japan and Korea?]," *Asahi Shimbun*, June 24, 1996.

51. "Shinrai taitō wo rōryū kyōchō [Roh-Style Politics Stresses Trust and Equality]," *Asahi Shimbun*, January 24, 2003.

52. "Rō daitōryō kokkaidemo miraishikō kyōchō [President Roh Again Stresses Future-Oriented Stance at Diet]," *Asahi Shimbun*, June 9, 2003.

53. "Luwuxuan danxin yingxiang xingxiang jujue yu xiaoquan gongyu [Roh

Concerned about Image and Rejects Bathing with Koizumi]," *Xinhua News Agency,* December 27, 2004.

54. "Koizumi jidai: 'Tsuyoi' okoto enjita gaikō [Koizumi Era: Diplomacy Staged by Unyielding Man]," *Asahi Shimbun,* May 3, 2006.

55. Ji, *Kankoku daitōryō retten,* 270.

56. "Nikkan shunō kaidan 'kako yori mirai 'tsuranuku' [Japan-Korea Summit: Stick to 'Future More Important Than Past']," *Asahi Shimbun,* June 8, 2003.

57. "Taitōna raibaru kankei no 'kōki' ['Prime Opportunity' of Equal Partnership]," *Asahi Shimbun,* September 24, 2003.

58. "Ajia gaikō: Yuzuranu shushō [Diplomacy toward Asia: Prime Minister Not to Make Compromise]," *Asahi Shimbun,* November 15, 2005.

59. "Koizumi jidai."

60. "Shushō san'nen tsuzuke yasukuni sanpai [Prime Minister Visits Yasukuni Three Years in a Row]," *Asahi Shimbun,* January 15, 2003.

61. Ibid.

62. Ji, *Kankoku daitōryō retten,* 234.

63. "Kankokudaitōryō: Tenno wa doitsu motoshushō wo minarai shazaisubeki [Korean President: Japanese Emperor Should Learn from Former German Chancellor and Apologize]," *People's Daily* (Japanese version), November 12, 2008.

64. Tosa, *Kawaru kankoku kawaranai kankoku,* 117–26.

65. Personal interviews with a Japanese Diet member, a senior Japanese television journalist, and a senior Korean newspaper journalist, August 1, 2004.

66. Otmazgin, "Contesting Soft Power," 94–95.

67. Sun-eh Park and Tsuchiya, *Nihon taishūbunka to nikkan kankei,* 189.

68. Ibid. See also Hosokawa and Otake, "Karaoke in East Asia."

69. "Rai'nichi shita kankokujin ga 'takeshima no hi' ni kōgikatsudō [Koreans Come to Japan to Protest 'Takeshima Day']," *NHK,* February 22, 2009.

70. "Miraishikō to kakokaifuku yureru nikkan kokkō 40nen [(40th Anniversary of Japan–South Korea Relations: Shaken by Collision between Future and Past]," *Asahi Shimbun,* June 20, 2005.

71. "Kan'nichi jichitai no kōryū ga aitsuide torikeshi: Chuncheon shi, Yamaguchiken hōfushi nado subete no jichitai to no kōryū wo chūdan [Local Exchanges between Korea and Japan Cancelled One after Another: Exchange between Chuncheon City (Korea) and Hōfu City of Yamaguchi Prefecture Was Halted Among Others]," *KBS News* (Korea), July 22, 2005.

72. Wan, *Sino-Japanese Relations,* 69.

73. Chang, "Gurōbaruka to minzokushugika no nagare no nikkan kankei," 16.

74. Human Rights Watch, "North Korea."

75. "China's North Korea Policy Unlikely to Change," *Korea Herald,* October 26, 2006.

76. Korea International Trade Association, *Statistics Bulletin.*

77. Embassy of the Republic of Korea in China, *Hanzhong jiaoliu tongji.*

78. Ibid.

79. "Qunian hanguo churujing renshu tupo siqianwanrenci daguan [Number of People Departing and Entering Korea Passes 40-million Threshold]," *Yonhap News* (Korea), January 5, 2010, http://www.icnkr.com/article-42404-1.html.

80. "Zhongguo Nüqu Yayun 2:1 Zhanshenghanguo duoguan [Chinese Women's Field Hockey Beats Korea 2:1 and Wins Gold Medal]," *Xinhua News Agency*, October 11, 2002, http://news.xinhuanet.com/asiangames/2002-10/11/content_593133.htm.

81. Chung, *Between Ally and Partner*, offers a rare glimpse into the two countries' process of approaching each other.

82. Zhao, "Zhonghan guanxi xiubu shengji."

83. Ruan, *Zhonghan jieji waijiao*, 43–50.

84. Ibid., 74.

85. "3213hao yuleiting pantao hanguo shijian shimo [The Case of No. 3212 Motor Torpedo's Defection to ROK]," *Junshiwenzhai*, September 2, 2010, http://military.china.com/zh_cn/history4/62/20100902/16122438.html.

86. "Zhongguo shouren zhu ganhuodashi: shenban yayun lajin zhonghan [China's First Ambassador to ROK: Bid for Asian Games Brings China and ROK Closer]," *Shijie Xinwenbao*, July 6, 2007.

87. Chung, *Between Ally and Partner*, 6–8.

88. The metaphor was used by Amsden, *Asia's Next Giant*.

89. Shu, "1970nian guoqingdadian Mao Zedong weihe yaoqing Sinuo shang tian'anmen?"

90. Jun Yang, "Zhonghan: you duizhi zouxiang jiechu [China and ROK: From Confrontation to Contact]," in Yang, *Zhongguo yu chaoxianbandao guanxi shilun*.

91. Zhao, "Pengzhuangzhong de zhonghan minzuzhiyi."

92. "Miraishikō to kakokaifuku yureru nikkan kokkō 40nen [40th Anniversary of Japan–South Korea Relations: Shaken by Collision between Future and Past]," *Asahi Shimbun*, June 20, 2005.

93. For a collection of Chinese leaders' ceremonial speeches praising the history and development of Sino-Korean exchanges, see Jinzhi Liu et al., *Zhongguo yu chaoxian bandaoguojia guanxi wenjianziliao huibian*, esp. speeches by Li Peng, 277, Hu Jintao, 474, and Jia Qinglin, 552–53.

94. Ying Jiao, "Li Changchun huijian hanguo jizhoudao zhishi, canguan xufugongyuan [Li Changchun Meets with Governor of Jeju and Visits Xufu Park]," *China National Radio*, http://www.cnr.cn/gundong/200904/t20090405_505294507.html.

95. China's entrenched fear of encirclement was vividly described in a speech by James R. Lilley, former U.S. ambassador to China, in a speech to the Graduate School of International Studies at the University of Denver, February 12, 2007.

96. "Hu Jintao zai hanguo guohui fabiao yanjiang [Hu Jintao Addresses Korean Parliament]," *People's Daily*, November 17, 2005.

97. "Lu Wuxuan gaosu bushi zhongguo cengjing qinlueguo hanguo shubaici [Roh Moo-hyun Tells Bush: 'China Is the Country That Invaded Korea Hundreds of Times']," *Phoenix News*, June 15, 2005, http://news.163.com/05/ 0615/13/1M9QVCLF00011248.html.

98. Overseas Korean Foundation, http://oaks.korean.net/n_bbs/5bbs.jsp?biID=STTOverseasKoreans&SK=&SW=&mode=V&bID=13010&SN=&SK=&SW=.

99. For a detailed analysis of the Goguryeo dispute, see Gries, "Goguryeo Controversy."

100. "South Korea and China Argue over Camelot Kingdom," *Times* (London), August 24, 2004. See also "Seoul Gets Tough over Koguryo Dispute," *Korean Times,* July 17, 2004.

101. Gries, "Goguryo Controversy," 8.

102. Ibid., 6.

103. Chinese Academy of Social Sciences, Research Center on the History of China's Border Regions. *Introduction to the Northeast Project.*

104. "Dongbeigongcheng yinfa gaogouli zhizheng [Northeast Project Triggers Dispute on Goguryeo]," *Phoenix News,* http://news.china.com/zh_cn/history/all/11025807/20050729/12525151.html.

105. "Kōshi mo kankokujin dattta toiu kankoku no gōman shuchō [South Korea's Arrogant Claim: 'Confucius Was Also Korean']," *Shūkanshinchō*, November 16, 2006. On the claim that Genghis Khan was ethnically Korean, see *Segye Times*, September 17, 2008, http://www.sgtusa.com/detail.php?number=4716&thread=25r03.

106. "Youkaishi yaomohua hanguoren le? [Are We Once Again Demonizing the Koreans?]," *Zhongguo Wang*, August 1, 2008, http://opinion.nfdaily.cn/opinionlist/content/2008-08/01/content_4508640.htm. See also Guanghui Li, "Zhongmei you zaoyao: Hanguo zhuzhang fei'erpusi you hanguoxuetong [Chinese Media Once Again Spread Rumor on Korean Claiming Phelps Has Korean Blood]," *Chosun Ilbo*, August 20, 2008, http://chn.chosun.com/site/data/html_dir/2008/08/20/20080820000027.html; "Liang'an fanhanchao: Chaoxian ma zaojia [Anti-Korea Wave on Both Taiwan and the Mainland: Korea Denounces Fabrication]," *United Daily News*, August 20, 2008, http://tw.news.yahoo.com/article/url/d/a/080820/2/14fuj.html.

107. Lisi Zhong, "Zhiyou yige zhongguo [There Is but One China]," http://www.xctax.cn/Article_Show.asp?ArticleID=4171.

108. "Riben jiangyu 2015nian miewang zhongguo, zhongguoren bi kan [Japan Will Eliminate China by 2015—Chinese Must Read This!]," http://qbar.qq.com/dahuajunqing/14525.htm.

109. "China Upset with 'Baekdu Mountain' Skaters," *Chosun Ilbo*, February 2, 2007, http://english.chosun.com/w21data/html/news/200702/200702020024.html. In another case of a sense of betrayal triggered by language barrier, Icelandic pop diva Björk shouted "Tibet Tibet!" at the end of a concert in Shanghai, but most audience members had no idea what she was shouting and felt shocked and betrayed when they later found out.

110. "Hanguo chongwudian gongran ruhua [Korean Pet Store Blatantly Humiliates China]," *Xinjingbao*, July 31, 2007, http://www.xici.net/b669493/d55898012.htm.

111. "Hanju chuxian mingxian rūua qingjie yinfa zhenglun [Korean Drama Has Apparent Scenes Humiliating China and Triggers Controversy]," *China News Network*, March 23, 2009, http://et.21cn.com/tv/huati/2009/03/23/6033455.shtml.

112. "Ruhe diyu zhonghan minjian hanliu [How to Stop the Cold Current at the People-to-People Level between China and Korea]," *Xianqu Luntan Daobao*, December 3, 2008, http://news.163.com/08/1203/09/4S7T7TID000120GU.html.

113. "Diaocha cheng hanguo zuitaoyan guojia wei sange jinlin, zhongguo paiming di'er [Poll Shows Korea Most Strongly Dislikes Three Neighbors, China Ranks Second]," *China News Network*, October 3, 2008, http://news.sohu.com/20081003/n259844183.shtml.

114. Personal conversation with a Japanese diplomat, March 2, 2009.

115. Wan, *Sino-Japanese Relations*, 69.

116. Kondo, *Nihon, chūgoku, kankoku.*

CHAPTER 4

1. Taiwan Affairs Office and the Information Office of the State Council, *White Paper on Taiwan Issue: The One China Principle and the Taiwan Issue*, February 21, 2000, http://www.gwytb.gov.cn:8088/detail.asp?table=WhitePaper&title=White%20 Papers%20On%20Taiwan%20Issue&m_id=4. See also "Wen Jiabao: Taiwan wenti chunshu zhongguo neizheng burong waiguo ganshe [Wen Jiabao States Taiwan Issue Is Purely China's Domestic Politics and Does Not Allow Foreign Intervention]," *Xinhua News Agency*, March 14, 2005, http://www.cctv.com/news/ china/20050314/101185.shtml.

2. Taiwan Affairs Office and the Information Office of the State Council, *White Paper.*

3. "Guojiazhuxi Hu Jintao tong meiguo dangxuan zongtong Aobama tong dianhua [President Hu Jintao Has Phone Conversation with U.S. President-Elect Obama]," *Xinhua News Agency*, November 18, 2008.

4. Office of the Press Secretary of the U.S. President, "President Bush and Premier Wen Jiabao Remarks to the Press," November 9, 2003, http://www.white house.gov/news/releases/2003/12/print/20031209-2.html.

5. Thomas J. Christensen, "A Strong and Moderate Taiwan," speech delivered to U.S.-Taiwan Business Council Defense Industry Conference, Annapolis, Maryland, September 11, 2007.

6. "Wangdiao Chenshuibian yuandanwengao de surprise! [Forget Any Surprise in Chen Shui-bian's New-Year Proclamation!]," *China Times*, December 30, 2006.

7. "Hu Jintao: Guanche jixiwangyu taiwanrenmin de fangzhen juebugaibian [Hu Jintao: Absolutely No Change to the Principle of Placing Hope on the Taiwanese People]," *Xinhua News Agency*, March 4, 2005.

8. The Taiwan Affairs Office of the State Council, *Welcome Message by the Minister*, http://www.gwytb.gov.cn:8088/detail.asp?table=Introduction&title=Intro duction&m_id=1.

9. Taiwan Affairs Office of the State Council, http://www.gwytb.gov.cn:8088/ list.asp?table=headlines&title=Headlines.

10. Tianyuan Chen, "Wang Yi: Waijiaoxinxing de minjian duben [Wang Yi: Unofficial Interpretation of a New Diplomatic Star]," *Phoenix Weekly* 158 (2007): 28. See also "Zhongguo zhuridashi Wang Yi: Cong zhiqing dao daxuesheng [Chinese Ambassador to Japan Wang Yi: From Rusticated Youth to College Student]," *People's Daily*, May 22, 2007.

11. The Anti-Secession Law lists three conditions under which "nonpeaceful means" will be used to solve the Taiwan issue: (1) if "Taiwan independence" forces, using whatever name or method, accomplish Taiwan's separation from China; (2) if a major event occurs that would lead to Taiwan's separation from China; (3) if all possibility of peaceful unification is lost.

12. Mainland Affairs Council of the Republic of China, "Minzhong dui dang-

qian liang'an guanxi zhi kanfa minyidiaocha (Minguo 97nian 8.22–24) [Survey on the Public Attitude on Cross-Strait Relations (August 22–24, 2008)]," http://www .mac.gov.tw/big5/mlpolicy/pos/9708/pos9708a.pdf.

13. Mainland Affairs Council of the Republic of China, "2008nian liang'an guanxi guo'nei gejie minyidiaocha zonghe fenxi [Combined Analysis of Public Attitude on Cross-Strait Relations in 2008]," http://www.mac.gov.tw/big5/mlpolicy/ pos/9802/po9802.htm.

14. Ibid.

15. For a collection of various polls on Taiwanese self-identification, see Mainland Affairs Council of the Republic of China, http://www.mac.gov.tw/big5/mlpo licy/pos/9802/12.pdf.

16. Mainland Affairs Council of the Republic of China, http://www.mac.gov .tw/public/Attachment/9762295476.pdf.

17. The status quo category includes four subanswers: To maintain the status quo permanently, to maintain the status quo and decide later, to maintain the status quo and then to reunite, and to maintain the status quo and then to become independent.

18. For the Hong Kong migration wave in the 1990s, see, for example, Skeldon, *Reluctant Exiles.* See also Jupp, "Tacking into the Wind."

19. Wanfei Lin, "Lian yeye, bie huilai le! [Grandpa Lien, Don't Come Back!]," *Lianhe Zaobao,* May 5, 2005, http://www.zaobao.com/special/china/taiwan/pages8/ taiwan050505d.html.

20. "China 'Will Not Have Democracy,'" *BBC,* March 9, 2009, http://news.bbc .co.uk/2/hi/asia-pacific/7932091.stm.

21. "Xiaohudui zaihuishou chunwan gaochao [Little Tigers' Return Climax of Spring Gala Show], *Xinmin Evening News,* February 14, 2010.

22. "Bai Yansong caifang Zhang Huimei [Bai Yansong's Interview of Zhang Huimei]," *CCTV,* July 17, 2004.

23. "A-mei Blasted for Not Taking a Stand," *Taipei Times,* August 27, 2004.

24. "Meng Guangmei yanxing bufuze zao baiwanwangyou fennushengtao [Meng Guangmei's Irresponsible Words and Deeds Trigger Furious Condemnations from Millions of Netizens], *Chongqing Shangbao,* September 4, 2006.

25. "Meng Guangmei: Wo daoxian bingbushi yinwei wo weiqu [Meng Guangmei: I Apologized Not Because I Felt Unfairly Treated]," *Nandu Zhoukan,* November 9, 2006.

26. "Meng Guangmei chengqing wuruneidi shijian: Wo congwei chaoxiao neidiren [Meng Guangmei Clarifies 'Humiliating Mainland' Incident: I Have Never Made Fun of Mainlanders]," Sina.com, September 23, 2006.

27. See, for example, Shambaugh, "China and Japan," 92–93; Green, *Japan's Reluctant Realism;* Mochizuki, "American and Japanese Strategic Debates."

28. For classical explications of liberalism and its implications for international relations, see, for example, Deutsch, Burrell, and Kann, *Political Community;* Keohane and Nye, *Power and Interdependence.*

29. Japanese Ministry of Finance, http://www.mof.go.jp/singikai/sangyokanze/ tosin/skl406mt_05.pdf.

30. Wakabayashi, "Taiwanese Nationalism."

31. Katsunori Nakamura, "Meishō, Taiwan sōtoku toshite no Kodama Gentarō

[Famous General: Kodama Gentarō as Governor of Taiwan]," in *Zoku: Unmeikyō-dōtai toshite no Nihon to Taiwan*, ed. Nakamura et al., 208–37.

32. Wakabayashi, "Taiwanese Nationalism," 9.

33. "Hu Jintao zai jinian zhongguo renmin kangri ji shijie fan faxisi zhanzheng shengli 60zhounian dahui shang de jianghua [Hu Jintao's Speech at the Conference Commemorating the 60th Anniversary of the Great Victory against Fascist Forces by the People of China and of the World]," *Xinhua News Agency*, September 3, 2005, http://news.xinhuanet.com/newscenter/2005-09/03/content_3438800.htm.

34. "Ma Ying-jeou: Taiwanren congwei wangji ziji shi huaxiazizun [Ma Ying-jeou States Taiwanese Never Forgot They Were Descendants of Chinese Nation]," *Huaxia Wang*, October 23, 2005, http://big5.huaxia.com/zt/pl/05-087/602102.html.

35. See, for example, Tsai, "Nihon tōchi jidai to kokumintō tōchi jidai ni mata-gatta taiwanjin no nihonkan."

36. Ibid., 23.

37. Uchida's official title is the director of the Taipei Office of the Interchange Association, Japan (IAJ). The IAJ, nominally a private organization, is authorized to carry out functions normally carried out by an embassy. It is headquartered in Tokyo and has offices in Taipei and Kaohsiung.

38. Uchida, *Nittai kankei*, 59–60.

39. Ibid., 195.

40. Ibid., 40–71.

41. There are numerous studies on the normalization process between Japan and China. For a detailed historical account, see, for example, Ogata, *Normalization with China*.

42. Shiba, *Taiwan kikō*, 400–411.

43. For the Japanese Cabinet Office's annual survey on Japanese perceptions of key foreign countries and regions, see http://www8.cao.go.jp/survey/h17/h17-gaikou/2-1.html.

44. Uchida, *Nittai kankei*, 50.

45. Between 1988 and 1989, the number of Japanese who felt friendly toward China dropped from 68.5 percent to 51.6 percent; by 2005, that number had fallen to 32.4 percent. See http://www8.cao.go.jp/survey/h17/h17-gaikou/2-1.html.

46. Japanese Cabinet Office, *Taigaikankei Tasukufōsu, 21seiki nihon gaikō no kihon senryaku: Aratana jidai, aratana bijon, aratana gaikō* [Japanese Foreign Policy Strategies in the 21st Century: New Time, New Vision, New Foreign Policy], http://www.kantei.go.jp/jp/kakugikettei/2002/1128tf.html.

47. Uchida, *Nittai kankei*, 98.

48. Wen Shen, "Luo Yang Dong Jie Yu Gang Shan de You Hao Guan Xi [Luoyang Freezes Its Friendly Relations with Okayama," *Zhongwendaobao* [Chinese Review Weekly], May 15, 2003.

49. The Japanese government referred to Chen as president but added quotation marks around the word as a sign of Tokyo's refusal to recognize Taiwan as a sovereign state. See Uchida, *Nittai kankei*, 188–92.

50. In August 2005, in a highly unusual gesture, Japanese ambassador to China Anami Koreshige sent an official telegraph urging Koizumi not to further antagonize Japan-China relations by visiting the controversial Yasukuni Shrine. Koizumi apparently ignored Anami's appeal, visiting the shrine in October.

51. Uchida, *Nittai kankei*, 80–81.

52. *Nihon Keizai Shimbun*, December 23, 2003.

53. In fact, Katō made a series of speeches to voice his objection to Koizumi's annual visits to the Yasukuni Shrine on the grounds that they might further antagonize China. A right-wing nationalist burned down Katō's house and adjoining office in August 2006. See *Asahi Shimbun*, August 17, 2006.

54. Uchida, *Nittai kankei*, 104.

55. Shu Chin-chiang, chair of the Taiwan Solidarity Union, paid homage to the Yasukuni Shrine on April 4, 2005, with other lawmakers from his party. The party is commonly perceived as a hard-line pro-independence party with former president Lee as its spiritual leader. For Shu's visit, see, "TSU Head Visits Controversial Shrine," *Taipei Times*, April 3, 2005.

56. Uchida, *Nittai kankei*, 68.

57. Zhou Xian, "Ma Yingjiu cheng zhongguodalu 'wei wo ling tu' [Ma Yingjiu Says Mainland China 'Belongs to Our Territory']," *Huanqiu Shibao*, October 8, 2008.

58. Uchida, *Nittai kankei*, 58.

59. Chinese foreign ministry spokesperson Liu Jianchao has confirmed that some Taiwanese fishermen were hanging Chinese national flags. He also stated that China "pays close attention to and actively protects Chinese fishermen's right for normal fishing in the area." See "Wai jiao bu jiu taiwan yu min xuan gua wu xing hong qi deng wen ti da wen shi lu [Foreign Ministry Answers Questions on Taiwanese Fishermen Hanging Chinese National Flag, etc.]," *China News Agency*, June 21, 2005.

60. "Taiwan qiangjing, riguan jugongdaoxian kaolü peichang zhuangchen yuchuan [Taiwan Toughens, Japanese Official Bows to Apologize and Considers Compensation for Sunken Fishing Boat]," *Ming Pao*, June 16, 2008.

61. "Xu Shikai yaoqiu jikezhunci, Ou Honglian huipi: jujue beixun feichang buyinggai [Ko Se-kai Demands Immediate Resignation, Ou Honglian Shoots Back by Criticizing Ko as Very Irresponsible for Refusing Legislative Questioning]," *NOW News*, June 16, 2006.

CONCLUSION

1. This sentiment also appeared in a 2009 bestseller, Song et al., *Zhongguo bugaoxing*, esp. 2–17.

2. "Bainian aoyun mengxiang licheng jianzheng zhonghuaminzu weidafuxing jiaobu [Journey of a Hundred-Year-Long Olympic Dream Witnesses Steps of the Chinese Nation's Great Revitalization]," *Xinhua News Agency*, August 6, 2008, http://news.xinhuanet.com/Olympics/2008-08/06/content_8980073.htm.

3. See the comprehensive coverage compiled by a leading news web portal, *Tengxun Xinwen:* "Zhuantibaodao: 2008 Chunyun Zhongguo, Kangjixuezai Huijiaguonian [Special Report: 2008 China's Spring Festival Mass Transportation—Fight Snow Blizzard and Head Home to Celebrate the New Year]," http://news.qq.com/zt/2008/chunyun2008/.

4. "Zhongguo wuyue baogao shouzukoubing siwang 40li, yiqing wenzhong youjiang [40 Deaths Caused by HFMD in China in May, Pandemic Stabilizes

with Minor Drop in Cases," *China News Agency,* June 10, 2008, http://health.sohu
.com/20080611/n257412311.shtml.

5. "Baoyuhongshui yizaocheng 169ren siwang 3800duowan ren shouzai [Tor-
rential Rain Hits 38 Million People and Causes 169 Deaths]," *Xinhua News Agency,*
June 16, 2008, http://news.qq.com/a/20080616/000077.htm.

6. "Shangdong lükelieche xiangzhuang zaocheng 71ren shenwang 416ren
shoushang [Passenger Trains Collide in Shangdong, Leading to 71 Deaths and
416 Injuries]," *China National Radio,* April 29, 2008, http://news.sina.com.cn/
c/p/2008-04-29/202515452505.shtml.

7. "Wenchuan dizheng daocheng zhijiejingjisunshi 8451yi, Sichuan zui yanzhong [Wenchuan Earthquake Causes Direct Economic Loss of 845.1 billion
yuan, Sichuan Hit Hardest]," *China News Network,* September 4, 2008, http://news
.qq.com/a/20080904/001668.htm.

8. Conversation with a group of Shanghai-based journalists, November 21,
2008.

9. Bob Tourtellotte and Paul Eckert, "Steven Spielberg Quits as Advisor over
Darfur," *Reuters,* http://www.reuters.com/article/domesticNews/idUSN1231478
420080212.

10. "Liu Guijin xiang meiti pilu Sipi'erboge cizhi zhenxiang [Liu Guijin Reveals to the Press the Truth Behind Spielberg's Resignation]," *Xinhua News Agency,*
February 20, 2008, http://news.qq.com/a/20080222/002082.htm.

11. "Olympic Child Singing Star Revealed as Fake," *Agence France Presse,* August 12, 2008, http://afp.google.com/article/ALeqM5gyXGZrP-fDoZSx-Ux
lHF3-tOElRA.

12. "China and Russia 'Approval Down,'" *BBC News,* February 6, 2009, http://
news.bbc.co.uk/2/hi/7873050.stm.

13. Private conversation with a Chinese professor of political science, January
19, 2009.

14. Private conversation with a Shanghai-based journalist, November 20, 2008.

15. "Olympic Flame Carried through Quiet New Delhi," *Associated Press,* April
18, 2008.

16. Madeleine Coorey, "China Urging Supporters to Attend Torch Rally: Australian FM," *Agence France Presse,* April 22, 2008, http://www.hindustantimes.com/
StoryPage/Print/306140.aspx.

17. "Seikarirei kōgi . . . bakanakoto no shishoku'in hatsugende Naganoshi ga
saitoni owabi keisai [Nagano City Apologizes on Website for Official's Remark on
Protesting Torch Relay as Stupid]," *Yomiuri Shimbun,* April 11, 2008.

18. Private conversation with a Japanese official working for the Asō cabinet,
March 2, 2009.

19. For a summary of competing views on the Asian values, see Subramaniam,
"Asian Values Debate." See also Philip Wonhyuk Lim, "Asian Values Debate Revisited."

20. One Japanese official stated that he felt China was "already democratic" and
that such a huge country would demand a heavy-handed approach. Private conversation with a vice ministerial official, March 2, 2009.

21. For a discussion of Lee Kuan Yew's impact on the Asian values debate, see
Barr, "Lee Kuan Yew."

22. Yoshida, *Nihon wo kettei shita hyakunen.*

23. The term *Xifang minzhu guojia* (Western democracies) frequently appears in both popular and scholarly discourses in China. Although the term's exact scope is vague, different versions invariably include the United States, Canada, the EU member states, Australia, New Zealand, and Japan.

24. Malcolm Moore, "China's Next Leader in Hardline Rant," *Daily Telegraph*, February 16, 2009.

25. Most criticism came from outside mainland China. Messages criticizing Xi were almost nonexistent on websites inside China as a result of monitoring. For reports that cover views on both sides, see "Xi Jinping Moxige jianghua yingqi shuomingle shenme? [What's behind Xi Jinping's Toughness in His Speech in Mexico?]," *Duowei News*, http://www.dwnews.com/gb/MainNews/Forums/Back Stage/2009_2_18_11_34_54_342.html.

26. Quite the contrary, Chinese leaders are often seen as ill prepared to deal with unexpected incidents. Hu Jintao was obviously caught by surprise when a Falun Gong protester posed as a journalist and began shouting political slogans at a White House ceremony to welcome Hu to the United States. Hu attempted to leave the podium before the ceremony officially ended, forcing President George W. Bush to pull on Hu's sleeve to keep him on the stage. See "In Pictures: Chinese Leader's U.S. Visit," *BBC*, April 20, 2006, http://news.bbc.co.uk/2/hi/in_pic tures/4927966.stm.

27. "Guanfang hao juzi dazao zhongguoban CNN, Xinhuashe jiang dangang [Government Injects Huge Investment to Create Chinese Version of CNN, Xinhua News Agency to Lead]," *Sintao Global Net*, January 16, 2009, http://www.stnn .cc/china/200901/t20090116_963358.html.

28. Mission statement available at Anti-CNN.com.

29. As of March 18, 2009, YouTube recorded 3,493,056 views for the video.

30. Manuel Valdes, "Hundreds Protest Dalai Lama in Seattle," *Seattle Times*, April 15, 2008.

31. "Zhongguo zai qihou fenghui dailing fazhanzhong guojia tuwei [China Leads Developing Countries to Break Encirclement at Climate Conference]," *CCTV*, December 17, 2009.

32. Mark Lynas, "How Do I Know China Wrecked the Copenhagen Deal? I Was in the Room," *Guardian*, December 22, 2009.

33. Hongmei Li, "U.S. Top Diplomat's Etiquette Needs Polishing," *People's Daily*, May 17, 2011.

34. David Barboza, "China Seeks to Stop Paris Sale of Bronzes," *New York Times*, February 16, 2009, http://www.nytimes.com/2009/02/17/arts/design/17auct.html.

35. Si Wang, "Wen Jiabao cheng bufangwen faguo zeren buzai zhongfang [Wen Jiabao States Responsibility of Bypassing France Does Not Lie on Chinese Side]," *Huanqiu Shibao*, February 2, 2002.

36. "Lu Kewen xianxiang zheshe zhongguo guoji yingxiangli buduanshang-sheng [The 'Kevin Rudd Phenomenon' Reflects Continued Rise of China's Global Influence]," *Xinhua News Agency*, November 26, 2007, http://news.xinhuanet.com/world/2007-11/26/content_7144970.htm.

37. Yongfeng Gao, "Lukewen zonglimen yanzheng zhongguo ruanshili [People Like Prime Minister Kevin Rudd Attest to China's Soft Power]," *Phoenix TV*, No-

vember 26, 2007, http://blog.sina.com.cn/s/blog_4e977df001000a0y.html 2010-6-2. Rui Chenggang, a popular host at China Central Television, referred to Rudd as Lao Lu and Kevin. See Chenggang Rui, "Wo he Lu Kewen de wangnian zhijiao [My Cross-Generational Friendship with Kevin Rudd]," *Hebei TV,* June 22, 2009, http://tv.people.com.cn/GB/39805/42848/9516458.html.

38. *Qinhua* literally can be translated as "pro-China," but Beijing applies the *pro-* or *anti-*label primarily based on the target's stance toward the Chinese government rather than the country of China. By implicitly equating the Chinese government with China, Beijing apparently seeks to gain popular acceptance of and support for such framings.

39. Ben Child, "Rebiya Kadeer Row Engulfs Melbourne Film Festival," *Guardian,* July 15, 2009.

40. "Aodaliya gaibian duihua zhengce beihou: zhengdang neidou da 'zhongguopai' [What's behind Australia's Changed China Policy: 'China Card' for Partisan Fight]," *Xinhua News Agency,* September 18, 2009, http://news.sina.com.cn/c/sd/2009-09-18/085418677899.shtml.

41. "Chuan rebiya ke'neng 8yue fang'ao; zhuanjia jinggao fanhuaqingxu jingpen [Rebiya Rumored to Possibly Visit Australia in August; Expert Warns of Eruption of Anti-China Sentiment]," July 27, 2009, http://news.qq.com/a/20090727/000416.htm.

42. "Wen Jiabao duncu riben liji wutiaojian fangren [Wen Jiabao Urges Japan to Release (Chinese Captain) Immediately and Unconditionally]," *Xinhua News Agency,* http://news.xinhuanet.com/mrdx/2010-09/23/c_13525991.htm.

43. For complete coverage of Chinese retaliation, see "Riben xunluochuan chongzhuang woguo yuchuan [Japanese Patrol Ship Rams Our Country's Fishing Boat]," http://news.sina.com.cn/z/zbxlcczzgyc/index.shtml. China's other leading web portals, including Sohu and Netease, also set up similar forums on this topic.

44. "Chūgoku ni hairyo shitawake dewa nai—Nihon kokumin he no eikyo jūshi—Naha chiken ['Not Because We Consider China'—Naha Prosecutor Stresses Impact on Japanese Citizens]," *Jiji Press,* September 24, 2010, http://www.jiji.com/jc/zc?k=201009/2010092400752.

45. "Zhongguo waijiaobu: Rifang xudui kouya yuchuan shijian daoqian peichang [Chinese Foreign Ministry Demands That Japan Apologize and Compensate for Placing Chinese Fishing Boat in Custody]," *Xinhua News Agency,* http://news.sina.com.cn/c/2010-09-25/042321163916.shtml.

46. For a review of scholarly and media debate on the gains and losses for Japan and China in this dispute, see the archive of Japan-U.S. Discussion Forum hosted by the National Bureau of Asian Research under the topic "fisheries dispute," http://nbrforums.nbr.org/foraui/list.aspx?LID=5.

47. The repeated usage of the words *happen to* are present in both Chinese and Japanese coverage (*ouran* in Chinese, *guzen* in Japanese). For an example of Chinese coverage, see "San Ouran cucheng zhongri shounao zoulang jiaotan [Three Happened to Assist Hallway Conversation between China and Japan]," *Phoenix TV,* October 5, 2010, http://www.sinovision.net/index.php?module=news&act=details&col_id=3&news_id=149481. For an example of Japanese coverage, see "Kurozuappu 2010: Nicchū shunōkaidan: mentsu mamori guzen enshutsu [Close-Up 2010: Japan-China Summit—A Staged 'Happen to' Act

to Save Face]," *Mainichi Shimbun*, October 6, 2010, http://mainichi.jp/select/opin
ion/closeup/news/20101006ddm003030061000c.html.

48. "Kan and Chinese PM Meet, Affirm Commitment to Improving Relations," *Mainichi Shimbun* (English edition), http://mdn.mainichi.jp/mdnnews/
news/20101005p2a00m0na007000c.html.

49. "Zhongri fangzhang dianti'ouyu jiaotan, xi zhuangchuan shijian hou shouci
[Chinese and Japanese Defense Ministers Happen to See Each Other in Elevator
and Chat, First Meeting after the Fishing Boat Collision Incident]," *Xinhua News
Agency*, http://news.sznews.com/content/2010-10/12/content_4988133_3.htm.

50. Japanese Ministry of Foreign Affairs, *Expanding Diplomatic Horizon*.

51. Tarō Asō, "Arc of Freedom and Prosperity: Japan's Expanding Diplomatic
Horizons," speech at the Japan Institute of International Affairs Seminar, November 30, 2006, http://www.mofa.go.jp/announce/fm/aso/speech0611.html.

52. Delegation of the European Commission in Japan, "EU Calls for Japan
to Abolish Death Penalty" (press release), February 16, 2001, http://www.deljpn
.ec.europa.eu/home/news_en_newsobj678.php.

53. International Whaling Commission, *Resolution 2007-1*.

54. In the BBC World Public Opinion poll, Japan received majority positive
reviews in both 2008 and 2009, while only 20 percent of respondents viewed Japan's
influence as negative. See BBC World Service Polls, http://www.worldpublicopin
ion.org/pipa/pdf/feb09/BBCEvals_Feb09_rpt.pdf.

55. "Nichi'in kankei [Japan-India Relations]," in Japanese Ministry of Foreign
Affairs, *Gaikō seisho*, 43.

56. For a list of Japanese diplomatic missions, see Japanese Ministry of Foreign
Affairs, http://www.mofa.go.jp.

57. Xiufeng Zhu, "Shixi riben de waijiaozhanlue—Ping 'ziyou yu fanrong zhi
hu' [Tentative Analysis of Japan's Diplomatic Strategy: Comments on the 'Arc of
Freedom and Prosperity']," *China Daily*, July 11, 2007; Xide Jin, "Jiazhiguan waijiao
= Yanse waijiao [Value Diplomacy = Color Diplomacy]," *Guojixianqu Daobao*, December 11, 2006.

58. See, for example, Silu Liu, "Anbei ezhi zhongguo de 'dayazhou' meng
nanyuan [Abe's 'Great Asia' Dream of Containing China Hard to Realize]," *Wenweipo* (Hong Kong), August 25, 2007, http://www.xici.net/u12502659/d57293036
.htm.

59. Hoshiyama, *21seiki nihon gaikō no kadai*, 212; personal conversation with a
senior Japanese diplomat, March 9, 2009.

60. Shinzō Abe, "Japan and NATO: Toward Further Collaboration," speech at
the North Atlantic Council, January 12, 2007, http://www.mofa.go.jp/region/eu
rope/pmv0701/nato.html.

61. Yuzo Saeki, "Japan Economy in Biggest Dive since 1974," *Reuters*, February
16, 2009, http://jp.reuters.com/article/topNews/idUSTRE51F04720090216.

62. Katzenstein, "East Asia."

63. News broadcast, *NHK*, February 24, 2009; *TV Asahi* news broadcast, February 24, 2009.

64. "Ozawa, gi'in 140nin hikii hōchū [Ozawa Leads 140 Lawmakers to
Visit China]," *Nikkei Net*, December 10, 2009, http://www.nikkei.co.jp/news/
seiji/20091211AT3S1001X10122009.html.

65. News broadcast, *NHK*, December 14, 2009.

66. Private conversation with three Japanese diplomats, December 8, 2009.

67. "Naikaku shijiritsu no sui'i [Trajectory of Support for Government]," *Jiji Press*, July 14, 2011, http://www.jiji.com/jc/v?p=ve_pol_cabinet-support-cgraph -past.

68. For a classical work that sees power as having little fungibility, see Keohane and Nye, *Power and Interdependence*. See also Bull, *Anarchical Society*, esp. 108.

69. Ramo, "Beijing Consensus," esp. 3–4.

70. For a review of the evolution of the Beijing consensus as a concept, see Dirlik, "Beijing Consensus."

71. Ibid., 2.

72. Some excellent single-country-based studies on this topic have been conducted. See, for example, Shirk, *China*; Gries, *China's New Nationalism*; Shinoda, *Koizumi Diplomacy*. But few comparative efforts have sought reveal any cross-national pattern and its interactive dimensions.

73. Kang, *Rīdā ha hanppomae wo ayuke*, 170.

74. "316 Confucious Institutes Established Worldwide," *Xinhua News Agency*, http://news.xinhuanet.com/english2010/culture/2010-07/13/c_13398209.htm.

75. Ding and Saunders, "Talking Up China."

76. Gill and Huang, "Sources and Limits."

77. I thank June Teufel Dreyer for sharing this insight with me. See also Leheny, "Narrow Place."

78. See, for example, Wu, *Zai faguo de waijiao shengya*.

79. Joseph Nye, "In Mideast, the Goal Is 'Smart Power,'" *Boston Globe*, August 18, 2006.

80. "Clinton: Use 'Smart Power' in Diplomacy," *CBS News*, January 13, 2009.

81. For a summary of presidential historians' assessments of the Bush presidency, see John Shaw, "George W. Bush's Global Legacy: Consequential but Deeply Flawed," *Washington Diplomat*, December 2009, http://www.washdiplomat.com/ index.php?option=com_content&view=article&id=6320:george-w-bushs-global -legacy-consequential-but-deeply-flawed-&catid=973:january-2009&Itemid=249.

Bibliography

A listing of media sources appears at the end of the this bibliography.

Allen, Christopher S. "Germany." In *Introduction to Comparative Politics: Political Challenges and Changing Agendas*, 5th ed., edited by Mark Kesselman, Joel Krieger, and William Joseph, 157–210. Boston: Wadsworth, 2010.

Amako, Satoshi. "Dui 21shiji zhongriguanxi de jianyi—Zai ganqinglun he zhanlüelun de jiafengjian [Suggestions on Sino-Japanese Relations in the 21st Century—Squeezed between Emotions and Strategies]." Translated by Jianbo Zhang, *Taipingyang Xuebao* [Pacific Journal], no. 8 (2005): 50–60.

Amsden, Alice S. *Asia's Next Giant: South Korea and Late Industrialization*. Oxford: Oxford University Press, 1989.

Arai, Toshiaki. *ASEAN to Nihon: Higashi Ajia keizaiken kōsō no yukue* [ASEAN and Japan: The Trajectory of the Construction of the the East Asian Economic Sphere]. Tokyo: Nicchū, 2003.

Art, Robert. "American Foreign Policy and the Fungibility of Force." *Security Studies* 8, no. 4 (1996): 7–42.

Association of Southeast Asian Nations Secretariat. *ASEAN Statistical Yearbook*. Jakarta: ASEAN Secretariat, 2006.

Baldwin, David. "Power Analysis and World Politics: New Trends vs. Old Tendencies." *World Politics* 31, no. 2 (1979): 161–94.

Barr, Michael D. "Lee Kuan Yew and the Asian Values Debate." *Asian Studies Review* 24, no. 3 (2000): 309–35.

Bull, Hedley. *The Anarchical Society: A Study of Order in World Politics*. New York: Columbia University Press, 1995.

Chang, Dal-joong. "Gurōbaruka to minzokushugika no nagare no nikkan kankei [Japan–South Korea Relations in the Midst of Globalization and Nationalization]." In *Nikkan kyōdō kenkyūgōsho 14 Sengo Nikkan kankei no tenkai* [Unfolding of Postwar Japan–South Korea Relations: Japan–South Korea Joint Research Publication, vol. 14], edited by Masao Okonogi and Dal-joong Chang, 11–34. Tokyo: Keiō University Press, 2005.

Cheng, Ruisheng. *Mulin youhao sishi nian* [Four Decades of Neighborly Friendship]. Chengdu: Sichuan Renmin Chuban, 2006.

Cheng, Yuanxing. *Waijiao wangshi: zhongguo shewai jiaowang miwen* [Diplomatic Memories: Hidden Stories of China's Foreign Affairs]. Beijing: Zuojia Chubanshe, 2006.

Chinese Academy of Social Sciences, Research Center on the History of China's Border Regions. *Introduction to the Northeast Project*. 2007. http://news .qq.com/a/20070501/000458.htm.

Chinese Communist Party Central Archive Bureau. *Deng Xiaoping nianpu (1975– 1997)* [Timeline of Deng Xiaoping (1975–1997)]. Beijing: Central Archive Publishing, 2004.

Chinese Communist Party Central Archive Bureau. *Mao Zedong waijiao wenxuan* [Selection of Mao Zedong's Works on Diplomacy]. Beijing: Central Archive Publishing, 1994.

Chinese Communist Party Central Archive Bureau. *Zhou Enlai nianpu (1949–1976)* [Timeline of Zhou Enlai (1949–1976)]. Beijing: Central Archive Publishing, 1997.

Chinese Communist Party Central Archive Bureau. *Zhou Enlai waijiao wenxuan* [Selection of Zhou Enlai's Works on Diplomacy]. Beijing: Central Archive Publishing, 1990.

Chinese Ministry of Education. *International Students in China*. 2009. http://www .study-in-china.org/ChinaEducation/PolicyLaws/2009726193544754.htm.

Chinese Ministry of Foreign Affairs. *Yafeihuiyi Wenjianxuanji* [Selected Documents of the Asia-Africa Conference]. Beijing: Shijiezhishi Chubanshe, 1955.

Chinese Ministry of Foreign Affairs. *Pro-Active Policies by China in Response to Asian Financial Crisis* (press statement). November 17, 2000. http://www.fmprc.gov .cn/eng/ziliao/3602/3604/t18037.htm.

Chung, Jae Ho. *Between Ally and Partner: Korea-China Relations and the United States.* New York: Columbia University Press, 2006.

Colbert, Evelyn. "Japan and the Republic of Korea: Yesterday, Today, and Tomorrow." *Asian Survey* 26, no. 3 (1986): 273–91.

Deng Xiaoping. *Deng Xiaoping wenxuan* [Selection of Works by Deng Xiaoping]. Beijing: Renmin, 2004.

Deutsch, Karl W., Sidney A. Burrell, and Robert A. Kann. *Political Community and the North Atlantic Area*. Princeton: Princeton University Press, 1957.

De Vries, Reinout E. "Self, In-Group, and Out-Group Evaluation: Bond or Breach?" *European Journal of Social Psychology* 33, no. 5 (2003): 609–21.

Diamond, Larry. *The Spirit of Democracy: The Struggle to Build Free Societies throughout the World*. New York: Times Books, Holt, 2008.

Ding, Shen, and Robert Saunders. "Talking Up China: An Analysis of China's Rising Cultural Power and Global Promotion of the Chinese Language." *East Asia* 23, no. 2 (2006): 3–33.

Dirlik, Arif. "Beijing Consensus: Beijing 'Gongshi': Who Recognizes Whom and to What End?" *Globalization and Autonomy Online Compendium* (2010): 1–8. http:// www.globalautonomy.ca/global1/posiPapers/PP_Dirlik_BeijingConsensus.xml.

Dreyer, June Teufel. *China's Political System: Modernization and Tradition*. 5th ed. New York: Pearson Longman, 2006.

Embassy of the Republic of Korea in China. *Hanzhong jiaoliu tongji* [Statistics of Korea-China Exchanges]. 2009. http://china.koreanembassy.cn/politics/politics_01b.aspx?bm=2&sm=1&fm=1.

Feng, Zhaokui, and Chang Lin. *Zhongri guanxi baogao* [A Report on the China-Japan Relationship]. Beijing: Shishi Chubanshe, 2007.

Ferguson, Niall. "Think Again: Power." *Foreign Policy* 134 (2003): 18–24.

Fraser, Matthew. *Weapons of Mass Distraction: Soft Power and American Empire.* New York: St. Martin's Press, 2005.

Fu, Ying. "Zhongri baleiwaijiao chongxian [Restaging of Sino-Japanese Ballet Diplomacy]." *Shijie xinwenbao* [World News Journal], March 2008. http://world.huanqiu.com/roll/2008–03/68829.html.

Fujisawa, Nobuyuki. *Fujisawa Nobuyuki tsuisō: Ajia ni michi wo motome* [Reflections by Fujisawa Nobuyuki: Quest for the Future in Asia]. Tokyo: Ronsōsha, 1985.

Fukuda, Takeo. *Kaiko kyūjunen* [Ninety Years in Retrospect]. Tokyo: Iwanami Shoten, 1995.

Fukuzawa, Yukichi. "Jiji shōgen" [Brief Comments on Contemporary Issues]. In *Fukuzawa Yukichi chosakushū* [Collection of Fukuzawa Yukichi's Works], vol. 8, edited by Jūrō Iwatani and Shunsaku Nishikawa, 226–29, Tokyo: Keiō University Press, 2003.

Gill, Bates, and Yanzhong Huang. "Sources and Limits of Chinese 'Soft Power.'" *Survival* 48, no. 2 (2006): 17–36.

Goto, Ko'ichi. *Kindai nihon to tonan'ajia: Nanshin no "shōgeki" to "isan"* [Modern Japan and Southeast Asia: Southward Policy's Impact and Legacy]. Tokyo: Iwanami Shoten, 1995.

Green, Michael. *Japan's Reluctant Realism: Foreign Policy Challenges in an Era of Uncertain Power.* New York: Palgrave, 2003.

Gries, Peter Hays. *China's New Nationalism: Pride, Politics, and Diplomacy.* Berkeley: University of California Press, 2005.

Gries, Peter Hays. "The Goguryeo Controversy, National Identity, and Sino-Korean Relations Today." *East Asia* 22, no. 4 (2005): 3–17.

Han, Han. *Guanyu Shanghai waiguoyu daxue Wu Youfu jiaoshou zuo de xuewen* [On the Scholarship by Professor Wu Youfu from Shanghai Foreign Studies University]. 2006. http://tieba.baidu.com/f?kz=152605915.

Han, Kyung-koo. "Nikkan no chiteki kyōryoku to kōryū [Intellectual Cooperations and Exchanges between Japan and South Korea]." In *Nikkan no kyōtsū ninshiki: Nihon wa kankoku nittote nannanoka?* [Japan and South Korea's Common Perception: What Is Japan in the Eyes of South Korea?], edited by Gyeongju Kim and Won-dok Yi, 131–46. Hadano, Kanagawa: Tōkai University Press, 2007.

Harding, Harry. Speech to the first U.S. Foreign Policy Colloquium, organized by the National Committee on U.S.-China Relations at George Washington University, July 2003.

Hatano, Sumio, and Susumu Satō. *Gendai nihon no tō'nan'ajia seisaku: 1950–2005* [Modern Japan's Southeast Asia Policy: 1950–2005]. Tokyo: Waseda University Press, 2007.

Hayashi, Natsuo. "Taishu bunka kōryū kara miru gendai nikkan kankei [Contemporary Japan–South Korea Relations from the Perspective of Mass Cultural Exchanges]." In *Nikkan kyōdō kenkyūgōsho 14: Sengo Nikkan kankei no tenkai*

(Unfolding of Postwar Japan–South Korea Relations: Japan–South Korea Joint Research Publication, vol. 14), edited by Masao Okonogi and Dal-joong Chang, 227–64. Tokyo: Keiō University Press, 2005.

Heaton, William R. "China and Southeast Asian Communist Movements: The Decline of Dual Track Diplomacy." *Asian Survey* 22, no. 8 (1982): 779–800.

Hobbs, Thomas. *Leviathan.* Oxford: Clarendon, 1909.

Hong, Jun. *Zhuxi yu ligu zhexue bijiao yanjiu* [Comparative Study of Zhu Xi's and Kuritani's Philosophical Thoughts]. Shanghai: Fudan University Press, 2003.

Hoshiyama, Takashi. *21seiki nihon gaikō no kadai: Taichūgaikō, ajia gaikō, gurōbaru gaikō* [Japan's Diplomatic Challenges in the 21st Century: China Diplomacy, Asia Diplomacy, and Global Diplomacy]. Tokyo: Sōfūsha, 2008.

Hosokawa, Shūhei, and Akiko Otake. "Karaoke in East Asia: Modernization, Japanization, or Asianization." In *Karaoke around the World: Global Technology, Local Singing,* edited by Tōru Mitusi and Shūhei Hosokawa, 173–96. London: Routledge, 1998.

Hu, Changming. *Zhou Enlai molüe daquan* [Complete Collection of Zhou Enlai's Strategies]. Xining: Qinghai People's Publishing, 1996.

Huang, Dahui. *Riben daguohua qushi he zhongriguanxi* [Japan's Power Build-Up and Sino-Japanese Relations]. Beijing: Social Sciences and Academic Press, 2008.

Human Rights Watch. "North Korea: Ending Food Aid Would Deepen Hunger." 2006. http://www.hrw.org/en/news/2006/10/09/north-korea-ending-food-aid-would-deepen-hunger.

In, Chun-go. *Jitsuroku: Shin'nichiha* [On the Record: Pro-Japan Faction]. Seoul: Torabege, 1991.

International Whaling Commission. *Resolution 2007-1: Resolution on JARPA.* 2007. http://iwcoffice.org/meetings/resolutions/Resolution2007-1.pdf.

Ishida, Yuji. "Cultural Genocide and the Japanese Occupation of Korea." Speech at Comparative Genocide Studies workshop, November 23, 2004. http://www.cgs.c.u-tokyo.ac.jp/workshops_e/w_2004_02_23_e.html.

Itō, Yō'ichi, and Takeshi Kōno, eds. *Nyūsūhōdō to shimin no taigaikoku'ishiki* [News Coverage and Citizens' Perception of Foreign Countries]. Tokyo: Keiō University Press, 2008.

Japanese Cabinet Office. *Gaikō ni kansuru yoron chōsa* [Annual Survey on Foreign Policy]. http://www8.cao.go.jp/survey/h21/h21-gaiko/2-1.html.

Japanese Diet Archive, nos. 140–45. 1995. http://kokkai.ndl.go.jp/SENTAKU/syu giin/140/0380/14002030380005a.html.

Japanese Ministry of Foreign Affairs. *Expanding Diplomatic Horizon.* 2009. http://www.mofa.go.jp/mofaj/gaiko/free_pros/pdfs/shiryo_01.pdf.

Japanese Ministry of Foreign Affairs. *Gaikō seisho* [Diplomacy Blue Book]. 1978, 2008.

Japanese Ministry of Foreign Affairs. *Key Notes of Meeting by Ambassadors to Southeast Asia,* March 12, 1973.

Japanese Ministry of Foreign Affairs. *Ni-ASEAN shuyōkyōryoku jigō* [Japan's Major Assistance Projects in ASEAN]. 2008. http://www.mofa.go.jp/mofaj/area/asean/j_asean/ja_skj_03.html.

Japanese Ministry of Foreign Affairs. *Nihon gaikō shuyō monshu nenhyō—2* [Major Documents and Chronology of Japanese Diplomacy—2], 1965.

Japanese Ministry of Foreign Affairs. *Proceedings of the Second Meeting on November 9, 1954.* Document A0136.

Japanese Ministry of Foreign Affairs. *Surveys on Southeast Asian Countries' Public Attitude toward Japan.* 2008. http://www.mofa.go.jp/mofaj/area/asean/pdfs/yoron08_02.pdf.

Japanese Ministry of Foreign Affairs. *Tanaka sōri no tō'nan'ajia gokkakoku hōmon ni tsu'ite* [On Prime Minister Tanaka's Visit to the Five Countries in Southeast Asia]. Document A433, January 23, 1974.

Japanese Ministry of Foreign Affairs. *Tokyo Declaration on Japan-ASEAN Partnership.* December 11, 2003. http://www.mofa.go.jp/mofaj/kaidan/s_koi/asean_03/sengen.html.

Japanese Politics and International Relations Database. *Nikkan kaidan "Kuboda Hatsugen" ni kansuru sangi'in suisan i'inkai shitsugi* [Senate Fishing Committee Questioning on "Kuboda Speech" at Japan–South Korea Negotiation]. University of Tokyo, 2009. http://www.ioc.u-tokyo.ac.jp/~worldjpn/documents/texts/JPKR/19531027.O1J.html.

Ji, Dongwok. *Kankoku daitōryo retten: Kenryokusha no eika to tenraku* [Biographies of South Korean Presidents: Rise and Fall of Power Holders]. Tokyo: Chuō, 2002.

Jiang, Lifeng. "Zhongri lianhe jinxingde shehui yulun diaocha [Survey of Public Opinion on the Progress of China-Japan Relations]." In *Riben Wenti* [Issues of Japan] 2 (1989). http://www.cnki.com.cn/Article/CJFDTotal-REED198902003.htm.

Jiang, Zemin. *Jiang Zemin wenxuan* [Selected Works by Jiang Zemin]. Beijing: Renmin Shuban, 2006.

Jin, Zhongji. *Zhou Enlai zhuan: 1949–1976* [Biography of Zhou Enlai: 1949–1976]. Beijing: Central Archive Publishing, 1998.

Jupp, James. "Tacking into the Wind: Immigration and Multicultural Policy in the 1990s." *Journal of Australian Studies,* no. 53 (1997): 25–35.

Kane, Robert G. "The Potential Futures of the U.S.-China-Japan Nexus." *Orbis: A Journal of World Affairs* 52, no. 4 (2008): 701–12.

Kang, Sang-jung. *Rīdā ha hanppomae wo ayuke: Kim Dae-jung toiu hinto* [Leaders Need to Take Half a Step Ahead: Kim Dae-jung's Hint]. Tokyo: Shūeisha, 2009.

Karaki, Kunikazu. "Chūgoku no taigaikaihō seisaku to tōnan'ajia bō'eki [China's Open-Door Policy and Trade with Southeast Asia]." In *Tō'nan'ajia ni okeru chūgoku no imeiji to eikyōryoku* [China's Image and Influence in Southeast Asia], edited by Saburō Matsumoto and Kunie Kawamoto, 392–427. Tokyo: Taishūkan shoten, 1991.

Katō, Junpei. *Japan's Cultural Exchange: In Pursuit of New Ideals.* Tokyo: Simul, 1988.

Katō, Kō'ichi. "Aji'a no seiki'no nicchūkankei [Japan-China Relations in the Asian Century]." In *Higashi Aji'a: Nihon ga towareteirukoto* [When Japan Was Questioned by East Asia], edited by Matsumura Takao and Takakusa Gikō'ichi, 55–66. Tokyo: Iwanami Shoten, 2007.

Katz, Richard. *Japan: The System That Soured: The Rise and Fall of the Japanese Economic Miracle.* Armonk, NY: Sharpe, 1998.

Katzenstein, Peter J. "East Asia—Beyond Japan." In *Beyond Japan: The Dynamics of East Asian Regionalism,* edited by Peter J. Katzenstein and Takashi Shiraishi, 1–36. Ithaca: Cornell University Press, 2006.

Kawashima, Yutaka. *Japanese Foreign Policy at the Crossroads: Challenges and Options for the Twenty-First Century.* Washington, DC: Brookings Institution Press, 2003.

Kazankai Foundation. *Nicchū kankei kihon shiryōshū* [Collection of Major Archives on Japan-China Relations]. Tokyo: Kazankai Foundation, 1970.

Keohane, Robert O. *After Hegemony: Cooperation and Discord in the World Economy.* Princeton: Princeton University Press, 1984.

Keohane, Robert O., and Joseph Nye. *Power and Interdependence: World Politics in Transition.* Boston: Little, Brown, 1977.

Khalid, Khadijah Md., and Poh Ping Lee. *Whither the Look East Policy.* Banji, Malaysia: Penerbit Ukm, 2003.

Kim, Young-jak. "Nihon(jin) toha Kankoku(jin) nitotte nan'nanoka? [To Korea (the Koreans), What Is Japan (What Are the Japanese)?]." In *Nikkan no kyōtsū'ninshiki Nihon ha kankoku nitotte nan'nanoka?* [Japan and South Korea's Common Perception: What Is Japan in the Eyes of South Korea?], edited by Gyeongju Kim and Won-dok Yi, 3–21. Hadano, Kanagawa: Tōkai University Press, 2007.

Kim, Yung-sik. "Problems and Possibilities in the Study of the History of Korean Science." *Osiris*, 2nd ser., 13 (1998): 48–79.

Kimiya, Tadashi. "Nikkan kankei no rikigaku to tenbō: reisenki no dainamizumu to tatsureisenki ni okeru kōzōhenyō [Political Dynamics of South Korea–Japan Relations and Its Prospects: From the Cold War toward the Post–Cold War]." *Shakai kagaku jānaru* [Journal of Social Science] II-B, no. 61 (2007): 5–25.

Kirshner, Jonathan. "States, Markets, and Great Power Relations in the Pacific: Some Realist Expectations." In *East Asian International Relations and the Asia Pacific*, edited by John G. Ikenberry and Michael Mastunduno, 273–98. New York: Columbia University Press, 2003.

Kishi, Nobusuke. *Kishi Nobusuke kaikoroku: hoshugōdō to anpokaitei* [Kishi Nobusuke's Memoir: Conservative Contract and Security-Alliance Reform]. Tokyo: Kōsaidō, 1983.

Koizumi, Jun'ichirō. "Japan and ASEAN in East Asia: A Sincere and Open Partnership." Speech delivered to the Institute of Southeast Asian Studies and published as *Singapore Lecture Series.* Singapore: Institute of Southeast Asian Studies, 2002. http://www.asean.org/2802.htm.

Kondo, Daisuke. *Nihon, chūgoku, kankoku: Juntōmeikankei* [Japan, China, South Korea: The Era of Quasi-Alliance]. Tokyo: Kobunsha, 2009.

Konno, Shigemitsu. "Sofuto pawā to nihon no senryaku [Soft Power and Japan's Strategy]." In *Imehji no naka no nihon: Sofuto pawā saikō* [Japan in Perception: Revisiting Soft Power], edited by Nobuto Yamamoto and Yutaka Ō'ish, 1–16. Tokyo: Keiō University Press, 2008.

Kōnō, Masao. *Heiwa kōsaku: Tai kanbojia gaikō no shōgen* [Work toward Peace: Testimony on Diplomacy toward Cambodia]. Tokyo: Iwanami Shoten, 1999.

Korea International Trade Association. *Statistics Bulletin.* 2009. http://www.kita.org.

Koschmann, J. Victor. "Asianism's Ambivalent Legacy." In *Network Power: Japan and Asia*, edited by Peter J. Katzenstein and Takashi Shiraishi, 83–110. Ithaca: Cornell University Press, 1997.

Krauss, Ellis, and Priscilla Lambert. "The Press and Japan's Attempts at Political and Administrative Reform." *Harvard International Journal of Press and Politics* 7, no. 1 (2002): 57–78.

Kurlantzick, Joshua. *Charm Offensive: How China's Soft Power Is Transforming the World.* New Haven: Yale University Press, 2007.

Kusuda, Minoro. "U.S.-Japanese Relations and the Nixon Shocks, 1969–1976." Remarks at Woodrow Wilson International Center for Scholars, the Smithsonian Institution, March 11, 1996. http://www.gwu.edu/~nsarchiv/japan/kusuda .htm.

Lee, Gee-won. "Japan's Expansionist Cultural Policy and Problems on the Penetration of Japanese Culture into Korea." In *New Japanese Hegenomism and Korea-Japan Relations,* edited by Shin Yon-hwa, 171–264. Seoul: Kim Yon, 1993.

Leheny, David. "A Narrow Place to Cross Swords: Soft Power and the Politics of Japanese Popular Culture in East Asia." In *Beyond Japan: The Dynamics of East Asian Regionalism,* edited by Peter J. Katzenstein and Takashi Shiraishi, 211–71. Ithaca: Cornell University Press, 2005.

Li, Yanhui. "Zhanhou zhongguo yu yinni de guanxi [Postwar Relations between China and Indonesia]." *Dongnanya Yanjiu* [Southeast Asian Studies], no. 4 (1991): 49–56.

Liberal Democratic Party of Japan. "Period of President Ikeda's Leadership." 2005. http://www.jimn.jp/jimin/english/history/chap4.html.

Lilley, James R. Speech to the Graduate School of International Studies at the University of Denver, February 12, 2007.

Lim, Jie-hyun. "The Antagonistic Complicity of Nationalisms—On 'Nationalist Phenomenology' in East Asian History Textbooks." In *Contested Views of Common Past: Revisions of History in Contemporary East Asia,* edited by Steffi Richter, Frankfurt: Campus, 2008. http://www.culturahistorica.es/lim/complicity_na tionalisms.pdf.

Lim, Philip Wonhyuk. "The Asian Values Debate Revisited: Positive and Normative *Dimensions.*" *Korea Journal* 40, no. 2 (2000): 365–85.

Lin, Daizhao. *Zhanghou zhongri guanxi shi* [History of Postwar China-Japan Relations]. Translated by Hideo Watanabe. Tokyo: UNI, 1992.

Lin, Zhenjiang. *Shounao waijiao* [Summit Diplomacy]. Beijing: Xinhua, 2008.

Liu, Jinzhi, Jingchu Pan, Rongying Pan, and Xiyu Li, eds. *Zhongguo yu chaoxian bandaoguojia guanxi wenjianziliao huibian: 1991–2006* [Collective Archive of Documents on China's Relations with Countries on the Korean Peninsula: 1991–2006]. Beijing: Shijiezhishi Chubanshe, 2007.

Liu, Wanzhen, and Qinggui Li. *Mao Zedong guoji jiaowang lu* [Record of Mao Zedong's Diplomatic Activities]. Beijing: Central Party History Publishing, 2008. http://www.uus8.com/BOOK/html/type2/09/02/10/009.htm.

Ma, Yong. "Li Guangyao de ribenguan [Lee Kuan Yew's View on Japan]." *Dongnanya Yanjiu* [Southeast Asian Studies], no. 2 (1996): 12–17.

Machiavelli, Niccolò. *The Prince.* Translated by N. H. Thomson, New York: Collier, 1910.

Mahathir bin Mohamad. *The Malay Dilemma.* Singapore: Asia Pacific, 1970.

Manabe, Kazufumi. "Nihonjin no chūgoku imēji: Ten'anmon jiken go no henka no kiseki [China's Image in Japanese Eyes: Post-Tiananmen Incident Trajectory]." *Yoron,* no. 66 (1990): 7–8.

Mao, Zedong. *Mao Zedong waijiao wenxuan* [Selection of Mao Zedong's Works on Diplomacy]. Beijing: Central Archive Publishing, 1994.

Mao, Zedong. *Mao Zedong wenxuan disijuan* [Mao Zedong's Works]. Vol. 4. Beijing: Renmin Chubanshe, 1996.

Mao, Zedong. *Selected Works of Mao Tse-tung*. Vol. 4. Beijing: Foreign Languages Press, 1969.

Matsumoto, Saburō. *Chūgokugaikō to tō'nan'ajia* [Chinese Diplomacy and Southeast Asia]. Tokyo: Keiō University Press, 1971.

McGray, Douglas. "Japan's Gross National Cool." *Foreign Policy* 130 (2002): 44–54.

Meng, Honghua. "Yali, renzhi yu guojixingxiang: Guanyu zhongguo canyu guoji zhidu zhanlüe de lishi jieshi [Press, Perception, and International Image: A Historical Explanation of China's Strategy on Participating International Institutions]." In *Zhongguo xuezhe kan shijie: Di si juan* [World Politics: Views from China], edited by Jun Nie, 4:157–69. Beijing: New World Press, 2006.

Miyagi, Taisō. *Sengo ajia chitsujo no mosaku to nihon: Umi no ajia no sengoshi, 1957–1966* [Exploration of Postwar Asian Order and Japan: A Postwar History of Maritime Asia, 1957–1966]. Tokyo: Sōbunsha, 2004.

Miyamoto, Kenji. *Nihon kakumei no tenbō* [Outlook for Japan's Revolution]. Tokyo: Shin'nihon shinsho, 1967.

Mochizuki, Mike M. "American and Japanese Strategic Debates: The Need for a New Synthesis." In *Toward a True Alliance: Restructuring U.S.-Japan Security Relations*, edited by Mike Mochizuki, 43–82. Washington, DC: Brookings Institution Press, 1997.

Mondejar, Reuben, and Wai Lung Chu. "ASEAN-China Relations: Legacies and Future Directions." In *China and Southeast Asia: Global Changes and Regional Challenges*, edited by Khai Leong Ho and Samuel C. Y. Ku, 211–27. Singapore: Institute of Southeast Asian Studies, 2005.

Nakamura, Katsunori, Kazuo Asano, Zhaotang Huang, and Hitoshi Tokuoka, eds. *Zoku: Unmeikyōdōtai toshite no Nihon to Taiwan* [Sequel: Japan and Taiwan as Destiny Community]. Tokyo: Waseda, 2005.

Nakasone, Yasuhiro, and Seisaburō Satō. *Tenchiyūjō: Gojū'nen no sengo seiji wo kataru* [History Has Passions: On Fifty Years of Postwar Politics]. Tokyo: Bungei shunjū, 1996.

Nam, Ki-jeoing. "Kankoku minzokushugi no tenkai to nikkan kankei [Development of South Korean Nationalism and Japan–South Korea Relations]." In *Nikkan no kyōtsū ninshikii: Nihon wa kankoku nittote nannanoka?* [Japan and South Korea's Common Perception: What Is Japan in the Eyes of South Korea?], edited by Gyeongju Kim and Won-dok Yi, 91–130. Hadano, Kanagawa: Tōkai University Press, 2007.

Nye, Joseph. *Soft Power: The Means to Success in World Politics*. New York: Public Affairs, 2004.

Office of the Korean Prime Minister. "Early Joseon Period." http://www.opm.go.kr/warp/webapp/content/view?meta_id=english&id=62.

Ogata, Sadako. *Normalization with China: A Comparative Study of U.S. and Japanese Processes*. Berkeley: University of California Press, 1989.

Ogura, Kizō. "Nikkan no shutaiteki jikoishiki to rekishi nin'shiki mondai [Japan and South Korea's Autonomous Self-identity Mentality and Problems of Historical Recognition." In *Nikkan no kyōtsū ninshiki: Nihon wa kankoku nittote nannanoka?* [Japan and South Korea's Common Perception: What Is Japan in the Eyes of South Korea?], edited by Gyeongju Kim and Won-dok Yi, 73–88. Hadano, Kanagawa: Tōkai University Press, 2007.

O'Neil, Patrick H., Karl Fields, and Don Share, eds. "Germany." In *Cases in Comparative Politics*, 3rd ed., 157–99. New York: Norton, 2010.

Otmazgin, Nissim Kadosh. "Contesting Soft Power: Japanese Popular Culture in East and Southeast Asia." *International Relations of the Asia-Pacific* 8, no. 1 (2007): 73–101.

Park, Cheol-on. *Nikkan kōryū kagede sasaeta otoko—Park Cheol-on no jinsei* [The Man Who Supports Japan–South Korea Exchanges: Life of Park Cheol-on]. Tokyo: Sankei Shimbun, 2005.

Park, Sun-eh, and Reiko Tsuchiya, eds. *Nihon taishūbunka to nikkan kankei: Kankoku wakamono no nihon imehji* [Japanese Popular Culture and Japan-Korean Relations: The Japanese Image among the Korean Youth]. Tokyo: Sangensha, 2002.

Qian, Qichen. *Waijiao shiji* [Ten Notes on Diplomacy]. Beijing: Shijiezhishi Chubanshe, 2007.

Qiao, Linsheng. *Riben duiwaizhengce yu dongmeng* [Japan's Foreign Policy and ASEAN]. Beijing: Renmin Chubanshe, 2006.

Qin, Yaqing. "Shijie gejü yu zhongguo waijiao [Global Pattern and Chinese Diplomacy]." Speech delivered to the Guangzhou Forum, May 26, 2005. http://wenku.baidu.com/view/df20f636f111f18583d05a9e.html.

Ramo, Joshua Cooper. "The Beijing Consensus: Notes on the New Physics of Chinese Power." *Foreign Policy Centre* (2004): 1–74. http://fpc.org.uk/fsblob/244.pdf.

"Record of Historic Richard Nixon–Zhou Enlai Talks in February 1972 Now Declassified." 2010. http://www.gwu.edu/~nsarchiv/nsa/publications/DOC_readers/kissinger/nixzhou/.

Ruan, Hong. *Zhonghan jieji waijiao: Zhuo Changren jieji'an yu hancheng tanpan neimu* [Hijacking Diplomacy between China and the ROK: The Case of Zhuo Changren's Hijacking and What Is behind the Negotiations in Seoul]. Beijing: Dangdai Chubanshe, 2009.

Russett, Bruce. "The Mysterious Case of Vanishing Hegemony; or, Is Mark Twain Really Dead?" *International Organization* 39, no. 2 (1985): 207–31.

Sai'onji, Kazuteru. "Inshōbukai Shūonraisōri no hanashi [Premier Zhou's Impressive Remarks]." In *Kiroku to kōshō: Nicchū seijōka, nicchū yūkō jōyaku teiketsu kōshō* [Documentation and Investigation on Japan-China Normalization and Negotiation on Japan-China Peace and Friendship Treaty], edited by Ishii Akira, Jianrong Zhu, Soeya Yoshihide, and Lin Xiaoguang, 249–55. Tokyo: Iwanami Shoten, 2003.

Sasaki, Masaharu. "Commercial Cultivation of Tradition." Paper presented at the Japanese Academic Society for Ventures and Entrepreneurs, 2007. http://www.venture-ac.ne.jp/seminar/detail/20070115155330.html.

Schneider, Cynthia P. *Culture Communicates: U.S. Diplomacy That Works*. 2004. http://www.clingendael.nl/publications/2004/20040300_cli_paper_dip_issue94.pdf.

Shambaugh, David. "China and Japan towards the Twenty-First Century: Rivals for Pre-Eminence or Complex Interdependence?" In *China and Japan: History, Trends, and Prospects*, edited by Christopher Howe, 83–97. Oxford: Clarendon, 1996.

Shiba, Ryōtarō. *Taiwan kikō* [Travel Essays: Taiwan]. Tokyo: Asahi Shimbun, 2005.

Shimane Prefectural Government. "Rontenseiri: Kindai kara gendai he [Overview of Arguments: From the Recent Past to the Contemporary]." *Kensei Kōhōshi* [Prefecture Chronicle]. 2009. http://www.pref.shimane.lg.jp/kochokoho/photo/161/.

Shimokawa, Kōshi. *Showa Heisei kateishi nenhyō* [Chronology of Family History during the Showa and Heisei Eras]. Tokyo: Katei Sōgōkenkyukai, 2001.

Shinoda, Tomohito. *Koizumi Diplomacy: Japan's Kantei Approach to Foreign and Defense Affairs.* Seattle: University of Washington Press, 2007.

Shirk, Susan L. *China: Fragile Superpower—How China's Internal Politics Could Derail Its Peaceful Rise.* New York: Oxford University Press, 2007.

Shu, Yun. "1970nian guoqingdadian Mao Zedong weihe yaoqing Sinuo shang tian'anmen? [Why Did Mao Zedong Invite Snow onto the Tian'anmen Gate at the 1970 National Independence Celebration Ceremony?]." *Zhong Qing Zai Xian*, October 17, 2007. http://news.163.com/07/1019/11/3R5NS HGU00011232_2.html.

Skeldon, Ronald, ed. *Reluctant Exiles or Bold Pioneers: Migration from Hong Kong and the New Overseas Chinese.* Armonk, NY: Sharpe, 1994.

Song, Xiaojun, Xiaodong Wang, Qiang Song, Jisu Huang, and Yang Liu. *Zhongguo bugaoxing: Dashidai damubiao ji women de neiyouwaihuan* [China Is Unhappy: The Great Time, Grand Vision, and Our Challenges]. Nanjing: Phoenix and Jiangsu Renmin Chubanshe, 2009.

Stuart-Fox, Martin. "Communism and the Cold War." In *China and Southeast Asia*, vol. 6, *The People's Republic of China and Southeast Asia*, edited by Geoff Wade, 1–27. London: Routledge, 2008.

Stuart-Fox, Martin. *A Short History of China and Southeast Asia: Tribute, Trade, and Influence.* Crows Nest, NSW: Allen and Unwin, 2003.

Subramaniam, Surain. "The Asian Values Debate: Implications for the Spread of Democracy." *Asian Affairs* 27, no. 1 (2000): 19–35.

Sun, Jing. "China as Funhouse Mirror: How Japanese National Dailies Watch China and Japan-China Relations, 1949–2004." Ph.D. diss., University of Wisconsin at Madison, 2005.

Sun, Jing. "China as Funhouse Mirror: The *Yomiuri Shimbun's* China Coverage during the Cultural Revolution." *Japanese Studies* 28, no. 2 (2008): 179–96.

Sun, Jing. "Covering a Non-Democracy: Analysis of Japanese Newspapers' Portrayals of China and Implications for Media Balancing." *International Journal of Communication* 1 (2007): 717–37.

Sun, Weiguo. *Daming qihao yü xiaozhonghua yishi—Chaoxian wangchao zunzhousiming wenti yanjiu (1637–1800)* [Great Ming's Banner Identity and Little China Mentality—Research on Korean Dynasties' Respect for Zhou and Ming Dynasties (1637–1800)]. Beijing: Shangwu Yinshuguan, 2007.

Suryadinata, Leo. "'Overseas Chinese.'" In *Southeast Asia and China's Foreign Policy: An Interpretive Essay.* Research Notes and Discussion Paper 11. Singapore: Institute of Southeast Asian Studies, 1978.

Suzuki, Kenji. *Nashonarisumu to masukomi* [Nationalism and Mass Media]. Tokyo: Iwanami Shoten, 1997.

Takeiri, Yoshikatsu. "Rekishi no haguruma ga mawatta, nagarekimeta Shū shushō no handan [Premier Zhou's Decision Determines the Moving Forward of History]." In *Kiroku to kōshō: Nicchū seijōka, nicchū yūkō jōyaku teiketsu kōshō* [Documentation and Investigation on Japan-China Normalization and Negotiation on Japan-China Peace and Friendship Treaty], edited by Akira Ishii, Jianrong Zhu, Yoshihide Soeya, and Xiaoguang Lin, 197–211. Tokyo: Iwanami Shoten, 2003.

Tanaka, Hitoshi, and Sō'ichirō Tahara. *Kokka to gaikō* [Country and Diplomacy]. Tokyo: Kōdansha, 2007.

Tarō, Asō. "A New Look at Cultural Diplomacy: A Call to Japan's Cultural Practitioners." Speech at Digital Hollywood University, Tokyo, April 28, 2006. http://www.mofa.go.jp/announce/fm/aso/speech0604–2.html.

Thand, Leng Leng, and S. K. Gan. "Deconstructing Japanisation: Reflections from the 'Learn from Japan' Campaign in Singapore." *New Zealand Journal of Asian Studies* 5, no.1 (2003): 91–106.

Tian, Heng, ed. *Zhanhou zhongriguanxi wenxianji* [Collection of Archives on Postwar China-Japan Relations]. Beijing: Chinese Academy of Social Sciences, 1997.

Tori'i, Tami. *Kōtakumin no sensō: "Hannichi"de ikinobiru chūgoku* [Jiang Zemin's War: A China that Hangs in by Hating Japan]. Tokyo: Sōshisha, 2004.

Tosa, Masaki. *Kawaru kankoku kawaranai kankoku* [Changing Korea, Unchanging Korea]. Tokyo: Yōsensha, 2004.

Tsai, Chin-tang. "Nihon tōchi jidai to kokumintō tōchi jidai ni matagatta taiwanjin no nihonkan [Taiwanese Perceptions of Japan during the Japanese and the Kuomintang Eras]." In *Sengō Taiwan ni okeru Nihon: Shokuminchikeiken no renzoku, henmō, riyō* [Japan in Taiwan's Postwar World: Continuity, Change, and Application of Colonial Experience], edited by Masako Igarashi and Yūko Mio, 19–59. Tokyo: Fukyōsha, 2006.

Tu, Zhen. "Zhou Enlai yu Mei Lanfang Ersanshi [A Few Anecdotes between Zhou Enlai and Mei Lanfang." *Renwu* [People], March 2008. http://news.sina.com.cn/c/2008–03–19/141615181247.shtml.

Uchida, Yoshihisa. *Nittai kankei: daijōbu ka? Taiwandaishi no honneroku* [Are Japan-Taiwan Relations Going OK? True Voice of Ambassador to Taiwan]. Tokyo: Sankei Shimbunsha, 2006.

U.S. Department of State. "Asia and the Pacific (in Two Parts)." In U.S. Department of State, *Foreign Relations of United States, 1951.* http://digital.library.wisc.edu/1711.dl/FRUS.FRUS1951v06p1.

U.S. Department of State. "China and Japan (in Two Parts)." In U.S. Department of State, *Foreign Relations of United States, 1952–1954.* http://digital.library.wisc.edu/1711.dl/FRUS.FRUS195254v14p2.

U.S. Department of State. *Dictionary of International Relations Terms.* 3rd ed. Washington, DC: U.S. Department of State Library, 1987.

U.S. Energy Information Administration. *World Oil Transit Chokepoints.* 2008. http://www.eia.doe.gov/emeu/cabs/World_Oil_Transit_Chokepoints/Background.html.

Wakabayashi, Masahiro. "Taiwanese Nationalism and 'Unforgettable Others.'" In *China's Rise, Taiwan's Dilemmas, and International Peace*, edited by Edward Friedman, 3–21. London: Routledge, 2006.

Wan, Ming. *Sino-Japanese Relations: Interaction, Logic, and Transformation*. Stanford: Stanford University Press, 2008.

Wang, Gungwu. "Early Ming Relations with Southeast Asia: A Background Essay." In *The Chinese World Order,* edited by J. K. Fairbanks, 34–62. Cambridge: Cambridge University Press, 1968.

Wang, Shuo. "Teshiteban: Hu Yaobang yu jingjitequ [Special Occasions Demand Special Measures: Hu Yaobang and the Special Economic Zones]." *Yanhuang Chunqiu,* no. 4 (2008): 36–40.

Wang, Weibin. *Chūgoku to Nihon no gaikō seisaku: 1950 nendai wo chūshin ni mita kokkō seijōka he no purosesū* [China and Japan's Foreign Policy: Process toward Normalization with the 1950s as the Focus]. Kyoto: Minervashobō, 2004.

Wang, Yongxiang, and Qiaoqiang Gao, eds. *Shū Onrai to Nihon: Kunō kara hishō he no seishun* [Zhou Enlai and Japan: A Youth from Despair to Soaring]. Tokyo: Hakuteisha, 2002.

Watanabe, Yasushi, and David McConnell, eds. *Soft Power Superpowers: Cultural and National Assets of Japan and the United States.* London: Sharpe, 2008.

Wen, Beiyan. "Zhongguo-yinni zhanlue huobanguanxi de xianzhuang he zhanwang [The Current Situation and Future Prospects of Strategic Partnership between China and Indonesia]." *Dongnanya Yanjiu* [Southeast Asian Studies], no. 1 (2007): 2–43.

Wen, Jiabao. Speech at the annual press conference at the conclusion of the second session of the Tenth National People's Congress, March 14, 2004. http://www.gov.cn/english/official/2005-07/26/content_17183.htm.

Whiting, Allen S. *China Eyes Japan.* Berkeley: University of California Press, 1989.

Wu, Jianmin. *Zai faguo de waijiao shengya* [My Diplomatic Career in France]. Shanghai: Sanlian, 2006.

Xu, Shanbao. "Zhongguo dongmeng guanxi sishinian fazhan de licheng jiqi qishi: Gongtong liyi de shijiao [The Development of China-ASEAN Relations in the Past Forty Years and Its Inspiration: From a Perspective of 'Common Interests']." *Dongnanya Yanjiu* [Southeast Asian Studies], no. 3 (2007): 54–59.

Xu, Xianfen. "Shoupi duihua riyuandaikuan de zhongri jueceyuanyin [Reasons Behind Sino-Japanese Decision on Japan's First ODA to China]." *Zhongguo yu Riben de Tazherenshi* [China and Japan's Mutual Perception as the "Other"], 202–33, Beijing: Shehui kexue wenxian chubanshe, 2004.

Yabuki, Susumu. "Nicchū gokai wa 'meiwaku' ni hajimaru: Kokkōseijōka 30 shū'nen zenya no shōkō [Misunderstanding between Japan and China Started as 'Causing Inconvenience'—A Short Contemplation Prior to the 30th Anniversary of Normalization of Relations]." Paper presented at the Japan-China Communication Studies Seminar, Beijing, November 23, 2001. http://www.21ccs.jp/china_quarterly/China_Quarterly_01.html.

Yamamoto, Nobuto, and Yusuke Takagi. "Tō'nan'ajia shokoku no nihon imehji saikō [Revisiting Southeast Asian Countries' Perceptions of Japan]." In *Imēji no naka no nihon: Sofuto pawā saikō* [Japan in Perception: Revisiting Soft Power], edited by Nobuto Yamamoto and Yutaka Ō'ishi, 155–86. Tokyo: Keiō University Press, 2008.

Yanagimachi, Isao. "Sengo nikkan kankei no keisei to sono keizaiteki sokumen—Niraitetachi no kōdō wo chūshin ni [The Formation of Japan-Korea Relations and Its Economic Aspect: The Role of Key Persons]." *Keizaigaku Kenkyū* [Journal of Political Economy] 71, no. 1 (2004): 51–72.

Yang, Jun. *Zhongguo yu chaoxian bandao guanxi shilun* [On the History of the Relationship between China and the Korean Peninsula]. Beijing: Shehuikexue Wenxian Chubanshe, 2006.

Yi, Won-dok. "Rekishi mondai wo meguru nikkan no kattō mekanizumu [Mechanism of the Japan–South Korea Dispute on Historical Problems]." In *Nikkan no kyōtsū ninshiki: Nihon wa kankoku nittote nannanoka?* [Japan and South Korea's Common Perception: What Is Japan in the Eyes of South Korea?], edited by Gyeongju Kim and Won-dok Yi, 25–88. Hadano, Kanagawa: Tōkai University Press, 2007.

Yoshida, Shigeru. *Kaisō jū'nen* [Ten Years in Retrospect]. Tokyo: Shinchōsha, 1957.

Yoshida, Shigeru. *Nihon wo kettei shita hyakunen* [The One Hundred Years That Shaped Japan]. Tokyo: Chūkōbunko, 1999.

Yu, Tianren. *Bing yan kan riben: 15nian liuri de guancha he sikao* [Japan in the Eyes of a Calm Observer: Observations and Thoughts during My 15-Year-Long Stay]. Beijing: Yuwen Chubanshe, 2009. http://military.china.com/zh_cn/history4/news3/11078476/20091102/15687321_1.html.

Zha, Daojiong, and Weixing Hu. *Building a Neighborly Community: Post–Cold War China, Japan, and Southeast Asia*. Manchester: Manchester University Press, 2006.

Zhang, Xizhen. "Dang qian taiguoren de zhongguoguan [How Contemporary Thais View China]." *Dongnanya Yanjiu* [Southeast Asian Studies], no. 6 (2007): 58–62.

Zhang, Xizhen. "Zhongtai guanxi sishinian [Forty Years of Sino-Thai Relations]." *Dongnanya Yanjiu* [Southeast Asian Studies], no. 2 (1990): 1–12.

Zhao, Boyuan. "Pengzhuangzhong de zhonghan minzuzhiyi [Chinese and Korean Nationalism on Colliding Course]." *Nanfengchuang*, May 30, 2008. http://www.nfcmag.com/articles/825.

Zhao, Boyuan. "Zhonghan guanxi xiubu shengji [Efforts to Repair China-ROK Relations Escalate]." *Nanfengchuang*, September 22, 2008. http://www.nfcmag.com/articles/1064.

Zhou, Ke. "Yaobang tongzhi bang wo pingfan [Comrade Yaobang Helps Me Regain Justice]." In *Fengyu qishinian: shidai dachao zhong de wo he wode yijia* [Seven Decades of Ups and Downs: My Family and I Through Trends of Our Time], edited by Ke Zhou and Xunzhong Gu, 279–83. Shanghai: Wenhui Chubanshe, 2006.

Zhou, Mingwei, ed. *Guojia xingxiang yanjiu luncong* [Collective Research on the Spread of the State Image]. Beijing: Foreign Languages Press, 2008.

MEDIA

Agence France Presse, 2008–11.
Asahi Shimbun (朝日新聞), 1954–2006.
Associated Press, 2008.
BBC World Service, 2006–9.
Boston Globe, 2006.
CBS News, 2009.
Central News Agency (Taiwan/中央社), 2009.

Chengdushangbao (成都商报), 2008.
China Central Television (中国中央电视台), 2004–8.
China Daily, 2007.
China National Radio (中央人民广播电台), 2009.
China News Agency (中国新闻社), 2004–9.
China Youth Daily (中国青年报), 2008.
Chosun Ilbo (South Korea), 2007–8.
Daily Telegraph, 2009.
Dongfangwang (东方网), 2008.
Dongfangzaobao (东方早报), 2005.
Duowei News (多维新闻), 2009.
Economist, 2007.
Guangzhou Ribao (广州日报), 1985.
Guardian, 2009.
Guoji Xianqudaobao (国际先驱导报), 2003–6.
Hebei TV (河北电视台), 2009.
Huanqiu Shibao (环球时报), 2002–9.
Huaxia Wang (华夏网), 2009.
Jakarta Post, 2005.
Jiefang Daily (解放日报), 2008.
Jiji Press (時事通信社), 2010–11.
Jijishimpo (時事新報), 1885.
Jingjicankaobao (经济参考报), 2005.
JoongAng Daily (South Korea), 2005.
Junshiwenzhai (军事文摘), 2010.
KBS News (South Korea), 2005.
Korean Herald, 1984.
Korean Times, 2004.
Kyodo News International, 2006.
Lianhezaobao (Singapore/联合早报), 2005.
Mainichi Shimbun (每日新聞), 2010.
Mingpao (Hong Kong/明报), 2008.
Newsweek, 1996.
New York Times, 1998–2009.
Nihon Keizai Shimbun (日本経済新聞), 2003.
Nikkei Net, 2009.
Nippon Hōsō Kyōkai, 2004–9.
NOW News (Taiwan/今日新聞網), 2006.
People's Daily (人民日报), 1953–2011.
Phoenix TV (凤凰卫视), 2005–10.
Renwu Journal (人物), 2008.
Reuters, 2009.
Sankei Shimbun (サンケイ新聞), 1972–2007.
Seattle Times, 2008.
Segye Times (South Korea), 2008.
Shūkanshinchō (週刊新潮), 2006.
Southern Weekly (南方周末), 2007.

Strait Times (Singapore/海峡时报), 1986.

Taipei Times, 2004.

Time, 1972.

Times (London), 2004.

TV Asahi, 2009.

United Daily News (Taiwan/聯合新聞網), 2008.

U.S. Joint Publication Research Service, 1985.

Washington Post, 2006.

Washington Diplomat, 2009.

Wenweipo (Hong Kong/香港文匯報), 2007.

World News Journal (世界新闻报), 2007.

Xianqu Luntan Daobao (先驱论坛导报), 2008.

Xinhua News Agency (新华社), 1949–2010.

Xinjingbao (新京报), 2009.

Xinwenchenbao (新闻晨报), 2006.

Yomiuri Shimbun (読売新聞), 1973–2008.

Yonhap News, 2011.

Zhongwen Daobao (中文导报), 2003.

Index

Note: Page numbers in italics indicate figures and tables.

Wang Renshu, 61–62
Wang Yi, 125
war reparations, 27, 39, 66, 91, 177n12
"*weixiao waijiao* (smile diplomacy)," 63
Wen Jiabao, 1, 124, 158, 159, 160
Western democracies (*Xifang minzhu guojia*), 21, 150, 177n46
Whiting, Allen S., 36–37
world-wide and regional and contexts for charm offensives, 17–18
Wu Youfu, 1

Xifang minzhu guojia (Western democracies), 21, 150, 177n46
Xi Jinping, 21, 49, 155–56, 165, 195n25
Xinhua News Agency, 26, 109, 156, 158, 159
Xu Fu, 112

Yagi Nobuo, 92
Yamamoto Nobuto, 76
Yanagitani Kensuke, 40–41
Yang Peiyi, 153
Yasukuni Shrine controversy: Japan-China relations in charm offensives and, 28, 37–38, 40, 46, 54, 145, 146, 192n50, 193n53; Japan-South Korean relations in context of charm offensives and, 100; Southeast Asia in context of charm offensives by Japan and, 82–83; South Korea in context of charm offensives by Japan and, 100; Taiwan in context of charm offensives by Japan and, 146, 193n55; Taiwan-Japan relations and, 143, 145, 146, 192n50
Yi Neng Jing, 133
Yi Yong-hui, 91
Yomiuri Shimbun (newspaper), 33–34, 35, 39–40, 41, 45
Yoshida Shigeru, 29, 31–32, 66, 68, 90–91, 155
Yuan Yue, 2
Yuk Young-soo, 94

Zheng Bijian, 2
Zhong Lisi, 117
Zhou Enlai: Africa's relations with, 162; Bandung Conference and, 62–63, 77; China-Burma relations and, 63; China-Thailand relations and, 62; China-U.S. relations and, 63, 182n24; cultural exchanges and, 50–51; on JCP, 178n37; Othering by China and, 31–32; "peace offensive" phase in Japan-China relations and, 23, 25–30, 37, 40, 44–45; "smile diplomacy" by, 63; statist actors' authority and, 25, 27–28, 169
Zhu Xi, 89